# Modern Mental Health

## Critical Perspectives on Psychiatric Practice

In memory of Thomas
Stephen Szasz (1920–2012)

# Modern Mental Health

## Critical Perspectives on Psychiatric Practice

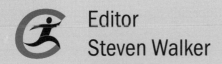 Editor
Steven Walker

First published in 2013 by Critical Publishing Ltd, St Albans

British Library Cataloguing in Publication Data
A CIP record for this book is available from the British Library

ISBN: 978-1-909330-53-5

This book is also available in the following e-book formats:
Kindle ISBN: 978-1-909330-54-2
EPUB ISBN: 978-1-909330-56-6
Adobe e-book ISBN: 978-1-909330-55-9

Cover design by Greensplash Limited
Project Management by Out of House Publishing
Typeset by Newgen Imaging Systems
Printed and bound in Great Britain by TJ International

Critical Publishing
www.criticalpublishing.com

# Contents

# Figures and Tables

## Figures

## Tables

# Foreword

We are in the midst of a massive cycle of difficulty and distress. The last time this happened was during the course of the first half of the twentieth century. Unbridled capitalism, colonialism, militarism and extreme totalitarian ideologies gave us two world wars, a great depression, holocausts and unprecedented global suffering. These terrible events also gave the UK the democratic force to create its welfare state, led to an ending of old empires and the creation of new nations and social values. But there was never really an enduring time of peace and calm and, since then, we have gone full circle, with new ideological struggles, new empire builders, new oppressions and a return to capitalism as unconstrained as in the nineteenth century. This is the age of neo-liberalism, globalisation, widespread war, unprecedented inequality and environmental disaster.

Yet as the external pressures on most of us get stronger and more destructive; as the impact of these forces penetrates deeper and more intimately into our lives, our minds, our relationships, our understanding of ourselves and each other, so dominant accounts increasingly emphasise that our ills are individual and of our own making – and so are their solutions. Neo-liberalism and psychiatry are now intimately and inextricably interconnected. Our problems and distress are increasingly explained by individualised psychiatric interpretations. The creation of more and more diagnostic categories reflects the expansion of psychiatry's empire and its solutions, while the poverty of its 'solutions', notably its over-reliance on chemical therapies, their damaging effects and large-scale failure, continue to be evidenced. If ever there were an area of medicine that could with justification be described as creating 'iatrogenic' problems, then it would have to be psychiatry. Few areas of medicine, let alone human service, create as great a fear as the problems that they are meant to address, as does psychiatry.

That is why this book can be seen as both valuable and helpful. Early on, its authors make clear that the book will:

*move away from that position of resigned helplessness in the face of government and psychiatric professional orthodoxy. Our inspiration is that of predecessors who have challenged the prevailing ethos and assumptions dictating mental health policy and practice.*

So while the odds may seem stacked against us, this book does not accept that things must stay as they are and that the current dominance of the medical model and Big Pharma is inevitable. Instead, building on a wide range of experience, of both service users and practitioners, it offers different ways of understanding and responding to the problems we now face and ways of overcoming them.

This response and resistance to psychiatry needs to be seen as work in progress. And so perhaps does this book. The contributors come from different experiences and offer different viewpoints, ideas, understandings and hypotheses. Doubtless there are internal inconsistencies and contradictions in what they say. Some authors challenge diagnostic categories, others include themselves in them. But that is where we are today. In challenging psychiatry from our different viewpoints, we are still at a stage of developing our thoughts, checking them out with each other, seeing how far we can reconcile and relate our different takes on our lives, responses to them and the world we live in. The last thing we need is another monolithic theory or ideology. This is a time of development and change and, of course, if the devil had all the best tunes, psychiatry rather than service users has most of the money and other key resources.

As the book makes clear, we are currently witnessing the collision of 'science' and neo-liberalism with madness and emotional distress – to all our cost. Now managerialism, the handmaiden of new right politics, is becoming as important as psychiatry as a force that inhibits and damages us and the two work in close association to magnify our difficulties. This book, relatively modest in size, nonetheless has a broad sweep that runs from the personal to the political as well as to the interrelations of the two.

It explores fresh ways of coming at loss and grief, culturally competent practice, shared decision making with service users and user involvement in decision making relating to psychiatric medication. There is a concern with helping as well as analysing. The book highlights human connection and the potential of reciprocal support and healing and the need to reclaim concepts appropriated from service users. It questions and challenges commercialisation, bureaucratisation and mental health law reform, as well as conventional public and private divides. It includes a wide range of human experience, from that of children and offenders and of women labelled with personality disorder, to a boy as a soldier and a girl invalided out of the services into the psychiatric system. It reports on trying to survive and user-led services, suicide, spirituality and dying. It brings to centre stage the importance of relationships, humanity, trust and the ordinary virtues, in supporting and restoring people who face cataclysmic difficulties or penalties from being seen as different.

Psychiatry, with its nineteenth-century emphasis on a cold kind of positivist science in both its theory and research, seems poorly suited to these complex, uncertain and ambiguous times. We must move on, and crucially that move must centrally involve the people who have been on the receiving end of both psychiatric 'explanation' and 'treatment'. Both are increasingly found wanting from many quarters, while carrying increasing political weight in reactionary times.

We are in the middle of a difficult period of change. We have to hope that this book can serve as part of the process of moving to better times. It may be one that people read from cover to cover or dip into favourite parts. If readers are anything like me, they will find some favourite phrases that will help them keep going and take things forward. And if the book can serve such purposes, then I think the authors will have done their task well, offering the rest of us another resource to help take forward our joint understanding of madness and distress, helping us to strengthen our understanding of each other and our solidarity and to take forward the struggle for people-centred support for people in distress, that sees us properly in our social, material, cultural, spiritual and political context.

**Professor Peter Beresford**

Peter Beresford OBE is Professor of Social Policy at Brunel University and Chair of Shaping Our Lives, the national disabled people's and service users' organisation and network. He is a long-term user of mental health services and has a background as author, activist, educator and researcher concerned with public participation. He is author of *A Straight Talking Guide to Being a Mental Health Service User* (Ross on Wye: PCCS Books, 2010).

# About the Authors

**Heather Castillo** worked for many years in Mind Organisations in Essex, developing advocacy for adults with mental health problems. She was also instrumental in setting up one of the first advocacy projects in the country for children and adolescents with mental health problems. Eight years ago she helped to set up, and became Chief Executive of, The Haven Project, a Department of Health National Innovation Site for the support and treatment of personality disorder. She has published a chapter in *The Art and Science of Mental Health Nursing* (2nd edition) titled The Person with a Personality Disorder (Open University Press). In 2011 she completed a doctorate about the process of recovery in personality disorder.

**Joanna Fox** is Senior Lecturer in Social Work at Anglia Ruskin University. Joanna identifies herself as a person with lived experience of mental ill health. Her lived experience plays a major role in her research, teaching and writing. Joanna has worked extensively in developing support services for carers, in implementing and supporting service-user and carer involvement in social work education and in PPI in health care. Areas of expertise include: the use of concept mapping in research and teaching, mental health caring, and recovery in mental health. She teaches mental health on the social work course at Anglia Ruskin University.

**Tim French** was until recently Senior Lecturer in Mental Health in the Faculty of Health, Social Care and Education, Anglia Ruskin University. He has had extensive experience working for the National Health Service in England as a community psychiatric nurse and has spent time caring for people within in-patient settings. He has a BA in Psychology, a Master's Degree in Sociology and Health Studies and a Post-Graduate Diploma in Jungian Studies from the Centre for Psychoanalytic Studies, University of Essex. Tim is currently working for a mental health trust in Eastern England in an Early Intervention in Psychosis service.

**R.D. Hinshelwood** is Professor in the Centre for Psychoanalytic Studies, University of Essex, and was previously Clinical Director, The Cassel Hospital, London. He has authored *A Dictionary of Kleinian Thought* (1989) and other books and articles on Kleinian psychoanalysis. *Observing Organisations* (2000) was edited with Wilhelm Skogstad and is among a number of texts on psychoanalytic applications to social science. In 2004, he published *Suffering Insanity*, a book on schizophrenia in psychiatric institutions. He founded the *British Journal of Psychotherapy* and *Psychoanalysis and History*. Currently he is completing *Research on the Couch: Single Case Studies, Subjectivity and Psychoanalytic Knowledge*, to be published in 2013, and a jointly edited book, with Nuno Torres, called *Bion's Sources: The Shaping of His Paradigms* (2013).

**Emma Kaminskiy** is a PhD student within the faculty of Health, Social Care and Education at Anglia Ruskin University. Her research is exploring collaborative psychiatric medication management. She holds an MSc in Organisational Psychology from City University, London, and has research interests in the areas of innovation, collaboration and mental health.

**Nicola Morant** is an applied social psychologist working in the field of mental health. She is Affiliated Lecturer in the Department of Psychology, University of Cambridge, and an honorary research associate in the Research Department of Mental Health Sciences at University College London. She also works in a freelance capacity as a qualitative research collaborator on a number of mixed-methods NHS-based research projects. These cover various areas of mental health, including acute and crisis care, psychiatric medication management, supported work environments, early intervention services and mindfulness-based cognitive therapy.

**Shula Ramon** is Emeritus Professor of Interprofessional Health and Social Studies at Anglia Ruskin University, Cambridge, and Professor of Mental Health Research at the University of Hertfordshire, Hatfield. A social worker and clinical psychologist by training, she has researched mental health extensively and internationally, focusing recently on recovery issues, and systematically involving service users in her research projects. Her recent publication is: Ryan, P., Ramon, S., Greacen, T. (2012) *Empowerment, Lifelong Learning and Recovery in Mental Health: Towards a New Paradigm* (Basingstoke: Palgrave Macmillan).

**Lena Robinson** is Professor of Social Work and Human Services at Central Queensland University, Australia. Previously she was Professor of Social Work at the University of the West of Scotland. She has also worked at the Universidade de Eduardo Mondlane, Mozambique. Professor Robinson has published and researched widely in the field of race, ethnicity, cross-cultural psychology and social work practice. She is a member of the Editorial Board of the *Journal of Ethnic and Cultural Diversity in Social Work* (from October 2003) and *British Journal of Social Work* (from January 2006–10). She is currently involved in a number of research projects, including an international study of mutual intercultural relations in plural societies and a study of suicide and parasuicide in India.

**Keverne Smith** was Course Director for BA Humanities at the University Centre, College of West Anglia, King's Lynn, from 2003 to 2011; this course was franchised from Anglia Ruskin University. His book, *Shakespeare and Son: A Journey in Writing and Grieving*, which examines the evidence that Shakespeare's later plays are affected by the loss in 1596 of his only son, Hamnet, appeared in 2011. He has also published articles on a variety of topics, including education (School to University: Sunlit Steps, or Stumbling in the Dark? and School to University: An Investigation into the Experience of First-Year Students of English at British Universities), religious history (To Sing or to Say: Dirges, Cymbeline, and the Reformers), and studies of loss (Tangled Up in Grief: Bob Dylan's Songs of Separation). His special interest is in interdisciplinary studies, especially involving Social History, Literature, Education and Psychology.

**James Trueman** is Senior Lecturer in Mental Health at Anglia Ruskin University, where he is the course leader for the Approved Mental Health Professional training programme, and theme leader for mental health law. Outside of his legal interests, a significant amount of his time is currently dedicated to leading and supporting the implementation of technology in education. His background is as a mental health nurse, with experience of working in both the NHS and private sector. His research interests include mental health legislation, professional, media and political discourse, and the history of medicine – commonly viewed through the theoretical lens of critical discourse analysis.

**Hannah Walker** was brought up on the Isle of Wight, where she also went to school. Hannah had the first of many breakdowns in London and was eventually diagnosed as being bipolar. She was unceremoniously chucked out of the RAF, got married and retrained as a psycho-therapist and hypnotherapist. She is Chair of the Dorset Mental Health Forum, a pan-Dorset charity which exists to improve the lives of service users in the county. Hannah is the co-editor of the book *Our Encounters with Madness*, published by PCCS Books, which is becoming a set text for nursing students. She hopes psychiatrists might read it as well.

**Steven Walker** trained as a social worker at the London School of Economics and Political Science. He qualified as a Systemic Psychotherapist in 1991 after studying at the Tavistock Clinic and the Institute for Family Therapy and Systemic Practice, London. He recently com-pleted his MPhil in Child and Adolescent Mental Health. Steven has worked extensively for the past 30 years with children and families in the context of child protection and child and ado-lescent mental health. He has authored or co-authored ten books, the latest being *Effective Social Work with Children and Families: Putting Systems Theory into Practice* (London: Sage, 2012). He has presented his research at many national and international conferences – the latest at the 2012 *European Conference for Dramatherapy and Psychotherapy* on the sub-ject of *Fidel Castro's Childhood*. Steven currently works for a charity offering a counselling service for troubled young people.

# Introduction

In the grand sweep of history, we can probably observe that the understanding, treatment and support for those experiencing mental health problems has improved dramatically in a relatively short space of time. From human sacrifice, the burning of witches, blood-letting, the Bedlam freak shows, lobotomies, electroconvulsive therapy and pharmacological regimes through to the era of encounter groups, talking therapy and mindfulness, it seems things are getting better. Or are they? Perhaps we have become complacent or resigned to the limits of ways in which human beings can be helped with their invisible suffering? Yet the stark reality is that the World Health Organization recently declared that mental illness was set to become the biggest public health challenge of the twenty-first century (WHO, 2010). *The Spirit Level*, published to critical acclaim in 2009, again demonstrated the connection between inequality and poor mental health, highlighting the link between increasing social divisions and the gap between a country's wealthier and poorer citizens and increasing levels of mental health problems (Wilkinson and Pickett, 2009). Globalisation, the rush to economic development, neo-liberal competitive practices and the fetish of conspicuous consumption propel people into a vortex of unhealthy working and living conditions that set the scene for emotional impoverishment and vulnerability to mental illness.

NHS managers in England were accused in the summer of 2012 of *shocking discrimination* in commissioning mental health services. The Mental Health Policy Group from the London School of Economics said three-quarters of people with depression or anxiety got no treatment. The group said that the NHS was guilty of injustice in its treatment of people with mental illness. The committee of senior academics and medical professionals described this as a *real scandal*. The committee is headed by economist Professor Lord Richard Layard and includes some of the country's most eminent mental health experts. Care Services Minister Paul Burstow said mental health should be treated as seriously as physical health issues.

The group's report found that among those aged under 65, nearly half of all ill health was mental illness. Six million people had depression or anxiety conditions and yet three-quarters got no treatment. This was often because NHS managers failed to commission properly the mental health services recommended in official guidance. They said the £400m earmarked by the government for psychological therapy was not always used for its intended purpose because there was no obligation on managers to do so. The committee concluded that mental health services should be expanded. But, if anything, they were being cut. Of particular concern is the recent news that child and adolescent mental health service provision is being reduced (Young Minds, 2010) after several years of real improvement. Untreated young people with mental health problems are the adults with mental health problems of the future, so this short-sighted saving will produce much more cost in the future.

It is easy to accept the logic and rationale of the bean counters and economists who mesmerise us with statistics and resource limits, hindering our thirst for new knowledge and innovative, person-centred care. So this book will move away from that position of resigned helplessness in the face of government and psychiatric professional orthodoxy. Our inspiration is that of predecessors who have challenged the prevailing ethos and assumptions dictating mental health policy and practice, such as Sontag, Szasz, Lacan, Laing and Foucault, to name only a few.

Anthony Clare, who as a psychiatrist was better placed than most to reflect on his profession and the prevailing complacency in psychiatry in the mid 1970s, voiced criticism from within the establishment in his seminal work: *Psychiatry in Dissent* (Clare, 1976). Feminist writers such as Segal, Friedan, Orbach, Greer and other radical voices, have been supplemented by authors such as Fernando, Bhugra, Young and Hall, whose thoughtful work on racism in psychiatry proved so unsettling to many practitioners resting on their laurels after the flurry of anti-racist and anti-discriminatory policies in the latter part of the twentieth century.

The publication of DSM-V, the latest version of the *Diagnostic and Statistical Manual*, used by psychiatrists to order, collate and regiment human suffering into neat linear classifications, in the same year as this book is as ironic as it is fortuitous. Like its cousin, the ISDM, it has metamorphosed over the years – always expanding to discover, register and rationalise the creation of yet more diagnoses and classifications of the human condition. Apologists within psychiatry admit its limitations but always say that they have to start 'somewhere'. But why not start with the person sitting in front of you? Answer: because it takes time, and time is money and in a global economic system which objectifies people into units of production, there is no space for the elasticity and complexity of individual experience. DSM-V symbolises all that is wrong with psychiatry and by attempting to corral the myriad of human experience into condensed descriptions and symptoms reveals its own paradox – how to offer individual care using a guidebook that does the very opposite. Even a member of the DSM V Personality and Personality Disorders Work Group has stated that *the DSM-5 proposal is a disappointing and confusing mixture of innovation and preservation of the status quo that is inconsistent, lacks coherence, is impractical, and, in places, is incompatible with empirical facts* (Livesley, 2010), characterising the overall effort as an expression of *incoherence and confusion*.

It is the pantomime ugly sister of Big Pharma – the enormous global pharmacological industry that now dictates policy and practice in mental health care, driven by an insatiable greed for profit rather than the needs of people. It is an industry monopolised by a handful of multinational corporations, with the incredible power of wealth, according to reliable data, amounting to multi-billion-dollar profits per annum. All too often, these mega-institutions are discovered to have been selective about their published data on efficacy and clinical trials of new drugs, and by their very nature, they are incapable of demonstrating long-term side effects or biological consequences because of the expense of mounting longitudinal studies and the media-fuelled demand from the public, who have been led to believe in the 'silver bullet' instant cure to all their ills, all wrapped up in sealed blister packs of medication.

The latest policy document from the UK government (Department of Health, 2009a) described the current mental health situation in the UK in terms of its impact on society. At any one time, just over 20 per cent of working-age women and 17 per cent of working-age men are affected by depression or anxiety. Approximately 5 per cent of men and 3 per cent of women can be assessed as having a personality disorder and over 0.4 per cent have a psychotic disorder such as schizophrenia or bipolar affective disorder. Half of those with common mental health problems are limited by their condition and around a fifth are disabled by it.

Mental illness accounts for more disability-adjusted life-years lost per year than any other health condition in the UK, and the figures for 2010 show that 20 per cent of the total burden of disease was attributable to mental illness (including suicide), compared with 16.2 per cent for cardiovascular diseases and 15.6 per cent for cancer. No other condition exceeded 10 per cent. No other health condition matches mental ill health in the combined extent of prevalence, persistence and breadth of impact. Importantly, the 'New Horizons' document highlighted an often neglected part of the population by revealing that mental illness begins early, with 10 per cent of children having a diagnosable mental health condition, and 50 per cent of lifetime mental illness is present by the age of 14. However, it failed to adequately address the mental health needs of children with learning disabilities, which is a serious deficiency and another indictment against the psychiatric establishment. Today's disturbed and emotionally vulnerable child is tomorrow's adult mental health patient unless intervention and support can quickly be brought to bear on an emerging mental health problem – the younger, the better.

The individual contributors to this book share a passion for needs-informed person-centred care for those people affected by mental ill health, and they feel a deep scepticism about the way help and support is organised and provided to the one in four people in the population who at some time will suffer mental health problems. The chapters include a diverse and rich mixture of stark personal testimony, reflective narrative, case studies in user-informed care, alternative models of intervention and support, rigorous empirical research and a forensic analysis of mental health law-making. Although the overarching philosophy of this book is critical of contemporary psychiatric care, each chapter offers an individual perspective on an aspect of provision.

And critical need not mean negative. We take the concept of critical to mean *subjecting to an interrogation from a different point of view than the prevailing orthodoxy*, in the manner of the Classical writer Socrates (Benson, 2000). The classical period in history witnessed the emergence of logical discourse with conventional beliefs and religious practices subjected to interrogation and a form of rationalism. This excerpt from Theophrastus, a successor to Aristotle at the Lyceum, illustrates the struggles to find an explanatory framework for human experience. In this case, a man who could be diagnosed with Obsessive Compulsive Disorder today is described thus then:

*Superstition is of course a kind of cowardice in the face of the divine. He washes his hands and asperses himself with water from the three springs and puts a laurel leaf from a temple-precinct in his mouth before going out for the day. If a cat runs across the road he refuses to budge till someone else has passed or he has thrown three pebbles across the road. If he sees a snake in the house he invokes Sabazios if it is red; if a sacred snake he establishes a shrine on the spot.* (Characters 16)

The French philosopher Voltaire captured an idea that is worth considered reflection when he said: *Uncertainty is not a pleasant condition. But certainty is absurd* (Voltaire, 1764). From this we can draw a valuable if uncomfortable conclusion – that the more psychiatrists seek the certainty offered by DSM-V, and are protected by status and wealthy legal protection against the weak, poor and suffering, then the less willing they are to be challenged, questioned and open to feelings of doubt and uncertainty. Even progressive and radical psychiatrists are hamstrung by employment constraints, career pathways and budget limits that inhibit creativity and suppress dissent. In the long run, the more uncertainty becomes acceptable, then the more the potential for real human growth and humane person-centred care can be revealed.

The book is a new addition to a corpus of existing literature that refuses to accept the status quo in psychiatry and is prepared to ask difficult questions. It will appeal to the hungry, inquisitive minds of junior doctors, newly qualified psychiatrists, nurses, social workers and all of those in a variety of educational and training contexts where they hope to qualify and acquire a professional status that allows them to intervene in the lives of the most vulnerable people in the population. This is an awesome responsibility which can weigh heavily. This burden can be relieved by withdrawing into certainty, procedures and prevailing orthodoxy, backed by insurance and employer control of information. It is called defensive practice and is understandable in the context of multiple external and internal stressors, the fear of making mistakes and the consequences for the patient and their family. However, within these chapters there lies the prospect of an exciting, invigorating, satisfying and fulfilling menu of resources to consider, digest, reflect upon and then put into practice. Doing something different – even a relatively small change inspired by what you read – could be liberating. Those people whose suffering you are trying to relieve will know the difference.

Steven Walker

# Part One
# The Human in the System

# 1 A Survivor's Story

## By Hannah Walker

## Introduction

My name is Hannah and I'm a survivor of the military mental health system, the NHS mental health system and a number of psychiatrists. I suffer from bipolar disorder and post-traumatic stress disorder (PTSD), and I was diagnosed 20 years ago. In this chapter, I will tell you some of my story.

I was adopted at four months into a loving upper-middle-class family who lived on the Isle of Wight. I have a sister, also adopted, who is six years younger than I am. Neither of us has ever wanted to trace our biological parents, because we were happy at home and didn't feel the need to go meddling. Both our adoptive parents are now dead, but they would have been quite happy had we wanted to seek our real mothers, but we thought not. No point.

I went to the local grammar school, and left at the age of 18 having been Head Girl and having collected a few O and A levels – nothing spectacular. When I was in the Upper Sixth, my best friend died; I later discovered that she had committed suicide. I had the first of what were to be many, many episodes of mania and depression after that event and had some time off school. The episode was curious – I didn't know what was happening to me and didn't really have the words to explain it to the GP. All I could tell him was that all the colours went bright outside, and I felt a rush of panic and fear as though I could no longer remain alive and deal with it. In that instant, I contemplated taking an overdose of painkillers – not so that I would die, but so that I could become unconscious and not have to feel the pain. I couldn't be alone, but I couldn't tell anyone what I was feeling as it was impossible to describe. The only time I felt 'well' was when I was driving a car. I slept with the light on as I couldn't bear to be alone in the dark with just my thoughts for company.

My parents hadn't any idea of what to do with me, so they sent me to my GP, and I tried to explain what had happened to me, without much success. He diagnosed an extreme grief reaction, without much in the way of a clue as to my illness. I became even more depressed and started self-harming, making up the most outrageous stories as to how I had cut myself. I spent hours with razor blades, slashing my arms to pieces, and telling the A&E Department that I had fallen through windows/dropped a glass which had shattered/been hit by a hockey ball. No one helped. No one asked me if I was OK – not even the medics who assiduously stitched me up every time. I was sent to an educational psychologist, but refused to talk to her as she had hinted to me that she thought I was self-harming. Far too ashamed to admit it, I reiterated my stories and told her that I was just very accident prone. She gave up.

I pulled myself together and carried on as though nothing had happened, which sowed the seeds of later episodes. I applied to join the RAF, having turned down a place at Warwick University to read Philosophy and Logic – having tried recently to read a book on philosophy, I can only say that it was for the best. I went to RAF Biggin Hill, the Officers' and Aircrew Selection Centre for a three-day assessment, and was accepted as a personnel officer.

In February, I joined the RAF as a cadet. The Officer Cadet Training Unit was at RAF Henlow in Bedfordshire – there were seven girls in a squadron of 60 people. It was hard and fast and we were pushed to the limits of exhaustion and beyond – I loved every minute. We carried telegraph poles up hills and down dales, using them to make bridges or stretchers, and falling, beyond tired, into sleeping bags at night. Classes were hard, especially for us new to the RAF (many of our number had come up through the ranks and knew all the stuff we were learning), and we had to assimilate information very quickly. I was extremely fit, but even I found it difficult. However, I graduated with the Sash of Merit for leadership, and was sent on detachment to RAF Gan, an island at the southern end of the Maldives.

We flew from RAF Brize Norton on a VC-10 to Cyprus, where we refuelled and went on to Gan. We arrived in the middle of a tropical thunderstorm. However, the weather cleared and we had a fabulous time in the sun – work was from 7.30am to 2pm and the afternoons were spent on the beach, water skiing or snorkelling. It was idyllic. Unfortunately, it was also due to close – transport aircraft had moved on and could get to Singapore and beyond without having to refuel at Gan, so it shut. However, the trip left me with an insatiable desire for more travel.

I did my professional training at the RAF College Cranwell; and after that I had a number of postings that weren't nearly as exciting as Gan. The MoD, RAF Stanbridge, Recruiting in Wales and Recruit Training at RAF Hereford followed, then RAF Coningsby, where I flew in a Phantom and a Lightning, and the Lancaster Bomber belonging to the Battle of Britain Memorial Flight. Germany next – two fantastic years – RAF Cottesmore and then, on promotion to Squadron Leader at the ripe old age of 29, RAF Waddington. I was considered a high flyer.

## Emerging problems

When I was 31, I was posted to the MoD as a military assistant to a general. It was a hard job, and we worked from 7.45am to well past 9pm. I didn't get much leave. And the episode that had been waiting to happen since the sixth form started to happen.

My personal life was a mess – I was having an affair with a married man and trying to do my job without it, or the relationship, suffering. With hindsight, I should have known something had to give, and give it did. After three years of punishing hours, and 18 months of waiting for the man to leave his wife, I started to come apart at the seams.

It began with not sleeping very well and feeling anxious all the time. I couldn't concentrate, and I couldn't see very well, strangely. Freddie, for that's what I shall call him, had left his wife and we were living together, but the Services take a dim view of extra-marital relation-ships, so it was all rather difficult. I began to be paranoid and to hear voices, and at that stage decided to go to the doctor.

I managed to walk in through his door and collapsed in a heap. I tried, as I had done at the age of 18, to explain my symptoms – anxiety, paranoia, low mood and lack of pleasure in anything – but once again, I didn't have the words. However, the doctor was marvellous and wrote me out a prescription for a drug that he said would help. It didn't, and I went back the following week. The doctor was a good man and gently said I needed to see a specialist. Ho hum, I thought – a shrink, I thought. Here we go, I thought.

I was referred to a very nice psychiatrist and went to see him the following week. Yet again I tried to explain my symptoms, and this time, someone understood. I said I had no pleasure in anything; that I couldn't concentrate and that I felt my life as I knew it had ended. I was bleak about the future and told him that I couldn't go on. He told me to imagine that my problems were a black dog – was the dog in the room, was it close to me? I replied that it was sitting on my lap, in an attempt to get him to see how near the edge I was. He prescribed an anti-depressant called Lofepramine, and told me to take two tablets daily. He said he'd see me every week.

By this time, I had moved jobs as well, and now worked for an irritable civil servant. The only bright thing on the horizon was his PA – a 60-year-old woman who would frequently wear her second-best teeth to the office, saving her others for 'best'. She and I would repair to a local pub every lunch time and come back late, giving the civil servant palpitations. However, Freddie was too senior for him to take any action. He contented himself with telling me I was late, and I infuriated him by agreeing. Eventually, I went sick and never returned.

I saw the psychiatrist once a week thereafter. Initially, he diagnosed me with situational stress, then with major depression. Freddie, who had been promoted again, didn't really understand, but asked the psychiatrist to brief him once a fortnight to help him make sense of the whole thing. After a month or two, the psychiatrist asked me if I'd ever felt like this before, and I suddenly remembered my school event. He then asked me if I'd ever had what he called an exuberant mood and, thinking back, I replied that I had, indeed, on many occa-sions, interspersed with periods of being quite solitary. After some lengthy discussions, he diagnosed me with manic depression.

In a way it was a relief – at last I had something to hang my hat on; a diagnosis and a reason for feeling the way I did. I read up on it, and the more I read, the more it all made sense to me. I devoured books, including *Darkness Visible* by William Styron, *House of Bread* by Amanda Nicol and *An Unquiet Mind* by Kay Redfield Jamison. The psychiatrist gave me a letter with 'Manic depressive psychosis' written in it, so I could take it back to the RAF GP. How he knew I was psychotic was beyond me – I had never declared hearing voices, but he was quite right. He decided that the best thing would be for me to retire from the RAF on medical grounds.

This next bit is difficult to write. I was phoned up by a man I had previously called a friend, who told me that I was to be discharged under the same regulations as alcoholics and drug addicts – 'Services No Longer Required'. When I tried to explain that manic depression was a mostly genetic illness, and that I was in no fit state to discuss this, he told me that it was all my fault for falling in love with a married man. This gave me such a shock that I didn't really know how to answer him – at this stage of the illness I was feeling suicidal, and Freddie was away in the Far East. This 'friend' told me I had to go to RAF Barnwood and make a statement in my defence. I suddenly realised that I was being punished – Freddie was too senior to have anything done to him – and that the RAF was no longer the supportive employer that I had been used to. While I was flying high, there was no problem; now that I was on my knees, others were very quick to condemn me. I had crossed boundaries by being with Freddie, and the RAF didn't take kindly to it.

## Institutional reaction

When one is invalided out of the services, one is entitled to a pension, enhanced and tax free if the reason for invaliding can be attributed to service. My psychiatrist had decided to invalid me; years later I discovered that he had been ordered to discharge me and that because I had committed 'social misconduct' I was to receive no pension. The RAF hadn't got the bottle to discipline me because of Freddie's rank – so they took it out on me by refusing to pension me off.

I was entitled to resettlement leave, and while on that, I slipped a disc. I went back to the RAF GP, only to be told that they would not treat me because I was being invalided. However, I couldn't register with a civilian GP because I was still in the RAF. Catch 22. So I struggled about, in agony, until I was discharged – I was immediately admitted to hospital and operated on the next day. To this day, because of the delay, I have trouble balancing on my right foot and my right calf is numb.

The sense of injustice was immense. I had given all I had to my career and to be summarily thrown out was devastating. I had no source of income and had to rely on Freddie for the simplest things – I, who had always earned my own living. We were living in Dorset at weekends and in London during the week; when I became too ill to travel, I stayed in Dorset.

I was referred to a new psychiatrist, who confirmed that I had bipolar disorder after she had spoken to the RAF consultant. I wasn't responding to the Lofepramine, so she changed my drugs – instead of feeling dreadful, I started to feel nothing at all, which was even worse. Freddie managed to finalise his divorce and we got married – he was still in the services, but was due to retire the following year. Despite desperately wanting to feel happy, I just felt numb and betrayed by the service I had loved.

I fought the RAF for a year. Letter after letter, phone call after phone call. During that year I began to feel more like myself, and Freddie and I were having fun. One day, I wrote to my old RAF psychiatrist, who had retired, and asked him for anything I could put in my next letter to the RAF. He responded with some fantastic quotes, which I forwarded. I got my pension – no word of an apology, merely a letter from some functionary giving me figures and saying that my illness was attributable to my service. At last, I thought, and went manic.

Freddie and I lived a happy life for a couple of years, going on holidays and spending a lot of time visiting friends. He was retired by now and had picked up a couple of consultancies. We bought a new house and did it up. I was happy – not manic and not depressed. We got two cats. However, the spectre – the Darkness Visible – was just around the corner.

I started a degree course in Applied Psychology and Computing Science, and lapped it up – I got a first in all subjects when I did my initial year. Freddie hated it – I refused to be the little woman in the home, where I felt unfulfilled and frustrated. Freddie's behaviour started to change; when I challenged him, he said that I was imagining it and that I must be getting ill again. It transpired that he was having an affair; not unusual for him – after all, he'd had an affair with me while married.

I cannot describe the betrayal that I felt. Freddie's delaying his divorce from his previous wife had partly been to blame for my breakdown when I left the RAF; I had given up a lot to be married to him and the needlessness of that rankled enormously. I gave him six months to change his ways and try to mend our relationship.

During that six months I had my first admission to a psychiatric hospital – I have had another 23 since. That initial admission was a complete eye opener to me with my rather sheltered background – mental illness is not a respecter of class. I discovered a lot of things, both about myself and about others – people who lived on the streets became friends and people who had the same diagnosis became confidants. I was terrified at first; I was put in a three-bedded dormitory with a small woman who never stopped puffing and a girl who regularly self-harmed (I hadn't done that since my teens). The main lounge was a nightmare – all the chairs had cigarette burns and the cues from the snooker table were constantly being broken in fights. The ward was a mess; long corridors and communal baths were of the essence.

I gradually got to know everyone. There was a row of armchairs in the foyer and that was where my friends and I sat, smoking furiously to pass the time. No one told me I was sup-posed to go to occupational therapy, but I was nevertheless reprimanded for not going. There was a drinks machine nearby, which was always being vandalised or tipped over by passing patients. The staff stayed in their offices, away from the patients, and very much left us to our own devices. We roamed the corridors and the grounds, looking for something to do.

The clinic was a modern add-on to a huge old asylum, built in the last century, which had been closed after disgorging its patients into the community or nursing homes. The old build-ings were shut and boarded up, but easily broken in to by agile patients, such as myself. I and another girl set about our illegal task with determination, dodging the elderly security guards and making our way through the barbed wire. We broke in through a window and found ourselves in a long corridor with wards going off it and a massive ballroom at one end. The sheer size of the place overawed us. The wards still had broken beds in them and the old stained mattresses were rotten. We walked slowly around the place, feeling the ghosts of the long gone. The ballroom was enormous, with huge windows – branches grazed the glass from outside, giving a creepy background sound to our meanderings. The whole place was scary and we left in rather a hurry, again avoiding the guards.

## Historical echoes

The lasting legacy of that asylum stays with people even today. Elderly men and women talk of it with anxiety; of the days when they had electric shocks given without anaesthetic. More worryingly, staff at the clinic still hark back to those 'good old days'; betraying a complete lack of awareness of how it must have been for the people incarcerated there. People who were treated there for any length of time display institutionalised ways of behaving. Having said that, it must have been a sanctuary for some who could not cope with the day-to-day hardships of living. Personally, it frightened the crap out of me.

Meanwhile, back in the clinic, Freddie said he was coming to visit, which filled me with a certain amount of trepidation – he had never understood my illness and didn't look as though he was going to start. I gathered the homeless and those with the twitches associated with long-term antipsychotics, and we sat and waited in ambush. After Freddie had gone, one of my friends asked me why I'd ever married such a plonker. I had no answer.

I was discharged, feeling no better, but having made a number of good mates – the kind who would come to your aid in a fight. I threw Freddie out of the house and told him to go and live with his girlfriend, and felt a lot better. By now I was on a potent cocktail of drugs prescribed at the clinic, including Haloperidol and Librium. I went to see my psychiatrist as a follow-up to discharge and he put me on lithium as well, telling me that it was a drug of last resort and if it didn't work, there was nothing else he could do for me. How cheering.

Lithium made me flat, boring and tired, and it took away my personality. It also gave me terrible side effects – thirst and hunger, weight gain, tremors, and made me more depressed and suicidal. I stopped taking it, and everything else, and suffered horrible withdrawal symptoms – I also went manic and had to be admitted again. I was put on Droperidol, which has since been banned, and Librium. I saw double all the time, and kept thinking I wasn't wearing my glasses. I must have walked miles every day to try and calm myself, but it didn't really work – the nurses told me afterwards that *only drugs will work*. I eventually came off the high and went home again.

My two cats were my lifeline, and one day one of them was run over and killed. I buried her under the chestnut tree at the bottom of the garden, and luckily had a friend who had two kittens that needed a home, so I took them. A month later, one was run over. Then, as if that wasn't enough, my older cat died of leukaemia. It goes almost without saying that I ended up back in hospital, this time in a deep depression.

Much has been written about depression. For me, it is the ending of life as I know it. I am devoid of all the things that make me a person with a soul, with hopes and dreams and with any kind of existence. It is vastly increased sounds and a sensitivity to everything – as though I were wearing my nerve endings on the outside. Sometimes it is a terrible silence – it is certainly absence. Nothing, but nothing, gives me any kind of pleasure. I avoid answering the phone and to think of calling someone myself is out of the question. What would I say? Who on earth would want to listen to a miserable nothing, an empty vessel, a walking shroud? I am terrified of everything and nothingness, and the desire to stop the pain is overwhelming. I have to hide tablets from myself and kid myself that it's all going to get better when I absolutely know it won't. Depression and the leaving of it is a series of false dawns – every day, the promise of a better one, followed by the immediate realisation that it's just the same. The voices tell me I'm shit and I believe them. Hospital is a sanctuary, however rough it is.

Mania, now, is on a completely different level. When one is depressed, time stops. When manic, there just isn't enough time to get everything done – life rushes past and I have no idea why other people can't keep up or can't follow my train of thought. It starts seductively, and the colours heighten – particularly natural colours, like those of trees and grass. There are portents everywhere – in the blue sky, in the sounds of birds; things begin to speed up. My mania starts with not sleeping – but is that the first symptom, or is it the cause? No one seems to be able to tell me, and I suppose it doesn't matter. I stay up later and later, pottering about with tasks of great importance, such as getting a pair of driving gloves in exactly the right shade of green. eBay calls me, with its wonderful website and the chance of nabbing a bargain. Eventually, I'm up all night, with no need for sleep – why waste a moment? Life is SUCH FUN. And as, for me, mania comes after a bad depression, it's worth waiting for. My friends tell me to take more drugs and I ignore them until it's too late and the high has its hold on me.

## Recurring patterns

I buy and buy – even the postman knows when I'm not well, as parcel after parcel arrives. I don't open a lot of them, as the fun is in the chase, not the winning. I make excellent puns and I have a flight of ideas. After about a week, I'm trapped in a no-sleep cycle – I start to become irritable and anxious if I don't do something about it. I constantly hear voices telling me I'm shit and I go from ignoring them to believing them. I'm tired and angry, but I can't sleep despite masses of tablets. Then comes hospitalisation and three weeks of coming down.

After just such a cycle, I was discharged yet again. Freddie kept phoning me and I kept ignoring him. I put all his things in two rooms and shut the doors – everything I could then see was mine and mine alone. After some time, I agreed to sell the house and I put it on the market – Freddie didn't offer to help with it, but we did agree to split the money half and half. I started looking for another house.

I looked everywhere in the county and gradually decided I wanted to live in the west. The details of a cottage called 'Restawyle' came through, but I couldn't bear the name. However, when the details came through for the fourth time, I went to have a look. I was hypomanic at the time, and I bought it. I had a house cooling party in the old house and moved to Restawyle.

My psychiatrist at the time was a weird woman – a Freudian analyst as well as a doctor. Unknown to me, she also suffered from bipolar disorder; all I knew was that she was moody as hell – one week I was her favourite patient, and the next she hardly spoke. I asked to go on sodium valproate and an antidepressant and she agreed – both turned out to be useless. She accused me of stopping my medication when it didn't work; I felt cowed by her and her anger. She put me on Risperidone, a powerful antipsychotic, and Sertraline, an antidepressant – my libido disappeared and my weight ballooned. There was no discussion of choice of medications, and no talk about the side effects. I was admitted to hospital yet again, in a mixed state – all the bad bits of mania and depression combined to make me anxious, sleepless and depressed. I was also extremely agitated. This time, I was sent to a small seven-bedded unit in the local town, rather than the clinic.

What a difference a place makes. It was an old house with nice rooms and lounges and friendly staff who actually asked how I was feeling. I remember that I cried a lot, mostly out of relief that someone cared. When I couldn't sleep, someone was always there to make me a cup of tea or just have a chat. The worst time was 4am – the body is at its lowest ebb and everything seems to be a disaster. During the day, I was often approached to have a simple word or two and the staff were visible and present. There was a garden. There was occupational therapy and this time I was asked if I wanted to go; I declined, but many people found it marvellously helpful. Once again I made friends. When I was discharged, the staff rang most days to see how I was doing, and I was able to ring during the night if I was feeling low.

Over the next three years, I alternated between mania and depression and was regularly hospitalised in the small unit. I did, however, then manage to get and hold down a job as a nursing assistant in an acute psychiatric ward – like calling to like, I suppose. I was considered an asset as I had first-hand knowledge of what it was like to be mentally ill. However, after a few years, I was struck down with a massive depression and hospitalised yet again. This time I stayed for 11 months.

I was completely suicidal; the only thing I could think about was killing myself. I had stored up 1,100 tablets for just such a moment, but well-meaning friends handed them in, taking away my only route out. I was furious with them as I'd planned to go on overnight leave and take the lot. Thwarted, I had to stay in the unit. Kate, my manager, came to see me every day – I apologise to her as I don't remember half of her visits. Every morning, I dragged myself out of bed and tried to face another day; every evening, drugged to the eyeballs, I tried to sleep away my fear. Weeks ran into months. I had electroconvulsive therapy (ECT) – ten sessions of it – all it did was wipe my memory clean. I had headaches from it and it failed to improve my mood. I am not against ECT per se; I've seen it work wonders and save lives, bringing people suffering from catatonia back to normality. I've had, over the years, three lots of ECT – the first time worked and the second and third didn't.

People with mental health problems will tell you that one of the most difficult things to deal with is change. Not that we are stuck in the past – merely that change, particularly swift change, is hard to cope with. And the hardest thing to do is change psychiatrists or your community psychiatric nurse (CPN). Having to tell your story again and again is soul-destroying and counterproductive – you are baring your soul every time you repeat yourself. Often, the things that make you ill – trauma, family dysfunction – are the things you have to deal with on a regular basis and the retelling of them repeats the trauma. So it was with a certain amount of trepidation that I learned I had a new psychiatrist and a new CPN.

I was still in hospital and thoroughly institutionalised. My new psychiatrist came to see me – another woman – and I fully expected to be psychoanalysed and taken to pieces again. Instead, she turned out to be a woman the same age as me, with a charming attitude and a can-do approach. I was wary at first – my experiences had not been good before. However, there was something quite uncluttered and normal about her. We discussed my drugs and side effects, and decided to put me on Olanzapine and another antidepressant – Venlafaxine. I was discharged on these tablets and nervously went back home to try to pick up the pieces of my life.

Antipsychotics are powerful drugs, mostly with unpleasant side effects, and I had a terrible reaction to the Olanzapine. My face swelled up and split open in places, and my hair fell out in lumps. I stopped the drug, but had to wear a wig for a month while my hair grew back. My psychiatrist and I had another think and eventually, she decided to try me out on a new anti-psychotic called Aripiprazole, or Abilify. When someone tells you that something is 'weight neutral', you immediately put on the pounds, and I did just that. However, wonder of wonders, I began to feel better, more like the person I had once been before drugs. I was on more than the maximum dose and on the top whack of Venlafaxine, but for the first time for a long time I was myself – my personality had been restored. I was also prescribed Lorazepam and Temazepam for sleeping, and Mirtazapine as an extra sedation and antidepressant at night. Nothing is foolproof in psychiatry and the drugs didn't stop me being admitted from time to time, mainly for hypomania. I was prescribed Chlorpromazine as well as the Abilify for hypo-mania and during my last admission was taking huge quantities of sedation at nights – and I still couldn't sleep. However, these admissions were shorter than the ones I had been used to, and I came off the high more quickly than I had before.

## Concluding thoughts

I currently take Abilify, Venlafaxine, Mirtazapine and Temazepam, and various anti-inflammatorics for arthritis. My liver seems to cope, but I'm overweight and sedentary, and a heavy smoker. When I'm high, I take Chlorpromazine and Lorazepam in addition, and when I get depressed, I put the Mirtazapine up. It's a huge cocktail, but it works for me and I haven't been in hospital for a couple of years – I used to have three to four admissions a year.

I've tried to analyse what has been helpful in my improvement. Firstly, I've had the illness a long time, and have got used to it. I now recognise, with the help of friends and family, the triggers that initiate mania and depression. For example, when I start making bad puns or getting flights of ideas that no one can keep up with, I start taking Chlorpromazine. I also try to regulate my sleep – not sleeping or sleeping badly can trigger an episode of mania. I don't suffer so badly from depression nowadays, but at the first sign, I take more drugs.

You will have gathered from this that I consider my illness to be biochemical in origin. As I understand it, bipolar disorder has a 70 per cent concordance rate, meaning that there's a 70 per cent genetic influence – the remaining 30 per cent is environmental. I have no doubt that both my earlier and later experiences contributed to my 'becoming' bipolar, and that any kind of stress is a precipitating factor. So I try, at all costs, to avoid stresses. I give myself time in the mornings and evenings to just sit and think, to plan my day and to come to from the drugs. Because I believe in the biochemical model, I have faith in the drugs I take, although I am thinking of reducing them or trying to come off them to see what happens. I can always go back on them.

Secondly, I have discovered the principles and practices of recovery. Not clinical recovery, because I will never be clinically better, but making the most of life beyond the catastrophic effects of my diagnosis. By taking control of my life and doing what I need to do to keep well, I have gained a much deeper understanding of myself. I live the life I want to the full.

Is there room for talking therapies in my biochemical model? I believe there is. I spent a year with a clinical psychologist, who diagnosed me with PTSD because of my RAF service, and she was excellent. I'm not sure that she did anything about the bipolar disorder, but I shed a lot of the baggage I'd been carrying for years, which certainly helped in the long term.

Finally, and I think most importantly, I have come to terms with having a 'severe and enduring' mental illness. It was a shattering diagnosis at first, but on the other hand, it meant I could research and learn about the illness and I do firmly believe that knowledge is power. My first admission, while being an eye opener, also gave me access to others in the same boat. I learned how to deal with the illness and recognise my relapse signatures. I still hate the lows and adore the highs, but I can see the destructive elements in the highs, and I try to moderate my behaviour.

So there you have it – a short memoir of madness. I hope it has gone some way to telling you what it's like to be mentally ill and constantly at the mercy of clinicians – if you're one, read this with care. The greatest snub of all is that of a psychiatrist who doesn't listen. After all, we're all a little mad, aren't we?

# 2 Service-User Insights into Recovery in Personality Disorder

## By Heather Castillo

## Introduction

Over two hundred years ago, doctors began to speak of *mania without delirium* (Pinel, 1801), defining what would now be called personality disorder, characterised by unexplained outbursts of emotion and impulsive actions in the absence of impaired intellectual function or delusion. For many years, doctors have known about a group of people who have been considered unusually difficult to treat, recognising that a thin outward veneer of integration can conceal a chaotic personality structure, which becomes highly erratic under stress, resulting in impulsivity, unstable moods, thoughts and interpersonal relationships.

Freud suggested that *a thing which has not been understood inevitably reappears, like an unlaid ghost, it cannot rest until the mystery has been resolved and the spell broken* (1909, p 137). An imperative for a problematic and misunderstood condition might be to attempt to master it by categorising it diagnostically. So much depends on a diagnosis in the field of health. It holds the key to therapy and prognosis and is a matter of great significance to the individual on whom it is conferred. The causes of organic diseases include traumatic, infectious or toxic origins. Such causes are comparatively limited and less controversial than those of psychiatry. The causes of psychiatric conditions are less clearly understood and their origins are not so easily traced. However, in psychiatry, classification and categorisation are central concerns. During the nineteenth century, doctors worked with a few obvious categories such as melancholia, general paralysis of the insane and dementia, for the sake of their asylum statistics (Shorter, 1997). In 1918, the *Statistical Manual for the Use of Institutions for the Insane* was published. This first edition of the psychiatric 'bible' was an invention of American psychiatrists linked to requirements in the USA to provide a diagnosis for insurance purposes (Kutchins and Kirk, 1997). The relationship between medicine and drug developments also led to new disease concepts. The assumption has been that classifications of mental disorders are well defined. However, this particular system has, at times, obscured more than it has clarified. The American Psychiatric Association has recently failed to agree a new system for diagnosing personality disorders for the next issue of the American Diagnostic Manual, DSM-5 (Aldhous, 2012). Work on revisions of the European Diagnostic Manual are also underway with the World Health Organization's International Classification of Diseases, ICD 11, due to be published in 2015. Here a rating scale regarding severity of symptoms is being considered. However, the diagnosis of personality disorder continues to be characterised by confusion and lack of agreement, and where understanding has been required, fear has emerged. The concern of psychiatry has been the classification of surface manifestations which have failed fundamentally to capture the experiences of the sufferer.

## Prevalence and impact

Coid et al. (2006) estimate that 4 per cent of people in Great Britain have a personality disorder. The British Psychological Society suggests that a higher proportion of the population, 10 per cent, meets the criteria for a personality disorder diagnosis and that prevalence is much higher among psychiatric patients. They highlight some studies which suggest that in excess of 80 per cent of psychiatric outpatients and between 50 per cent and 78 per cent of adult prisoners meet the criteria (Alwin et al., 2006).

The National Institute for Health and Clinical Excellence issued guidelines for the treatment and management of borderline personality disorder (NICE, 2009a). The Guidelines represent suicide attempts as a defining feature of the diagnosis, with some studies suggesting that suicide rates can be as high as 10 per cent. The Department of Health (2009b) estimates that 5 per cent of the population have a personality disorder and that 47 per cent to 77 per cent of suicides will have the diagnosis. NICE also highlights the economic impact of personality disorder. Guidelines outline a significant financial cost to the health care system, social services and wider society, and estimate the annual cost to the NHS at approximately £61.2 million, 91 per cent of this accounted for by in-patient care. They also estimate that people with personality disorder cost primary care services alone an average of £3,000 per person per year.

## Service users questioning and developing services

Following is an account of a group of service users in north-east Essex with a personality disorder diagnosis, who became involved in a study that has begun to create a synthesis of human development and recovery theory, which is new and important for people with a personality disorder diagnosis.

In 1998, I embarked on an earlier study together with local service users in north-east Essex, where we formed a research group involving 50 people who had attracted the diagnosis. Our aim was to carry out research about personality disorder from service users' perspectives.

In a climate that emphasised issues of risk and danger, and where personality disorder was considered untreatable in many quarters, part of the purpose in carrying out our study was to engender some kind of compassion and understanding in relation to this diagnosis. The study highlighted the origins and traumatic causes of such conditions and described the inner world and sufferings of those who had attracted the diagnosis. It was eventually published as a book (Castillo, 2003) and by then we had linked with the national agenda. At this time the Department of Health began to talk about investment in community pilot projects for the support and treatment of people with personality disorder. Now our local group of service users began to explore, in earnest, what ingredients would comprise a service that could really meet their needs. This service was to become The Haven.

# The Haven: concept

The concept of The Haven began essentially as dissolution of earlier models and responses to care and treatment for personality disorder in our area. It sprang from a shared vision and creativity which, from the outset, aimed to be proactive and responsive to lessons and the need for change. This was not a service model imposed on an area but one coming out of the local user-involved research (Castillo, 2003; Ramon et al., 2001). The Department of Health, as a daring response to the disappointment of previous service models, gave us carte blanche and, if our proposals for a service were agreed upon, we would receive the funding to pursue a pilot to test and develop our ideas for the care and treatment of personality disorder.

Planned around the ideas and aspirations of local service users, The Haven was created with some distinctly new and different features. It espoused aspects of the therapeutic community model where members would come together to explore emotional and psychological issues and exercise their decision making and personal responsibility while taking advantage of peer accountability (Campling and Haigh, 1999). Although the original concept of the therapeutic community suggested a retreat, over time the ethos of such communities embraced different models, some created as therapeutic community day units where participants could attend the programme while retaining links to their home area. In the 1990s, crisis houses began to appear in different parts of the country, offering short respite at difficult times. Not specialising in personality disorder, they were represented as a kind of asylum in the community; an alternative to psychiatric hospital. Faulkner et al. (2002) championed the efficacy of the crisis house model, highlighting the user-led nature of such services and the emphasis on human interaction rather than drug treatments. Uniquely, The Haven was created as a blend of models combining a therapeutic community with a crisis house element. Therefore, participants could remain in their own geographic area, but also have the benefit of a short-stay residential component within the service.

The Haven aspires to be a sanctuary with a sense of home, a place of refuge and protection (Bloom, 1997). It is housed in an old rectory in Colchester and its décor is warm and inviting. The services offered include a therapy and group programme from Monday to Friday, 24-hour crisis phone and text lines and a Safe Centre where those in crisis may come for a few hours, at any time of the day or night, on any day of the week. There are also five bedrooms, which constitute the crisis house element, where people may find respite from outside pressures for one night or up to three weeks.

As a new service set up in 2004, The Haven began with the intention of meeting needs; but to what degree did it do so and to what extent has it been successful in effecting social inclusion for clients with a personality disorder diagnosis? Internationally, there was no agreed rationale of recovery for those diagnosed with personality disorder and few researchers had sought the views of service users regarding this (Stalker et al., 2005). Examination of the psychotherapeutic, social and material aspects of the process of recovery was needed, from the perspective of those with a diagnosis of personality disorder. This is what our study set out to do.

**Table 2.1** *The first 50 clients to complete one year at The Haven (2006)*

| Service area/ intervention | Annual average use over two years prior to Haven* | Annual average use over two years prior to Haven* | Percentage reduction in use of service/ intervention |
|---|---|---|---|
| Section 136 | 42.5 times | 18 times | –57.64% |
| Other sections | 11 times | 4 times | –63.63% |
| Psychiatric in-patient admissions | 55 times | 8 times | –85.45% |
| Use of day hospital | 32 clients | 14 clients | –56.25% |
| Use of Community MH Team | 36 clients | 14 clients | –61.11% |
| Use of NERIL (MH Helpline) | 1,264 times | 317 times | –75.92% |
| Use of Crisis Team | 187 times | 42 times | –77.54% |
| Criminal Justice MH Team | 0 | 0 | 0 |
| Assertive outreach | 0 | 0 | 0 |
| Trust Eating Disorder Service | 56 times | 14 times | –75.00% |
| Psychology/psychotherapy/ counselling | 30 clients | 21 clients | –30.00% |
| Annual use of GP | 611 times | 459 times | –24.87% |
| Annual use of A&E | 141 times | 77 times | –45.39% |
| General hospital admissions | 47 times | 37 times | –21.27% |
| Police/probation/prison | 12.5 times | 2 times | –84.00% |
| Children's Social Services | 14 clients | 6 clients | –57.14% |
| Debt agencies | 7 clients | 1 client | –85.71% |
| Housing/homelessness | 11 clients | 2 clients | –81.81% |
| Substance Misuse Voluntary Agency | 4 clients | 1 client | –75.00% |
| Eating Disorder Voluntary Agency | 5 clients | 1 client | –80.00% |
| Mind advocate | 39 clients | 11 clients | –71.79% |

* Column 2 represents a one-year average of two years' use of the wider service area prior to The Haven, eg 42.5 detentions under Section 136 mean 85 over a two-year period.

## Service and cost savings

By 2006, an analysis of use of the wider service area, for the first 50 Haven clients who had been with the project at least one year, showed a drop in all services measured (Table 2.1). Notably, psychiatric hospital in-patient admissions had dropped for the first 50 clients by 85 per cent. Although continuing to represent a burden for GPs and the A&E Department, use had still dropped by 25 per cent and 45 per cent respectively.

Calculating the reduction of the use of the wider service area against health and social care figures, in national tariff documents, showed that the project had saved £220,000 per annum, over and above the cost of The Haven, for the first 50 clients. We had by then registered 110 clients, and extrapolating savings to this number showed that in excess of £480,000 per annum could be saved. The cost per week, per client, for Haven services was around £100, compared to costs ranging from £223 to £1,250 per patient per week, for personality disorder day units or the hospital therapeutic community, in other parts of the country (Chiesa et al., 2002).

Showing that the service is continuing to produce similar reductions, The Haven once again carried out a more recent update of service and cost savings in 2012 (Table 2.2).

Reflecting on the initial service and cost savings calculated in 2006, it became clear at that time that The Haven had fulfilled its original promise to engage the client group in our area and to prove cost savings in the wider service area. However, in 2006, concerns began to be expressed about whether the project would create a new kind of dependency. Most of the 110 clients who had registered were still with us and, although many were no longer subject to hospital admission, questions were asked about whether they could move beyond the stability achieved at The Haven. These questions also had a bearing on capacity at the project and the need to continue to register new clients. Therefore, in response to these concerns and as a result of emerging findings of this study, The Haven developed a new way of working called Transitional Recovery and opened a Social Inclusion Unit at the service. This meant that, with a client group which had now grown to 160, costs were further reduced from what was £100 per client per week in 2006 to £78 per client per week in 2012. These developments are described later in relation to the research findings and recovery in personality disorder.

## What is recovery?

Nehls (2000) suggests that, although some advances have been made, psychological approaches developed in treating personality disorder are not consistent with the concept of recovery as a vision constructed by the client, and that a new vision of treatment, based on recovery, will require a fundamental shift in control from professionals to the person who is recovering. Therefore, it was important in this study to examine the underpinning values, in the field of mental health, in relation to the possibility of recovery, and to identify the important factors in recovery for those diagnosed with personality disorder. In their study of recovery in borderline personality disorder, Katsakou et al. (2012) also concluded that professionals needed to devise more individualised treatment targets and outcomes which would include priorities important to service users.

The word recovery has a range of meanings, suggesting that conceptual clarity is necessary. Slade et al (2008) identify two classes of meanings. First is the traditional concept of recovery as cure. This locates the concept within an illness framework. Second is the personal definition of recovery, which has emerged from service-user narratives. These accounts emphasise an understanding of recovery as something other than the absence of mental illness. Recovery requires hope and opportunity. It is about building a future and recovering or discovering social roles and relationships that give value to life. The essence of the personal can be destroyed within psychiatric services because the recovery context, as defined by service users, has rarely existed within it. Wallcraft (2005), Coleman (1999) and Deegan (1996), writing from the perspective of service-user activists, see recovery as a process rather than a goal. Therefore recovery might best be defined as 'the journey of recovery'. It is a unique journey, personal to the individual who has embarked on it.

**Table 2.2** *The last 33 clients to complete one year or more at The Haven (2012)*

| Service area/ intervention | Annual average use over two years prior to Haven* | Annual average use over two years prior to Haven* | Percentage reduction in use of service/ intervention |
|---|---|---|---|
| Section 136 | 20 times | 1 time | –95.00% |
| Other sections | 10 times | 1 time | –90.00% |
| Psychiatric in-patient admissions | 25 times | 4 times | –84.00% |
| Use of day hospital/partial hospitalisation | 22 clients | 2 clients | –90.90% |
| Use of Community MH Team | 18 clients | 9 clients | –50.00% |
| Use of NERIL (MH Helpline) | 405 times | 156 times | –61.48% |
| Use of Crisis Resolution Home Treatment | 42 times | 5 times | –77.54% |
| Criminal Justice MH Team | 2 times | 1 time | –50.00% |
| Assertive outreach | 0 | 0 | 0 |
| NEEDAS (Drug and Alcohol Team) | 17 times | 5 times | –70.58% |
| Trust Eating Disorder Service | 6 times | 0 | –100.00% |
| Psychology/counselling (not at Haven) | 21 clients | 5 clients | –76.19% |
| Annual use of GP | 443 times | 304 times | –31.37% |
| Annual use of A&E | 72 times | 34 times | –52.77% |
| General hospital admissions | 30 times | 14 times | –53.33% |
| Police/probation/prison | 10 times | 5 times | –50.00% |
| Children's Social Services | 11 clients | 8 clients | –27.27% |
| Debt agencies | 8 clients | 3 clients | –62.50% |
| Housing/homelessness | 8 clients | 1 client | –87.50% |
| Substance Misuse Voluntary Agency | 8 clients | 0 | –100.00% |
| Eating Disorder Voluntary Agency | 2 clients | 0 | –100.00% |
| Mind advocate | 5 times | 0 | –100.00% |

A 16-year study of a large sample with borderline personality disorder was carried out by Zanarini et al. (2012), who concluded that remission of symptoms is more common than full recovery. Turner et al. (2011) highlight the complexity of the recovery debate and how it has travelled a long way from its roots in the survivor movement. Here the emphasis for service users has become one of self-discovery rather than recovery. They consider that the notion of recovery is a concept hijacked by mainstream services in a way that is unrealistic because it fails to acknowledge the challenges of living with the ongoing legacy of trauma and the need to conceive of the journey as a process rather than a goal.

# Aim, approach and method

The study aimed to find out how those with a personality disorder diagnosis define recovery; what factors are important in the recovery process for those with personality disorder; and whether The Haven, as a project, contributes to this process, and if so how? The research approach was emancipatory, where the study of a problematic or oppressive reality is not carried out by experts but primarily by those experiencing the problem (Freire, 1970). Here, service users became researchers in the study, with control over the selection of issues to be researched, data collection, analysis and dissemination (Ramon, 2003). The study used a Participatory Action Research framework which enabled cycles of action and reflection (Reason and Bradbury, 2001). The core issue underpinning its action research nature was to bring about change in the direction chosen by participants.

The research group, with a membership of nine Haven clients and me as Chief Executive of The Haven, was a primary vehicle in this process, and methods employed for data collection included not only focus groups and individual interviews but background data used to inform and illustrate results, combining data streams representing a rich amount of information. The potential sample for the study included 166 clients registered at the service by the time data collection was complete in 2009, and any associated family members and carers. The 66 participants involved in the study were first identified by self-selection followed by a degree of purposive and theoretical sampling. Thematic analysis was the method used for data analysis. This was a way of identifying and analysing patterns within data rich in detail and searching for themes across the entire data set (Braun and Clarke, 2006).

# Findings: mapping the process of recovery

Findings from the groups and interviews in the research transcripts, together with all data collected during the study, were subject to the thematic analysis. An examination of emerging themes within and between transcripts and questions, and the interplay between themes, gave insight into what respondents considered to be the key steps in the journey of recovery for someone with a personality disorder diagnosis. Themes are presented diagrammatically in Figure 2.1 as a pyramid representing a hierarchy of progress. Each level of the pyramid is discussed in sequence, from the base upwards.

## A sense of safety and building trust

Basic trust is associated with secure attachment. Campling (1999) proposes that severe personality disorder is related to insecure and disorganised attachment, where an infant may freeze on separation and be unable to sustain organised patterns of behaviour. She suggests that such experiences yield a future generation of people with personality disorder. Therefore, in working with someone who has a personality disorder diagnosis, trust has to be created in a very tangible way. Our clients have come to The Haven robbed of central aspects of identity, memory and feelings, sometimes resulting in widely swinging emotions,

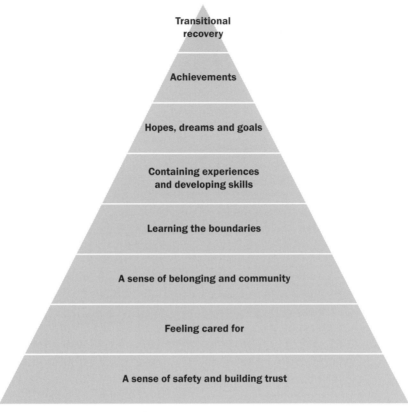

**Figure 2.1** The journey of recovery for personality disorder

chronic hyper-arousal, terror, rage, despair, hopelessness, guilt and shame. Thoughts can be incomprehensible and overwhelming and the need for physical and psychological *safety* may be palpable. The first lesson in our study was that participants were able to define the component parts of a *safe* place and how this related to an increased ability to protect them from the harm they might do to themselves.

*You can feel it when you walk in that door, you can feel that safety. It's a safe place. It helps you to be safe.*

The 24-hour nature of the service emerged as a crucial factor that could be internalised, even if one were not physically present at the service. It existed and it could be conceived of.

*It makes me feel very safe and secure to know it's always there. To me it's safe 24/7, it's a haven. That's what it really means.*

Feeling *safe* was related to learning to *trust*, and *trusting* meant that it was *safe* to show one's pain and talk about difficult emotions and experiences.

*The Haven has taught me to trust again. I don't have to hide behind a smile anymore. I can come in and cry. The important thing is that coming here makes you safe enough to change.*

The perspectives of family members and carers also emphasised the importance of *safety* and *trust*.

*It's helped my daughter. It's somewhere safe for her to come, somewhere without any bad memories.*

*I knew that I could probably go to sleep and that he was going to be okay and safe.*

## Feeling cared for and creating a culture of warmth

The study also revealed the importance of *feeling cared for* and participants described a component of *care* in terms of first contact and acceptance; acceptance no matter what. They knew about the affection that can exude from a smile and the warmth that can be felt from a hug or simply being made a cup of tea.

*They always look pleased to see you coming through the door.*

*It's been excellent, a kind ear, a cuddle, cup of tea, respite when I need it.*

*I don't do hugs, but I do now.*

*One of the most important things is the humanness of The Haven staff and other clients, there's a kind of warmth and compassion.*

They spoke of being listened to and treated as if they were important, and the touch of pampering and complementary therapies, and of interconnectedness and humanness.

*As a family member, I have to say that I just think The Haven is just a calm, happy, just a caring place. To be honest I found the hospital a hustle and bustle, and just total chaos. I have to say, I might have a tear in a minute, I have to say that The Haven is just, it's a wonderful place really.*

## A sense of belonging and community

Secure early attachment gives an infant a consistent experience of existence, which is internalised and provides a greater ability to face later life experiences (Bowlby, 1969). When emotional development has not provided secure attachment for a child, the first step in treatment is to re-create a secure attachment (Haigh, 1999). Our families are supposed to provide a place in which we feel safe and learn to trust, where we feel cared for and where we develop and learn to be spontaneous and creative. Clients at The Haven had often found this not to be the case and they came to us instead with a legacy of abuse, neglect and abandonment or a lack of emotional responsiveness. The next finding to emerge from the study was about the *sense of belonging* that the *community* generated. This was experienced as a reciprocal relationship where common ground was identified: you are broken like me.

*I isolate and can't mix with people, but I can see people in The Haven, you are the same as me.*

The community was seen as a place where decision making was shared, bonds of friendship were made, where there was fun, where shared realities were negotiated, where there were experiences of uniting in a common purpose.

*It's all about human contact. I think a lot of people here realise what it's like to be lonely, we all know what it's like so we all make an extra effort to be friendly.*

*It's about social interaction, it's about learning; I haven't laughed as much in years at the last Friendship Group I came to here.*

*A Sunday roast because it was my birthday on Sunday made me feel really good and happy. It was one of the best birthdays I ever had.*

*I don't think I've ever been any place where there's been people that have got mental health problems and there's been such a good strength of community.*

Winnicott (1965) suggests that a facilitating environment acts as a container where the gap between the container and the contained starts to open up and the individual can begin to explore autonomous identity:

*What I have found is that other people can like me. I am less serious. I have rediscovered my sense of humour and I have rediscovered my ability to make other people laugh. I rediscovered the fact I am good.*

Clearly voicing their newly developed sense of healthy attachment, participants began to regain, or gain for the first time, a sense of home and family:

*The Haven community, it's like having a family all under one roof.*

*It's the family I never had.*

## Learning the boundaries – love is not enough

Norton and Bloom (2004) emphasise the importance of ensuring that the culture of a therapeutic community is not eroded by difficult behaviours, suggesting that tolerance should have its limits.

For someone who has experienced early attachment difficulties, healthy attachment may be longed-for but also feared. The concept of attachment becomes idealised as an individual yearns for unconditional love. Haigh (1999) describes this process as a journey through the developmental phases of attachment in a therapeutic community. As an individual struggles with sadness, fear, pain and anger, savage mechanisms can sometimes come into play. The ability to be honest may be blocked by feelings of shame and humiliation. Here, denial, lying, projection and splitting begin to be demonstrated. Someone may display unconscious impulses to envy, spoil, steal or destroy what is good:

*Community isn't all about harmony and everyone loving each other and that sort of thing, because life is full of challenges and difficulties and rubbish and so inevitably that comes up within the community.*

Family-member participants set the scene with some of their observations about behaviours:

*She was stoned on Wednesday before we turned up. I'm also aware she's sold drugs, I caught her out at Christmas time drug dealing to children.*

*She tried to kill herself desperately under the care of the hospital and previous regimes.*

Living too long with untenable emotions and in a state of chronic hyper-arousal, people with a personality disorder diagnosis frequently adopt dysfunctional behaviours to numb unbearable feelings and to swiftly bring their mood down to a manageable level. Hurting the body can create temporary calm because of endorphin release. Such behaviours include self-harm and substance misuse. This is how people have coped and, for many, it has become a deeply ingrained coping strategy. Although containment is achieved through holding someone's distress, that distress may trigger unacceptable behaviours. Bettleheim (1950) suggests that *love is not enough* and that the damaging expression of pain needs containing measures. All this represents boundary setting and the social and moral limits that need to be present to create a safe community. Whatever rules and boundaries are negotiated in an organisation, the vital issue is that the boundaries are clear to everyone and that they are agreed, known and understood:

*I feel safe at The Haven because I know you're not allowed to get away with stuff, are you, like cutting while you're here, which means I don't try. It's about being protected from the negative parts of yourself.*

*I do get a real sense of freedom here, but I know that if anybody doesn't toe the line then they will be pulled up and they'll be at a meeting about it, yeah.*

The process of democratically setting and applying boundaries is cited by Hinshelwood (1996) as a learning process which addresses respect, not just for the reality of self, but also for the reality of others, enabling an individual to ultimately find the self as the seat of agency and to begin to take control and responsibility.

*We understand why people want to come in, for example, under the influence. We understand the struggle and the difficulties but we have, on those occasions, stood together as a community and we have said 'this is unacceptable'. People aren't abandoned at such difficult times, but the learning is about what is acceptable and unacceptable to the community and what is healthy and positive for the individual. We all take responsibility for The Haven Community but, at the end of the day, the message is that each person has to take responsibility for themselves, with our support.*

Evidencing the efficacy of *learning the boundaries*, over two-thirds of participants in the study reported a reduction in their use of negative coping strategies and over one-third described a dramatic reduction:

*Before I came to The Haven I used to overdose on a reasonably regular basis, I used to cut myself when anything went wrong, and I used to stop eating when anything went wrong. Basically, it was a whole host of maladaptive coping mechanisms and since coming to The Haven I have sort of redressed these. A lot of the reason has been because of the ruling about coming in when you have cut, or coming in when you have drunk alcohol. So you have to respect the values of the place. I now don't cut. To me to cut would be such a backward step I don't even want to go there.*

These first four findings concerned developing healthy attachment in terms of safety and trust, feeling cared for, a sense of belonging and learning acceptable boundaries, limits and behaviour. The next finding revealed that only when these were in place, and sufficiently consolidated, did respondents begin to learn to *contain* their past experiences and build necessary *skills* to progress. Meaningful therapy cannot take place, no matter how desperately it is needed, if trust does not exist and if behaviour is chaotic, risky and destructive. Overleaf, in Figure 2.2, the pyramid of progress can be viewed in an alternative way, where the first four layers represent the foundation stones, or pillars, on which progress in the higher levels is built.

*Before I came to The Haven nearly every other day I was tying things around my neck, overdosing, cutting myself and since coming to The Haven I don't tie anything round my neck, I've had maybe one overdose and I've learned to talk and, when things get really bad, to phone and ask for support instead of acting on impulsive thoughts.*

**Figure 2.2** The Haven hierarchy of progress

The finding that second-stage progress for clients relies on the 'pillars' of the first four lessons provides answers to why someone with a personality disorder diagnosis may be progressing, while someone else may not.

## Containing experiences and developing skills

Re-creating healthy attachment opens the door to therapeutic work. Healing is about integrating experience by making sense of what has happened. Prior to this stage, reality has often proved to be unbearable, and making sense out of traumatic experiences and child abuse is a difficult thing to do. This finding marked the long process of beginning to reframe traumatic experience.

*I had ten years of psychotherapy and I still managed to avoid the Issues. With the counselling I think it's the fact that it's here. It makes me feel safer which makes me take more risks than I ever have.*

*I'm clean and have stayed clean. I could have gone back to using without even knowing it was wrong, which I have done in the past, whilst I've been psychotic still. Kind of like instead of popping a pill, I come here. Stopping drugs, feeling the emotion and learning from it.*

Participants also began to express a new ability to mentalise: to separate out from their mental processes and reflect on them (Bateman and Fonagy, 2004).

*I think my new skills have fundamentally been to be able to stop and question the reality of the situation and the most logical conclusions, and the most logical assumptions, and to think the whole situation through, rather than jump into the first panic-stricken thought that comes into my head and act on it. It's the actual stopping and analysing the situation for what it really is, not what emotionally it's built itself up to be.*

# Hopes, dreams and goals and their relationship to recovery

Although dealing with symptoms and developing skills had an important place in the journey, they were not an underpinning principle in the user-defined concept of recovery. Waiting until all symptoms have subsided before trying to discover and use one's abilities could take a very long time and hope for a cure can overtake other ambitions.

*We spend too much time looking for a cure when there is none, we can only learn to live alongside our illnesses by re-thinking the way we think, to re-train the way we go about our daily lives and to learn to use our past experiences to guide us to where we want to be in life rather than carrying on the way we do.*

A focus on a deficit in skills can create a sense of hopelessness, a feeling easily triggered in the face of past trauma. Deegan (1990) characterises this 'giving-up', indifference and apathy as a way of surviving and protecting the last vestiges of the wounded self.

*Things that have happened to me when I was in care and on the streets ... the world I was in before was so black, and that was hard, I was petrified of becoming well and then failing every time, failing myself again, I just couldn't take that anymore.*

A sense of *hope* and realistic, attainable *dreams and goals* emerged as the next finding. *Hope* is a mysterious thing in that it can transcend life's catastrophes. Here some participants said they had begun to conceive of *dreams and goals* for the first time. Others began to link *hope* to a concept of the future and a range of specific *dreams and goals* began to be envisaged by participants.

*Before The Haven I wanted to die. Now I want to live.*

*I want to get on a bus and breathe at night without panic.*

*I look to the future more than I ever did. It exists now. My vision has changed. I didn't even think about the future before I came here. It was as much as I could do to survive today. I hated the thought of tomorrow. I never wanted it to come. I feel I am learning a lot and I would like to put that to some use.*

*My goal is to get through college and do my degree.*

# Achievements, identity and roles

What respondents felt they had accomplished emerged as a finding about *achievements*. This included both internal and external *achievements*. This interplay between the development of personal qualities, such as confidence and self-esteem, and their external expression, characterised their responses. Beginning from what was usually a high degree of self-loathing, during the course of the study 75 per cent of client participants answering a question about their internal sense of self reported positively regarding disliking oneself less. The majority who answered positively had been attending The Haven for two to three years, suggesting that building self-esteem, even in a hope-inspiring environment, takes time.

*I think I used to dislike myself a lot. I don't actually dislike myself now, although I dislike my behaviour at times, which is a massive difference and I'm actually able to go out and buy new clothes.*

*Although there are still good days and bad days, if you learn to love yourself you can begin to help others.*

Participants spoke of external *achievements* in terms of homemaking, parenting, leisure activities, education, voluntary work and employment, and how these *achievements* had contributed to growing confidence, gaining a sense of purpose and being able to separate out from the identity of their diagnosis.

*The change is due to actually learning who I am, I've been something else before now.*

*Just mundane things like going to the bank, I can actually speak to people behind the counter without just standing there and grunting at them.*

*I think how far I have come. When I think of that, I think no, I have done really well, and I know now, it's not an excuse, things that happened to me while I was in care and on the street, it wasn't my fault.*

*One of the biggest new skills I'm learning is how to be a Mum, learning to love you could say.*

*Before I came to The Haven I was locked up in a secure unit. I used to wake up every day wanting to die, trying to find a way to actually harm myself, to actually end it all, and now I'm actually going to college.*

*I'm actually working now and earning a reasonable amount of money. Working gives me a sense of purpose. It's very easy to slide into the diagnosis and not try to do anything. Although it has been difficult, so difficult, my self-esteem and confidence have risen massively.*

Employment may be a goal highly valued by both professionals and service users. However, lessons of The Haven have shown that a range of leisure and vocational pursuits are needed as building blocks to employment and that, even then, the proportion of Haven clients in paid employment, although much higher than 3.4 per cent, the national average for those with a personality disorder diagnosis, is as yet only 15 per cent.

## Transitional recovery and how to maintain healthy attachment

Liberman and Kopelowicz (2005) make a distinction between *recovery* and *recovering*, and show that it is not easy to separate the process from the outcome. Davidson (2003), within his definition of recovery, makes a distinction between living well with the illness and living beyond the illness. This concept suggests that the journey of *recovery* requires that the person does something rather than having something done to him or her by others.

Such constructs are consistent with the last finding in this study. *Transitional recovery* emerged as both a concept and a vehicle. It embraces all other findings, in that clients can continue their journey of *recovery* by defining and pursuing their unique goals and dreams, while still having a choice about whether to remain registered at The Haven or not. Participants feared losing their base and sense of home if they *recovered*. Many of the respondents had not developed a safe base in life and had no family or wider network of support to turn to if necessary. Some had achieved this at The Haven for the first time in their lives.

*When I think of recovery I get very frightened because I think recovery is like being on the top of a mountain and if I've recovered it means that I won't need The Haven anymore, and I cannot imagine having no more contact with The Haven.*

*One of my first questions when I very first came here, I said, is this a conveyor belt to chuck us in and chuck us out, get us well, I said, or is this a firm base that stays here forever? Just hold my hand on my bad days.*

*I hope that's not too much to ask.*

Because the word *recovery* could potentially become synonymous with the idea of loss, and the pursuit of *recovery* could lead to withdrawal of crucial support, it became vital to define what came next in a way that was going to work. As a result, the concept of *transitional recovery* was born, meaning that progress would be defined as a journey of small steps and that progression would not be penalised by discharge but rather rewarded by continued support, resulting in less use of the service over time but a choice about whether to remain part of it.

*I don't think we should clip our wings, we just need a nest to come back to.*

*If you feel well rooted then, like a tree, you can kind of branch out and blossom.*

The *vehicle* for implementing *transitional recovery* became the Social Inclusion Unit at the service, where clients are able to work specifically on personal development skills related to their aspirations and achievements outside of The Haven. Allowing an increase in numbers at the service meant that participants who had embraced the concept and structures of transitional recovery began to use the service less, while remaining registered at The Haven. Control over this decision rests crucially with the individual.

## The uniqueness of a service-user-informed model

The Haven has emerged as a unique model where therapeutic community principles have been combined with those of a crisis house. The 24/7 nature of the service has been cited by respondents as a vitally important dimension. The entire structure of the service at The Haven had been suggested and refined by its users. Their unique knowledge about what would best support them and help them to progress has shown that crisis support, therapy services and social inclusion development can all co-exist in a very effective way, as a continuum of support under one roof. The type of service model and the lessons on the journey of recovery show that it is possible to work effectively with a relatively large number of people with personality disorder, well in excess of a hundred at one time, many of whom had not made progress in other service settings, resulting in significant financial savings to the health, social care and the criminal justice system.

As an alternative to the historically sequential path of rehabilitation and proposed recovery, this study offers a new, socially inclusive way of working with people who have a personality disorder diagnosis, in which they may choose to retain a haven while continuing to develop and progress on their chosen path in the wider world.

## Conclusion

This study concerns an organisation that arose in a relatively enlightened pocket of time. It is an organisation that required a redefinition of leadership to *servant leaders*, where leadership is intrinsically collective (Kofman and Senge, 2001). This requires a value system that embraces leadership as a decision to serve and, at The Haven, has involved eight years of power sharing with its service users. Servant leaders choose to serve one another and a higher purpose. Kofman and Senge (2001) also propose that organisational learning is engendered by groups who espouse capabilities beyond the traditional: empathy, compassion, even love, they would say; practices that generate conversation, dialogue and collaborative action, and which have the capacity to see work as a system which is a flow of life. The Haven as an organisation has attempted to espouse such principles and, until now, has remained a living, learning and changing community.

A key part of this learning has concerned the need to reinforce and surround the organisation with robust structures for reflection. Hinshelwood has written at length, here in this book and elsewhere (Norton and Hinshelwood, 1996), about the potentially destructive impact on staff of working with severe personality disorder. This, of course, has an equal and opposite detrimental effect on the service users they are attempting to care for. The Department of Health (2007) has developed far-reaching programmes, such as the KUF, the Personality Disorder Knowledge and Understanding Training Framework (www.personalitydisorder.org. uk/training/kuf/), to aid the national workforce in understanding and best helping those with this diagnosis. Any staff team wishing to survive working with a client group who wrestle with unconscious impulses and employ savage mechanisms to cope, and who struggle with the ability to mentalise, must be able to create a team space for its clients in which to reflect, until they have developed the capacity to do so for themselves. This requires team openness, cohesiveness, trust, and a developed reflective capacity. At The Haven we call this triangulation or creation of the third space (Keval, 2003).

Scanlon and Adlam (2012) have opened an important dialogue concerning challenges to the therapeutic milieu and they examine many facets of the difficulties surrounding the care of those considered to have disordered personalities. In addition to their discourse regarding the internal pitfalls and challenges to services who work with severe personality disorder, they also reflect on the demise of some established organisations such as the Henderson Hospital, suggesting this was due to an oversimplification of the notion of the psychological complexities of personality disorder on the part of commissioners (Wrench, 2012). There is no doubt that this research study concerning The Haven shows that long-term work and long-term investment are vital. Something good and workable has been created. It emerged and grew in an organic way, informed by service users and responsive to organisational change. But it now exists in a difficult social and economic climate and is subject to the realm of necessity which is monetary, involving austerity measures and welfare reforms, which may leave little time and resources to acknowledge the psychological complexities of this diagnosis and the nature and length of the work needed to effectively respond to it.

Concerns currently exist regarding the future of health care and fears that recent legislation will open the door to turning health care into a market, without the proof that it is suitable for market mechanisms. The cost of health and social care may be considered unsustainable but this does not necessarily mean that a business model with a competitive ethos is going to provide a successful solution. As all sectors leap to respond to the next competitive tender, our greatest hope for the maintenance and proliferation of successful services in the future lies with the voice of service users. In relation to the dialogue with policy makers and commissioners, it is service users who are best able, with our support, to powerfully define themselves and their needs.

# 3 Exploring Shared Decision Making for Psychiatric Medication Management

## By Emma Kaminskiy, Shula Ramon and Nicola Morant

## Introduction

This chapter draws on two concurrent research projects[1] to explore how shared decision making is conceptualised by both practitioners and service users for psychiatric medication management. Selected similarities and differences in key themes between the stakeholder groups of psychiatrists, care co-ordinators and service users will highlight some of the crucial barriers, as well as some of the potential facilitating factors, to achieving a truly shared decision-making process that currently exist in UK mental health services. Shared decision making (SDM) promises to offer opportunities for recovery-oriented practice in mental health medication management, acknowledging the different forms of expertise needed in decision making and making explicit the ideal of involvement of both service users and practitioners in decision making. It is hoped that shedding light on the experiences and perceptions of the barriers and facilitators to SDM voiced by service users and practitioners will encourage reflection and change towards a more equal 'meeting of experts'.

There is a broad acceptance that there is an over-reliance on psychiatric medication in mental health treatment programmes in the UK (Healy, 2009). Most people's contact with psychiatric services revolves around medication-related discussions (Moncrieff, 2009). Yet there is a growing body of evidence which shows that the efficacy and helpfulness of antipsychotic medication, in particular, has previously been overestimated (Morrison et al., 2012). This, in conjunction with growing concerns over polypharmacy and the enduring and life-impeding side effects associated with many medications on offer, suggests that increased choice, involvement and open dialogue are essential to the psychiatric encounter.

The concept of SDM sits within the larger move towards recovery-based practice in mental health (Schauer et al., 2007), which, along with 'patient-centred care' is now considered to be core components of the UK mental health system (Department of Health, 2009b;

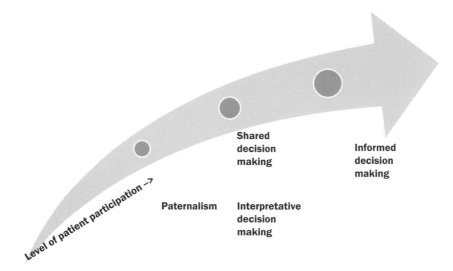

Shared
decision
making

Informed
decision
making

Paternalism

Interpretative
decision
making

*Level of patient participation* ⇢

**Figure 3.1** Shared decision making on the spectrum of service-user participation

National Institute for Mental Health in England, 2005). SDM for medication-related decisions, then, is one tool in a larger system or approach which focuses on giving the mental health service-user choice, freedom and partnership with practitioners in their individualised treatment plan (Davidson et al., 2010).

To date, very little research has been undertaken in mental health that explores service-user involvement in decision making and SDM relating to psychiatric medication. The studies that have been conducted show that mental health service users are keen to participate in decision making and desire greater involvement (Hamann et al., 2006; Loh et al., 2007). Practitioners also express a cautious willingness towards SDM (Patel et al., 2008). Positive impacts of SDM have been shown in terms of improved treatment adherence, satisfaction, knowledge, and involvement in decision making, reduced depressive symptoms and a trend towards reduced hospitalisation (Hamann et al., 2006).

In terms of levels of service-user involvement and responsibility in decision making, SDM has been proposed to occupy the middle ground between paternalism and informed choice (Figure 3.1). There is a considerable overlap between SDM and constructs with similar connotations, such as concordance, evidence-based patient choice, enhanced autonomy and mutual participation (Makoul and Clayman, 2009; Wirtz et al., 2006), and these concepts have been proposed to sit within the wider shared decision-making model (Coulter and Collins, 2011).

Charles et al. (1997, 1999) provide a useful and widely cited definition of SDM. Here, SDM includes four elements: (1) involving both practitioner and patient, (2) both parties sharing information, (3) both expressing treatment preferences, and (4) a consensus and agreement on treatment decision being reached. Expanding on this, Montori et al. (2006) argued that SDM may be carried out differently in chronic care conditions, where decisions may be delayed, or modified from visit to visit, without the delays leading to harm. Central to these broader conceptualisations of SDM is the importance of the relationship between the provider and patient. Through information exchange and sharing of preferences, the parties come to know each other, trust is formed and service users are treated as individuals with expertise.

This chapter will explore how service-user involvement and SDM is conceptualised in the context of medication management in community mental health services in the UK today, highlighting similarities and differences between care co-ordinators', psychiatrists' and service users' perspectives. First, a more detailed picture of the context in which medication management in the UK mental health system takes place will be presented.

# The landscape of psychiatric medication management in the UK

SDM as a strategy in the UK health system came first to primary care in the 1990s as an import from the United States. Clinicians have been asked to adopt it as a clinical practice principle. Its introduction was justified in terms of enhancing collaboration between patients and clinicians, with the aim of facilitating commitment to the relevant treatment decisions by both stakeholders. Much of the research conducted in primary care focused on observing the degree of SDM in doctor–patient consultations, and developing professional competencies for SDM (Edwards and Elwyn, 2009). In many of these studies, patients' views about their own experience, or about SDM were not elicited, and no training was provided to patients to help them participate in SDM.

SDM in the realm of mental health also arrived from the USA in the 2000s, but was developed mainly by service-user activists who also have clinical qualifications. It has evolved as an integral component of the recovery approach, with emphasis given to enhancing being in control of one's life. Being in control and having ambitions, as well as making one's own choices, are key elements in the recovery journey which is aimed at living well with the illness and beyond it (Anthony, 1993; Davidson, 2003). This new meaning of recovery implies the ability to be in recovery even if one continues to have symptoms of mental illness and crisis. It is predicated on the belief that people experiencing mental ill health have strengths as well as weaknesses, and that enhancing their potential strength is much more important than focusing on their deficit (Rapp and Goscha, 2012). This belief relates closely to the social model of disability developed by activists with physical disabilities in the 1980s in both the USA and the UK (Oliver, 1996).

The US emphasis has been on service users learning how to contribute to the process of SDM in the context of psychiatric medication management. This involves them using their experience of taking psychiatric medication as relevant information to be shared with their clinician, learning to be positively assertive in their contact with service providers, and treating psychiatric medication as one possible intervention among several which relate to personal medicine and well-being (Oades et al., 2011). The concept of 'personal medicine' introduced in the mid 2000s by Patricia Deegan (2005) remains important because it puts the service user at the centre of the recovery journey, and treats medication as one well-being tool among others. This has enabled the move to treating SDM itself as part of an overall well-being strategy within the recovery journey. Personal medicine strategies include a variety of everyday ways of coping with stress, derived largely from experiential knowledge.

The concept of personal medicine makes good sense to most service users, but not necessarily to clinicians, especially those who continue to view medication as the most important intervention, or the only one with sufficient scientific evidence of effectiveness. The fact that this evidence highlights the adverse effects of such medication, often belittled by naming them 'side effects', is known to both service users and providers in the USA and the UK (Whittaker, 2010). Thus it is likely that the dominance of the medical model in psychiatry is one key barrier to the acceptance of SDM between service users and clinicians regarding medication.

Experiential knowledge of medication and of other well-being strategies is highly valued within this relatively new approach to SDM. In fact, all types of SDM are predicated on the assumption that each partner to the process of SDM has unique knowledge they can contribute to the process and the decisions that follow. The concept of Expert in Experience, coined by UK service-user activists in the National Institute of Mental Health England (NIMHE) in the mid 2000s (Wallcraft, 2005), encapsulates the view that mental health service users have relevant knowledge pertaining to their experience of mental ill health and of the mental health service system, which complements the knowledge professionals bring. SDM has been justified in the USA as an effective strategy to enhance collaboration between people who use mental health services and their clinicians, as an ethical practice, and as a right of any citizen to have a say in major decisions related to their lives (Schauer et al., 2007).

The UK, too, has adopted the new meaning of recovery as one of its key policies in mental health (Department of Health, 2001), alongside the accepted bio-psychosocial model of mental illness. Yet the more traditional medical-model approach in which mental illness is perceived as a disease with bio-genetic aetiology, and where medication is treated as the most important intervention, continues to be a dominant feature of UK practice. This contradiction perhaps explains part of the identified paucity in the implementation of the recovery approach (Boardman and Shepherd, 2012; Ramon, 2011). The difficulty of changing professional and organisational cultures has led to current attempts to demonstrate how it can be done more constructively (see the Im-Roc project, Shepherd and Perkins, 2012).

Within the recovery approach there is a focus on personal recovery as against clinical recovery (Slade, 2009) and a growing awareness that without a reasonable degree of social inclusion (Secker, 2010), and reduction in both external and internalised stigma (Thornicroft, 2006), it is not possible to achieve recovery. While not objecting to psychiatric medication as one possible intervention within a range, recovery protagonists and researchers coming from a social-science perspective are concerned with the frequent and lasting negative effects of such medication (Pilgrim et al., 2011; Whittaker, 2010) and are searching for a much wider range of intervention options.

Alternatives to medication include the hearing voices network (Romme et al., 2009), in which service users act as peer supporters by sharing experiences of hearing voices and effective coping strategies for the negative effects of such voices. More emphasis on self-help, dialogical work (Seikkula et al., 2011), the Soteria therapeutic communities (Calton et al., 2008), psychotherapeutic interventions and social inclusion strategies which encourage service users to take up education, vocational training and employment also constitute part of this list of interventions. The introduction of peer support workers, who work alongside professionals mainly in a befriending capacity, to a growing number of mental health trusts in the UK symbolises this change in focus and in the credibility given to the user's experience and abilities (Repper and Carter, 2011).

The co-existence of biomedical and recovery-oriented approaches is problematic in that while the majority of service managers and practitioners would claim to adhere to recovery principles, their everyday practice tells a rather different story. This is one of inherent pessimism towards the likelihood of real improvement in the service users' quality of life and pursuit of wishes and ambitions, together with an ongoing focus on risk avoidance, leading to a preference for compliance with medication without users having a say in the decision-making process. In parallel, we have pockets of exemplary recovery-oriented practice, of people whose lives have indeed changed for the better despite the prevailing pessimism around them (Castillo, 2010; Coleman, 1999; Repper and Perkins, 2003).

More recently, SDM has been mentioned as part of the focus on choice for all people using mental health services and interventions provided by statutory services (Department of Health, 2008, 2011; NICE, 2009b). This emphasis relates on the one hand to the current government agenda aimed at introducing private service providers to the UK health system, where the choice will be between more than one service provider. On the other hand it relates to the growing recognition by policy makers that the effectiveness of clinical and non-clinical interventions is very limited if the patient does not become an active agent in promoting their own health, be it physical or mental. At present, the governmental documentation does not contain guidelines as to the implementation of SDM in everyday health- and social-care practice.

The use and misuse of psychiatric medication in the UK provides a good example of the limitations of the current system in encouraging good collaborative working relationships or SDM between clinicians and service users. Existing evidence suggests that polypharmacy is frequent, and that psychiatric medication prescriptions are not reviewed often enough to ensure effective prescribing in terms of choice of medication, dosage, duration of use, reduction of side effects and use of alternatives to medication. Furthermore, 50 per cent of service users are reported to stop using medication without notifying their clinicians (Nose et al., 2003), a finding illustrating insufficient collaboration and lack of SDM within the mental health system.

There are several UK and non-UK studies on the process of making decisions about and using different types of psychiatric medication by service users (Day et al., 2005; Malpass et al., 2009). Contrary to the assumption heard often from clinicians, service users rarely rush to an impulsive decision to discontinue medication. Instead, the decision may be made within a process of calculating the benefits and adverse effects that taking such medication entails. This process might be better conceptualised as meaning-making or decision making within a *medication career* or a *moral career* (Malpass et al., 2009). Within SDM it is of central importance to understand how service users reach their decisions, and to accept that stopping medication may represent a positive self-management choice if taken as a thought-through decision.

Approaches to risk within the mental health system are central to the possibility of having an SDM policy and practice. Presently, most UK mental health providers focus on risk avoidance interventions, in which the reliance on medication is paramount. However, this approach contradicts common sense and recovery-oriented thinking and practice in which it is necessary to take calculated risks if the person is to begin and remain on the recovery journey (Ramon and Williams, 2005).

At present, it is left to individual psychiatrists to decide if they wish to focus on improving their working relationships with their patients in the context of psychiatric medication management and use SDM in this context. The Royal College of Psychiatrists has recently developed an online training module for its members on this issue (June 2012), which can be accessed only by members of the college. Otherwise, there are no authorised training schemes for SDM or Trusts with a working strategy for how to encourage this in everyday practice.

It can be argued that current training in communication skills for psychiatrists may facilitate SDM, as may training service users to communicate with providers. However, additional communication training needs to be specifically focused on SDM in the sensitive context of medication to achieve this objective.

In summary, while pockets of exemplary recovery-oriented practice and SDM exist in the UK, many organisational and cultural barriers remain. The remainder of this chapter will present findings from the two studies, further shedding light on both the barriers and facilitators of SDM in the UK, by exploring similarities and differences between psychiatrists', care co-ordinators' and service users' perspectives on this issue.

# Background to the research

Two research projects are being conducted within Cambridgeshire and Peterborough NHS Foundation Trust (CPFT), by Anglia Ruskin University. Project A (2010–13), a PhD study conducted by Emma Kaminskiy, is concerned with how mental health service users are involved in decisions about their psychiatric medication, exploring both current practice and views of collaborative models of decision making. This study took place in the Intake and Treatment care pathway that provides community-based services for adults with moderate to severe mental health problems. Project B (2011–14), the 'ShIMME' project (Shared Involvement in Psychiatric Medication Management and Education), is a three-year independent research project funded by the National Institute for Health Research.

The project is led by Professor Shula Ramon from Anglia Ruskin University, with Dr Nicola Morant as the qualitative adviser to the project. It is based in the Rehabilitation and Recovery Service of CPFT, which provides longer-term community-based support and interventions for adults with mental health problems. ShIMME aims to develop, deliver and evaluate a training intervention for practitioners and service users focused on the process of shared decision making in psychiatric medication management (see www.shimme.arcusglobal.com for further details).

Both studies have included in-depth explorations of how different stakeholder groups (psychiatrists, care co-ordinators and service users) value and conceptualise service-user involvement in decisions about psychiatric medication.

Uniquely, this chapter presents findings from two research projects that have taken place con-currently in the same mental health trust but in different community-based teams, and in the same university, exploring how shared decision making is perceived, experienced and valued by key stakeholder groups. Very little previous research on this topic has explored both practi-tioner and service-user perspectives alongside each other, and none of it in the UK.

# Data

The data we draw on in this chapter consist of the following. For Project A: 30 individual inter-views conducted with psychiatrists ($n = 7$), community psychiatric nurses (CPNs; $n = 8$) and service users ($n = 15$). These interviews covered the following topics: general understanding of how decisions are made about psychiatric medication and different stakeholder groups' roles in the decision-making process; how service users should be involved in decisions, including barriers and facilitators; and an in-depth exploration of critical incidents (both posi-tive and negative) where decisions about psychiatric medication were made. For Project B: eight focus groups conducted with service users (four groups, $n = 27$), psychiatrists (two groups, $n = 4$), CPNs (one group, $n = 10$), and care co-ordinators from a range of professional backgrounds (one group, $n = 8$), and four individual telephone interviews with psychiatrists, making a total of 53 respondents. Discussions were structured around four broad topics: how decisions about psychiatric medication currently happen; how respondents thought these decisions should be made; factors that might facilitate SDM between professionals and service users; and perceived barriers to shared forms of decision making for psychiatric medication. Thematic analysis using NVivo software was used to analyse data from both research studies. Due to limitations of space, we will focus in this chapter on the principal similarities and differences between stakeholder groups (psychiatrists, service users and CPNs/care co-ordinators) that were detected across the two projects.

# Findings

## Similarities between stakeholder groups

On the whole, across both projects, there was a genuine desire to involve people / be involved in decision making about psychiatric medication. Service users taking increased ownership in the decision-making process and honest, open dialogue during discussions about medica-tion were seen as important by both practitioners and service users. SDM as an ideal model of practice was valued by all key stakeholder groups.

### *Service-user involvement varies*

However, across both studies, all stakeholder groups emphasise that involving service users in discussion and decision making about psychiatric medication varies according to how well the person is at the time. Limitations in the possibility of exchanging information and express-ing preferences during the acute stages of mental health crises are recognised as important barriers to fully participating, with acknowledgement that a more paternalistic approach may often be more appropriate when the person is acutely unwell. Indeed, increased guidance during these more difficult periods is valued by service users.

**Service user 3, Project A**: *I think when I was particularly ill, I found the meetings very difficult, I didn't know what to say, I really didn't know how to express how I was feeling, and at that point I was very much led by the consultant*

**Service user 12, Project A**: *I didn't feel in the right place / frame of mind to be able to go away and search on the internet about all these different options and weigh it up.*

**Psychiatrist 2, Project B**: *I think in more acute situations when maybe the decision making is more difficult and it's sometimes already part of relapse plan, but when people are well and they have a, are able to make decisions and have discussions with their partners or families to make the decision in advance. Ok, so people come unwell, what happens, what treatments would be acceptable to me? Which ones would I continue taking? And (erm) That would be helpful I think for the acute situation when you maybe can't be involved in decision-making decisions and discussions as such.*

Interestingly, in the quote by the psychiatrist above, the acceptance that decisions are more difficult in periods of crisis is directly followed by an acknowledgement that certain tools, such as advance directives and relapse plans, can assist greater involvement during these more difficult periods.

## The therapeutic relationship

The beneficial role of a supportive, trusting relationship between the service user and the practitioner is mentioned by the majority of participants in both research studies. A good therapeutic relationship appears to enable broader collaborative decision-making processes, mitigating against the problems of being involved during periods of crisis. Thus during periods of crisis, all participants seem to value increased guidance from practitioners. However, if based on trust, support and mutual understanding, the longer-term goals of service-user ownership and enhancing control and involvement are not necessarily impeded during these more difficult periods, when potentially important decisions about psychiatric medication are made. As such, being supported, feeling cared for, having trust and being honest and open seem to be facilitating factors for meaningful shared dialogue. This greatly assists at times of crisis when equal sharing of knowledge and information becomes more difficult. In the quotes below, the importance of developing a partnership over time and building longer-term goals is explored as assisting shared understanding. The importance of continuation of support from the same person is seen by some as especially important, with familiarity encouraging feelings of safety.

**Service user 4, Project B**: *I think that the thing that has made the difference between then and now is the relationship. So having constant and continued support from the same person and continuity of care with the same doctor, so that you feel that you're not battling it alone and it's not a battle then of the doctors and the patients, it's that you've got somebody there.*

**Service user 1, Project A**: *... rather than it just coming from a stranger, like you should take that, that, they don't even know the person and it's just, you know, if you're in such a state that you need to have the decision taken out of your hands. Having some stranger telling you what you should be taking, it's not good; you need familiarity to feel safe.*

Importance is often placed on the concept of walking a shared journey over time in partnership. Crucially, the participants stress the importance of being able to trust someone during the more difficult periods, both in trusting them to take more control of decisions during periods of crisis, and in having an open and honest dialogue and respecting each other's opinions.

**CPN 8, Project A**: *I think the thing that probably stands out for me about the job I do is how much of it is about standing shoulder to shoulder with the service user, it's not ... it can't be them and us, it has to be about [pause] this journey I walk by your side with, because I can't tell you how to get better.*

**Service user, group 4, Project B**: *So it's good to have a good relationship with somebody that knows a lot about your history and what you've been through and somebody that you trust to make decisions for you when you are unable to.*

**Psychiatrist, group 2, Project B**: *I think we mentioned before, trust is important, so is sincerity and honesty (erm) respect for each other's opinions I think.*

## Fear of coercion as a barrier

A key barrier to SDM to all stakeholder groups is the acknowledgement of power inherent in the mental health system and the resulting fear of coercion experienced by service users. This is seen as a barrier to being able to achieve an honest and open dialogue where power is truly shared and where a 'meeting between experts' can take place.

Interestingly, both studies were conducted in community settings where, in the most part, contact with mental health services is voluntary. However, there appears to be an underlying awareness by both practitioners and service users in this setting of the legal framework within which mental health services operate and the potentially coercive roles practitioners serve in the modern mental health system. This awareness can sometimes prevent service users from disclosing information about their mental health symptoms or personal use of medication:

**Service User 10, Project A**: *... so I was quite intimidated about talking to the doctor about that [hearing voices] because I've got children, and I was worried I was going to get sectioned and my children were going to get taken off me because I was completely insane and stuff like that, so that was a difficult conversation for me just for that reason.*

**Service user 7, Project B**: *Fear, because then you just don't tell the truth. I mean in my case I spent four years just not telling the truth and so then I hadn't got anyone to talk to and when I did tell the truth I was penalised for it. And in other words not wanting to be on medication was a sign of mental illness, and I couldn't say that actually I haven't been on it anyway for years! And so fear prevents shared decision making.*

# Differences between stakeholder groups

## Valuing different forms of expertise

All stakeholder groups highlight the role of the professional as being an 'expert' in medication management, valuing formal knowledge of medicines and their evidence bases, but also placing importance on expertise in practice.

**Service user 12, Project A**: *They are the ones who know about the pros and cons. The doctor is the expert to tell about pros and cons and the psychiatrist is the person you talk to about medication. You work on the basis that the psychiatrist has seen loads of other people who have taken pills and they know the pros and cons.*

However, psychiatrists on the whole were less likely to mention service users' expertise, or to suggest that service users' experiential knowledge might form part of the decision-making process. In comparison, CPNs, care co-ordinators and service users acknowledge that in addition to the expertise of professionals in medication management practice, there is also expertise brought to the process by service users. These respondents talk of service users having valuable experiential expertise in taking medication, sometimes over numbers of years, which can make a valuable contribution to discussions and shared decisions. This was linked to the acknowledgement that decision making for psychiatric medication requires greater discussion than other areas of health care and that multiple options are often available. Individuals' responses to medication differ, and medications vary in degrees of risk and side effects. Working to achieve the best type and dosage of medication for an individual over time, through exploration of service-user preferences and experiences is essential.

**CPN 1, Project A**: *I think that one of the things I've learnt is that patients tend, on the whole, to know themselves pretty well, you know, no matter how unwell they are. They often know each other, they know themselves quite well, and if they say that a particular medication is no good for them, you know, well maybe we have to listen to that, and I think we are getting better at that, I really do, I think everybody's getting better at that.*

**Service user 4, Project B**: *So it's the respect and being listened to and having expertise about ourselves that's going to help isn't it.*

## Differences in descriptions of being ill as a barrier

Lack of insight into mental illness was seen by most practitioners as a barrier to involvement in decision making. The person not understanding they are ill during periods of crisis was seen as the most problematic barrier to a shared dialogue:

**Care co-ordinator 5, Project B**: *I think it all gets more difficult when people aren't insightful particularly ... I think it all gets much more difficult for everybody when someone maybe doesn't accept their diagnosis but appears very unwell and then it becomes difficult for the team, difficult for them.*

In comparison, while on occasion referring to problems of lacking insight, service users were overall less likely to emphasise this as a key barrier.

**Service user 3, Project B**: *Some people believe that patients just don't want to take their medication as that being part of the symptoms of their illness. I mean most of the time they're complaining about how unwell they feel on medication.*

More often, service users describe problems in terms of the impact of illness on cognitive abilities such as concentration, memory and motivation, as well as the impact of distress in periods of crisis on being able to fully participate in the decision process. These problems can affect their ability both to communicate and to process information:

**Service user 3, Project A**: *I think when I was particularly ill, I found the meetings very difficult, I didn't know what to say, I really didn't know how to express how I was feeling.*

**Service user 10, Project A**: *When I first turned up at the GPs, I wasn't feeling very well at all, so um, it was actually physically hard for me to have a conversation, communicate and understand what was being said to me really.*

When practitioners suspect that a service user 'lacks insight' or does not agree with a diagnosis, they may tailor the way they present information to avoid conflict around the issue of the nature of the person's problems, and to increase the likelihood that they might agree to take medication:

**Psychiatrist 6, Project A**: ... who often are very distressed about their symptoms but don't necessarily see it as a mental health problem, so a lot of the work is around trying to get some sort of joint understanding. That's really hard because often most of their involvement with mental health services to prove that they are not ... then it becomes quite difficult to involve people um on the same level, because you have to walk a fine line between giving information that is correct and factual um but also if you, you start talking about this is an antipsychotic drug ... People start saying, but I'm not psychotic and so it's often about a fine line. It's not about giving the wrong information but giving information that would lead people to consider perhaps the options more carefully rather than being immediately backed off.

Of note, however, is that while this theme emerged across both studies, one psychiatrist talks about how insight should not be a barrier to full ownership.

**Psychiatrist 5, Project A**: It's not about insight, I think if someone hasn't got an insight and I feel that very strongly he suffers from a mental illness he needs to take medication, again it would be a decision made by him if he doesn't want to take, he doesn't take it.

## Doctor–patient power

Service users often talk about the unequal power base during the psychiatric encounter, feeling inferior and patronised in the conversation:

**Service user 2, Project A**: No, I don't work well when I'm obviously not her equal, she has more training but I don't work well when I'm being treated as, you know, an inferior... I'm an intelligent person, if like ... I don't know, I don't really, I can't think what it would be, a parent, child I suppose is what it feels like when ... but they seem to have this; I'm God, you're the patient.

**Service user 13, Project A**: Yeah, I think basically it's like, I don't know how you feel, but the way I feel sometimes, you come to see a doctor and you can feel very uncomfortable. Well, I do, I feel as if I'm thick and mental because I'm so ill sometimes when I come in and I feel sometimes that I get ... I'm being spoken down to and not at that way, that level.

This power imbalance was also acknowledged among CPNs and care co-ordinators. Psychiatrists, on the other hand, did not generally mention unequal perceptions of the doctor's and patient's roles and status as a potential barrier to SDM. Indeed, one psychiatrist below notes that they find it strange that service users perceive a power imbalance in their relationships with psychiatrists and in decision-making processes:

**Psychiatrist 6, Project A**: And you know often people come here and say, oh you're not going to tell me to take or reduce my drugs or take this. And I find that a very interesting view because I wonder where that comes from, this idea that I am going to tell them what to do, with certainty I never tell people what to do. Even when I detain people I tell people that this is the only choice I have now, so I find that very interesting, that because you have a prescription pad you have the power to make them take things, and actually you never can.

# Discussion

On the face of it, we have found broad support for the ideals of collaborative ways of managing psychiatric medication across all key stakeholder groups. A non-specific conceptualisation of SDM, where individual decisions are part of a longer-term and adaptable process, similar to that proposed by other authors (Entwistle and Watt, 2006; Montori et al., 2006) is widely supported by care co-ordinators, CPNs, psychiatrists and service users in these findings. Service users acknowledge and value more guidance in times of crisis, and strongly believe that SDM can only happen in the context of walking a journey together in a trusting, supportive and honest long-term relationship with a practitioner. As such, opportunities to move towards a more recovery-oriented approach to prescribing and medication management in community mental health services appear to exist. The importance of the therapeutic relationship was also apparent across all participant groups. A long-term process, where trust is gained over time and a partnership is formed, appears to be essential to establishing key principles of an SDM approach to medication management. This fits with the literature exploring what service users see as important to the decision-making process. For example, in a US study by Davidson et al. (2008), who undertook qualitative interviews with mental health service users, the decision-making process was often a protracted process of trial and error in finding both the right doctor or nurse, and then the right medication. The right prescriber was someone who listened to the person, was willing to try different things, and who viewed medication as one of many possible strategies to consider. It takes time to discern the benefits of a medication as change is often incremental and slow. These results also support findings suggesting that service users show a preference for a two-stage process, which first prioritises autonomy, but then, if that is not possible, defers to the clinician's judgement in more challenging or complex decisions.

The current system in which service users are unlikely to have frequent routine appointments with psychiatrists as standard, but rather on an 'as and when' needed basis, is perhaps not conducive to such a partnership being forged, at least between the psychiatrist and service user. It may be, then, that the role of other care co-ordinators, including CPNs, occupational therapists and STR workers (Support Time and Recovery) – many of whom, in our research, view themselves as on a journey with service users – could be usefully oriented towards encouraging SDM for medication management in mental health.

Findings presented in this chapter point to some paternalistic practices in current community-based mental health services, and SDM is at present far from being an integral part of mental health medication management systems. These findings are in line with recent research suggesting that decisions in medication management rarely reflect both parties' contributions and preferences in the outcome. For example, Matthias et al. (2012) show that while 61 per cent of recorded consultations reflected the practitioner perspective, less than 10 per cent reflected both service-user and practitioner perspectives.

The barriers to collaborative practice identified in these findings may go some way to explaining the gap between policy ideals and current practice. Fear of coercion acts as a key deterrent to achieving SDM, instead encouraging greater passivity and 'false compliance' (Chamberlin, 2005). In other areas of health, capacity may be limited by service users' knowledge of medical conditions and treatments, but their ability to reason is not in dispute. In mental health, the capacity to reason and make effective decisions is brought into question, and is often defined by others rather than by the person themselves, thus removing a significant determinant of choice and control. Part of this is defined in legislation and part through the social construction of professional practice in mental health (Morant, 2006).

Therefore, until risk, accountability and the wider contexts of legislation and organisational culture are acknowledged in a more open manner, system-level change towards a more democratic and risk-taking culture of honest shared dialogue and collaboration between service users and practitioners is unlikely. Perhaps the fact that both practitioners and service users expressed and reflected upon these barriers in these two research projects is, in itself, a step towards recognising these underlying fears and positively embracing a way forward towards the ideals of an honest, open dialogue. However, the lack of value given by psychiatrists to service users' experiential knowledge of medication may indicate that there are strong underlying obstacles to SDM being implemented. Perhaps the consistency of CPNs positioning themselves more alongside service users and less alongside psychiatrists reflects a move of this group away from full adherence to the medical model and a broadening in the types of knowledge they see as valid. A potential alliance of CPNs – now the largest professional group in UK mental health services – with service users may promise a shift in attitudes to SDM.

Differences between what service users conceptualise as important for SDM and what psychiatrists and care co-ordinators think important are also worth consideration. Service users often describe feeling patronised, feeling like a child and being spoken down to. The perception that the doctor knows best is still common in modern-day psychiatric practice, together with an explicit notion that users of services may not have the capacity to decide for themselves, or that their understanding of the situation is not valid. The prevalence of these views in current mental health services is not recognised as much by psychiatrists, and hence alternative positions may be difficult for them to accept, as these challenge what many might see as the psychiatrist's fundamental role within the mental health system.

A second interesting difference between stakeholder groups in our data concerns how illness symptoms are conceptualised. Psychiatrists and care co-ordinators are very clear that lack of insight, perceived as a deficit, is a key barrier to service users engaging in collaborative dialogue. They acknowledge that, when working with a person deemed to lack insight, they may change their communication style, provide less information, and at times use discursive practices that could be understood as subtle forms of deception and persuasion during the psychiatric encounter (Seale et al., 2006). For service users, on the other hand, lack of insight is not seen as so important for full participation in decisions. Instead, they place more emphasis on increased distress and lower levels of concentration and other cognitive functions such as memory and motivation as by far the biggest challenges to both feeling involved and fully participating in a shared and open dialogue. These may either be consequences of the illness itself or side effects of taking medication, although the latter appears not to be recognised as a barrier to SDM by practitioners in our studies.

This discrepancy needs further exploration. Despite practitioners' reservations, insight into illness should not in itself be seen as a prerequisite to engaging in SDM. Indeed, evidence shows that service users are capable of participating in most decision-making situations (Loh et al., 2007). Hamann et al. (2006) have demonstrated that SDM for medication can be successfully understood by inpatients on an admission ward using a simple manual and support from ward nurses. Decision aids and communication tools, then, may well be important ways of supporting service users to participate in SDM.

The emphasis placed by practitioners on lack of insight as a barrier may also point to the continuing dominance of the medical model in UK psychiatric practice today, moving experiential knowledge into the periphery of the decision-making process, and diagnosis, labelling and *othering* to the forefront. Decisions in mental health are also peculiar in that the acceptance of a mental illness diagnosis can be stigmatising and potentially lead to loss of control. There may be stigma not only from friends, family and society generally, but also self-stigma (Thornicroft et al., 2009; Yanos et al., 2011), and the worry that a diagnosis may interfere with job prospects and life chances more generally. 'Lack of insight', so termed by the practitioners in our respective research projects, while being described as a symptom of the mental health problem in question, could also be seen as a 'symptom' of the wider system and one tool in the existing power structures of a psychiatric system dominated by the medical model.

In summary, a number of obstacles specific to psychiatry appear to hinder the development of fully collaborative relationships between practitioners and service users. At the forefront of these is the central issue of competence or insight, judgement of which remains in the hands of psychiatrists, who, because of their specific training and background, are more likely than other mental health professionals to adopt a medical approach to assessment.

Research suggesting the importance of a respectful culture which recognises service-user expertise and communicates belief in individual potential is supported by these findings (Tee et al., 2007). In addition, while not objecting to psychiatric medication as one possible treatment strategy within a range of interventions, recovery protagonists and researchers from a social-science perspective are concerned with the frequent and lasting adverse effects of such medication (Pilgrim et al., 2011; Whittaker, 2010), and are searching for a much wider range of intervention options. In such a model, SDM sits at the centre of the therapeutic encounter, encouraging dialogue and discussion in an open forum.

## Conclusion and looking forward

Numerous diverse aspects of the current UK mental health system suggest potential opportunities for further development of SDM relating to psychiatric medication management. These potential facilitating factors include policy guidelines, the focus on implementing recovery-oriented approaches, the increased autonomy of care co-ordinators within the system, and the existing skills of some practitioners in forming and maintaining strong and enduring therapeutic relationships with clients.

Implementation of SDM could also be facilitated by the increased involvement of service users in service delivery, planning and audit, as well as training and research, and by the desire among many service users and some professionals to see SDM as an integral part of mental health practice.

Government focus on choice has led to the planned introduction of SDM strategies in a few Trusts, but real choice is still a long way from becoming embedded in practice. Barriers include poor implementation of policy makers' intentions; the need to change attitudes towards the value of service users' experiential knowledge and recovery potential; insufficient lay information about psychiatric medication that service users find easy to access and understand; service organisation and structures that are not conducive to forming therapeutic bonds between professionals and service users; and the lack of research evidence on shared decision-making processes in the context of psychiatric medication management.

The ShIMME project described in this chapter aims to contribute to this evidence base, and presently constitutes the only UK evaluated pilot intervention delivering parallel training programmes for service users, psychiatrists and care co-ordinators focused on SDM in psychiatric medication management (www.shimme.arcusglobal.com). Evaluation findings will be known in late 2013. Encouragingly, several other projects are working on themes central to the implementation of SDM in relation to psychiatric medication management. Devon Mental Health Trust has devised a strategy for recovery-oriented prescription, which includes SDM as a method. Although yet to be implemented, it provides a useful and comprehensive guide (Baker et al., 2013). An RfPB (Research for Patient Benefit) NIHR-funded project conducted in north-east London and led by Dr Joanna Moncrieff focuses on developing a tool for reviewing and recording experiences of taking antipsychotic medication, constructed on the basis of interviews with service users. Jordan and Slade (2012) are carrying out more generic research on SDM in mental health services in five EU countries, entitled CDIS (Clinical Decision-making Involvement and Satisfaction). The tool developed measures the extent to which SDM principles are applied according to both clinicians and service users. Interestingly, preliminary findings highlight differences in ratings of the same situation by clinicians and service users. Thus, a number of small-scale initiatives developing the implementation of SDM are now in existence, illustrating the increasing interest in this issue in the UK. However, a lot more progress is needed if SDM is to become an integral part of our mental health services.

The key challenges in the findings we have presented here suggest over-reliance on an approach that does not value the experiential knowledge of service users and gives preference to the medical model of psychiatry. Fear of coercion is one possible outcome of a clash of perspectives between service users and professionals, in which the latter have a much more powerful position as part of their social mandate. Thus SDM within mental health needs to be explored in terms of its implications for power sharing and ownership of the decision-making process, and not as a narrow model of the procedural actions necessary. SDM should be understood as embedded within long-term therapeutic relationships and the contextual constraints and facilitating factors of the current mental health system. Through making these systemic barriers and facilitators more explicit, developing and evaluating initiatives to promote SDM, and encouraging open dialogue between practitioners and service users about how to achieve shared decision making, it is hoped that change towards increased power sharing and collaboration will emerge.

## Acknowledgements

Sincere thanks to Amy Li, who helped direct the content of this chapter and provided relevant findings from the ShIMME project. Thanks to Rod Rivers for assisting with the discussion.

The contributions from other members of the research team are also acknowledged: Sheena Mooney, Carole Morgan, Fiona Blake, Sarah Rae, Mudassir Miah, Geoff Stone and Furhan Iqbal were co-researchers and facilitators for ShIMME and the PhD research project presented in this chapter. We are grateful to all those who shared their views and experiences with us in the interviews and focus groups we have discussed in this chapter.

# 4 The Recovery Concept: The Importance of the Recovery Story

## By Joanna Fox

## Introduction

The care and treatment of people with schizophrenia has been dominated by the biomedical model of mental health, emphasising the importance of medication, treatment compliance and the expertise of the doctor (Bogg, 2010; Campbell and Davidson, 2012). In the last 20 years, the traditional psychiatric model has been challenged and a model of recovery has emerged (Anthony, 2003; Deegan, 1996). This focuses on the service user's abilities to live well with and even beyond the label of schizophrenia by using their own strengths to manage their symptoms and to control their own lives (Spaniol et al., 2002). The recovery concept does not reject the role of medication in care but emphasises the importance of a life that is defined by the service user, rather than a life that is limited by a diagnosis and managed by compliance with treatment.

In this chapter the biomedical model of mental health is introduced. It is suggested that this model is underpinned by a practice that potentially limits the service user's own ability to control and self-manage their mental ill health. The new model of recovery is described and the role that the concept of recovery plays in allowing service users to define the limitations and boundaries of their lives is explored. I differentiate between the traditions of clinical recovery and personal recovery. It is argued in this chapter that clinical recovery reflects some of the difficulties encountered with the biomedical model and removes the expertise from the service user in defining their own recovery.

The concept of personal recovery is introduced, along with the potential it has to enable service users to define their own successes. I illustrate this with a story of personal recovery by describing my own journey to live beyond the disability (Spaniol et al., 2002) and explore what hindered and helped me. It is argued that allowing service users to define their own recovery journey (Brown and Kandirikirira, 2006; Ridgeway, 2001) gives space for them to define their limitations and their strengths; to manage their symptoms by taking responsibility for their lives; and to live well and successfully on their own terms. I describe the difference between the *process of recovery* and the *attainment of recovery*, and how this contributes to an understanding of the recovery concept.

I examine the staged models of recovery suggested by Spaniol et al. (2002) and Andresen et al. (2006). It is suggested that these models have the potential to contribute to service users' own understanding of the journey of recovery, enabling them to have insight into the process and journey their own lives may follow. The staged models of recovery contribute to an understanding of the quality of the recovery journey, rather than quantifying it into a set end point. I conclude by reflecting on how this can promote recovery in the lives of service users.

## The background

The development of the science of psychiatry based on the dominant biomedical model gave mental health experts increased power to diagnose and treat patients with mental health problems (Bogg, 2010; Campbell and Davidson, 2012). The Diagnostic Statistical Manual (DSM) and The American Psychiatric Association's (APA's) Practice Guideline for the Treatment of Schizophrenia (Lehman et al., 2004) are used to categorise the nature of mental ill health and define the treatment that should be given. Indeed, the new DSM-V is currently being developed amid much controversy, with the designation of new categories of mental disorder which widen the diagnostic umbrella of psychiatry. (This topic is too broad and complex to be discussed here; however, this debate is very current.)

The development of a science of psychiatry gave mental health professionals the legitimate power to detain service users who were deemed to pose potential harm to themselves or others, through the institution of mental illness statutes.[1] It is undeniable that mental health laws can promote public protection and support service users in distress; however, there is no other law which gives such power to detain people who have the *potential to harm themselves or others*, rather than those who have been *convicted of harming others* (Golightley, 2011). Indeed, in certain countries without the checks and balances that are involved in the 2007 Mental Health Act in England, the diagnosis of mental ill health has been used as a political tool to detain people contending the state (Bentall, 2003).

Slade (2009) questions the validity of the medical model, asking wider questions about the medical conceptualisation of mental ill health. Mental illness, he argues, is different to a physical illness. A diagnosis can *explain* the symptoms of a physical disease, whereas the diagnosis of a mental illness can only provide an *understanding* of its symptoms and causation. It cannot be said that bereavement causes depression; it may be one of many factors. A person may have symptoms of depression that are related to lifestyle, environmental factors, social factors, biomedical factors or psychological factors; therefore, it is difficult to say that depression implies a way of *explaining* a service user's reaction to these factors. In a similar way, schizophrenia has a number of causes which are not yet understood or definitively identified (Bentall, 2003; Slade, 2009); in this way it is hard to accept the biomedical model of schizophrenia, or any other model. Rather it is better to comprehend a diagnosis as an *understanding* of symptoms of mental distress, rather than a discrete illness *explained* by a set of symptoms. Indeed Walker (2006, p 74) reflects on this:

*When we are talking about a person's thoughts and feelings we are essentially talking about their identity (which includes values, beliefs, memories, fears, and desires). This is not like something physically wrong with part of their body. A 'disorder' of thought or feeling is a labeling of a person's identity. The labeling of subjective experience feeds on itself and perpetuates itself.*

The medical model of care fails to recognise the role that service users have to play in self-managing their symptoms, in taking control and responsibility for their lives, and in the agency and choice they have about their own lifestyles, medical treatments and residency issues. Beresford (2005, p 110) argues that the medical model is derived from a deficits model *which is based on assumptions of the inherent deficiency and pathology of 'the mentally ill'*. Dell'Acqua and Mezzina (1998) argue that once a diagnosis of schizophrenia is given a posteriori, then the definition of a person's character is tied up in their illness and no longer in their life experiences. The diagnosis of mental ill health defines a person's life and they become a 'schizophrenic', a 'manic depressive' or a 'depressive'. They absorb the stigma of mental ill health (Yanos et al., 2008) and their hopes and dreams are dominated by the label and the stigma they have internalised.

The writing of service users in the 1960s (Kesey, 1962) began to challenge the politics of mental health care, influencing the rise of anti-psychiatry (Laing, 1965, 1967; Szasz, 1961) and service-user involvement in mental health (Chamberlin, 1978). The influential stress-vulnerability models of schizophrenia (Zubin and Spring, 1977) posited that the prognosis of schizophrenia was responsive to social and environmental factors in the person's life. The development of normalisation and the principles of social role valorisation (Wolfensberger, 1972) and the concomitant moves to care in the community were associated with the shifting power balances in care and treatment. The process of de-institutionalisation, a subject too complex and broad to be addressed here, began to recognise in practice the new theory base that was emerging.

This slow but perceptible shift of power in the care and treatment of people experiencing mental ill health was further driven by the conception of the social model of disability and the growing rejection of the medical model of mental health care (Oliver, 1996). Indeed, the development of the strengths model (Rapp, 1998) in the case management of those with mental ill health challenged practitioners' persistent focus on their clients' deficits. It reminded them of the need to encourage practice based on empowerment and enablement: an emphasis on risk taking to enable service users to build on their strengths rather than focusing on risk avoidance based on a culture of paternalism. Davidson et al. (2005) describe a different approach to the *diagnosis-led medical model*. They focus on the idea of *wellness* in the day-to-day lives of those living with serious mental illness. It is not necessarily the absence of symptoms or the *holistic assessment* of global functioning that defines a person's wellness, but what they do with their lives. A mental health service user bowling with friends in a bowling alley is not judged by the status of their mental health, but by how good they are at bowling. Similarly, people should be judged by their active involvement in life, rather than clinical judgements of their lives. The recovery model builds on these different traditions and begins the journey of grasping back the experience of mental health for the service user, recognising their own role in the journey of recovery.

## The recovery concept

In this section, the recovery concept is discussed more fully and the evidence base that developed this notion is described. The nature of the concept is explored by highlighting the traditions of *clinical recovery* and *personal recovery* which emanate from different models of theory and practice. These two notions influence the ways practitioners from different backgrounds understand mental health, develop interventions for service users and develop underpinning theories to their practice.

## Clinical recovery

The model of recovery first posited in the work of Bleuler (1968) has since been strengthened by several studies that show that recovery from schizophrenia can and does happen (Ciompi, 1980; Harding et al., 1987; Harrison et al., 2001; Huber et al., 1975; Ogawa et al., 1987; Tsuang et al., 1979). In Harding et al. (1987), of the 262 individuals in their study, between 46 and 68 per cent of patients met criteria for recovery. However, Harrison et al. (2001, p 14), although presenting data that supported the premise that patients with schizophrenia might recover when measured at 15- and 25-year intervals after first diagnosis, also stated some concerns about the recovery concept:

*Working concepts of recovery require qualification as well. Our study relied heavily upon absence of symptoms, social disability, and resource utilization. This should not be equated with level of function achieved before the onset of illness, and even less with the recovery of lost potential.*

The working concept of recovery used by Harrison et al. (2001) is based on a biomedical model, where mental illness is perceived as a neurological disease.

Many researchers (Harrison et al., 2001; Liberman and Kopelowicz, 2005) argue that any kind of recovery model or improvement in illness outcome should be based on an empirical, evidence-based operational model. Successful recovery must include the ability to:

- function independently;

- take care of one's own personal care;

- manage one's own medication, health and money without regular supervision (Liberman and Kopelowicz, 2002).

The DSM describes recovery as a complete recovery to pre-morbid levels of functioning (APA, 1980) or a complete return to full functioning (APA, 1994). The APA Practice Guideline for the Treatment of Schizophrenia identifies a period of two years' absence of relapse and status of stability as an empirically convincing period that demonstrates recovery. This form of recovery derived from the medical model has been referred to as *clinical recovery* (CSIP, RCPsych, SCIE, 2007; Slade, 2009). Clinical recovery has been defined by Slade (2009, p 29) as being:

- an outcome or a state;

- observable by the clinician (ie it is objective not subjective);

- rated by the expert clinician, not the service user;

- invariant across individuals.

This is differentiated from *personal recovery* derived from the service-user movement.

# Personal recovery

The service-user movement proposes a new meaning of recovery in which living well with mental health problems dominates the agenda, not necessarily complete cure from symptoms (Anthony, 1993; Repper and Perkins, 2003). A life lived beyond the label of schizophrenia has been posited (Davidson, 2003), where the experiences and symptoms of mental ill health are synthesised through a process to live well and successfully with this diagnosis, beyond merely managing its symptoms.

Indeed, recovery is a process, a concept, an ideology that means many different things to different people. As already discussed, professionals have long argued that treatment for schizophrenia is based on a cure model, not a recovery model (Repper and Perkins, 2003). Service users have gone on to argue that complete reduction of symptoms is not necessarily a cure to them, nor is it what they are necessarily seeking (Coleman, 1999; Repper and Perkins, 2003). Repper and Perkins (2003, p 18) write that the model of recovery defines a *continuing process of growth of and adaptation to disability as opposed to time-limited interventions directed at symptom removal.* Anthony (1993, p 13) defines recovery as:

*a deeply personal, unique process of changing one's attitudes, values, feelings, goals, skills and/ or roles. It is a way of living a satisfying, hopeful and contributing life even with limitations caused by the illness. Recovery involves the development of new meaning and purpose in one's life as one grows beyond the catastrophic effects of mental illness.*

Anthony focuses on the personal attributes of recovery as an individual journey of development. According to Deegan (1997), recovery from mental illness is not necessarily defined by one group or another; it is a personal journey of individuality. She draws out the political aspects of recovery as derived from the service-user movement. Recovery should embrace all people's experiences and needs. It is not necessarily a continuing positive development, but may be a spasmodic process of recovery, accepting failures along the way (Deegan, 1996, p 97):

*We must have the opportunity to try and to fail and to try again ... In order to support the recovery process, mental health professionals must not rob us of the opportunity to fail.*

Recovery is defined as a journey that can reflect a life journey. As each person's life journey is individual, so is each person's recovery journey. Recovery is described and defined through different perspectives: service users, professionals, carers and policy makers. However, it is only through engaging with the *experience of schizophrenia* that it is possible to begin to understand the notion of recovery. By returning to service users' narratives of their life stories, a framework for understanding schizophrenia emerges which illustrates the importance of recovery as a concept. It shows how a service user can *live recovery* rather than necessarily always *attain* recovery.

In the next section, I reflect on my own experience of mental ill health, returning to the story of recovery and highlighting what helped and hindered me in this process. This personal narrative is used to represent in a larger sense the factors of recovery that are identified by the service-user community as common experiences among the wider group of people with mental health issues.

# A personal journey of recovery

I was brought up in a very stable family living both abroad in New Zealand and in my home country of England. I worked hard at school and was very successful in my studies, gaining very good marks. I enjoyed school but was always a bit of an outsider, having travelled extensively, with few roots and few long-term friends. I was always a little different from other people and escaped to books, homework and succeeding at school. I had many ambitions and enjoyed life as a well-adjusted and happy young person at school.

When I finished school, I lived abroad for a gap year at 18 years of age before going to university. I fell in love while I was abroad – a love which was unrequited. I was lonely, had little idea of how to make friends, little idea of how to live well by myself and was overwhelmed by the freedom of an unstructured life with little to do. I worked, but often had little to occupy me, so I had too much time to think and feel. During this time abroad, I had the first occurrence of strange thoughts and the start of a belief that certain signs and symbols were significant to my life – when they actually had no significance. This time of stress was the beginning of my mental ill health.

At the age of 19 I returned from Germany and went to Durham University to study Philosophy and Politics. I started a downward spiral of becoming mentally unwell. I had a frightening period of breakdown, with the experience of hearing voices, of paranoia, of chaotic thoughts constituting terror and anxiety as I responded to these moments of confusion and being out of control. I had a short period of voluntary hospitalisation. I was prescribed mental health drugs which served as a clinical cosh – deadening the symptoms but also deadening my emotions and thoughts. I no longer had thinking that flowed smoothly and quickly like water over obstacles, but thought processes that were slow, dull, difficult and laborious.

I had moments of terror. I can remember climbing up Hadrian's Wall with my parents, who had taken me out for the day from hospital. My legs seized up and they had to carry me back down the hill. Moments of fear overwhelmed me. Was this a further punishment from God? No, it was the side effects of the medication, which nobody had informed either me or my family about. Other side effects were to follow: increased appetite, leading to significant weight gain, anxiety, lethargy, and being clinically and mentally sedated. I left hospital after three weeks of voluntary admission.

I returned to university part time, spending half the week at home and half the week at university – a university that was 200 miles from home but connected by a fast train route. I struggled to work and struggled with anxiety whenever I sat at a desk. I had thought that recovery would come as quickly as the mental illness had come, but I was to learn that recovery was a patient experience of long-suffering pain, depression, paranoia and regrowth. Friends and family supported my recovery by helping me to occupy my unstructured days. I began to build my concentration by sitting for short periods at my desk, not always reading books, but physically sitting still and trying to concentrate. I found it very difficult to sit and work, and would hop up and down from the desk with the attention span of a butterfly. I slowly increased this time from five minutes to ten minutes, to increasing times of sitting still. This trained me to begin to learn how to concentrate again. I still experienced periods of very bad paranoia, depression, lethargy, occasional voices and a very damaged psyche. I finished my degree without taking any time off, getting a respectable 2.2.

I began to rebuild my life and my mind slowly and steadily over the next ten years. I had to hold onto a belief that something good had to come out of this illness, and eventually trained as a social worker. It was with difficulty that I passed the social work qualification and slowly continued to build my recovery. I was mentored by both Professor David Brandon, a professor who was himself a service user, and later by Professor Shula Ramon, both of whom recognised the potential in me. Potential that was there but just had to be dug up again and revealed from the quagmire in which experiences of mental ill health had buried it. It was a long and laborious and sometimes painful recovery underpinned by a belief that change was possible, that mental illness wasn't a life sentence of negativity, and by people who were willing to invest their time in a broken person.

I had been fed messages that recovery was possible. I met discrimination from others who stereotyped people with schizophrenia as mad, bad and ugly, but my family and mentors around me never let me accept that. They only let me concentrate on the positives and on the rebuilding – the process of recovery not necessarily the outcome of recovery. They believed in a life that could be rebuilt beyond the label of schizophrenia. This message was a key to my experience of recovery.

Now as a senior lecturer in social work, teaching the potential social workers of the future, working with colleagues who teach other students, my dreams of influencing practice and work are being realised. My recovery is ongoing, with moments of stress, paranoia, side effects from medication, but my hopes and dreams are being realised. I am living beyond my experience of mental ill health and telling my experiences to others to inspire hope and the dream of recovery (Spaniol et al., 2002).

## What experiences are central to describing the journey of recovery?

In this section, I identify the key components that are essential to *experiencing* recovery. The experience of recovery may be very different from the *attainment* of recovery. The former relates to the personal journey of recovery, emphasising that process is as important as outcome, while the latter refers to the notion of clinical recovery that describes measurable outcomes of independent living. For the purposes of this chapter, I focus on the process of experiencing personal recovery, although it is acknowledged that, for some, the attainment of recovery, however unreachable it may be, is more important than the journey.

Brown and Kandirikirira (2006) compiled a report investigating how mental health service users in Scotland described their own journey of recovery. They used a narrative story-telling approach with service users to enable them to talk about what helped and hindered their journey to recovery at the present time. Service users identified that taking part in this process was an empowering and deeply powerful experience. Service users identified the following as affecting their journey to recovery (Brown and Kandirikirira, 2006, p 3):

- hope, confidence and optimism;

- diagnosis;

- self-acceptance, responsibility, belief and esteem;

- self-efficacy;

- self-awareness;

- negative identity and low expectations;

- stigma – spoiled identity;

- thriving – growth beyond the label;

- powerlessness – removal of identity;

- reclaiming power and self-determination;

- physical image;

- sexual identity;

- creative identity;

- cultural, social and community identity;

- group identity – activism;

- spiritual identity.

The experience of stigma and discrimination was reported to hinder the journey towards recovery. Narrators further reported that negative attitudes to their mental ill health further lowered their sense of self-esteem, while, unsurprisingly, positive messages helped them to foster a positive self-image. Service users reported the need to take risks in their lives. Other narrators reiterated the need for self-determination, or 'agency' to increase their sense of well-being and good mental health. Brown and Kandirikirira (2006, p 20) concluded:

*For many, identity focussed upon being valued as an individual irrespective of, or indeed, in spite of their mental health problems, whilst for others the experience of ill health and recovery had been embraced and had been a focus of value to them. From the narratives gathered in this project, it was evident that much of the subject of identity appeared to be about the issue of personal growth and development and change internally. This challenge can make a belief in the possibility of recovery difficult for some. Given the complex interaction between identity and recovery which we have described, it is clearly not possible to impose recovery on people. People must be willing, ready, able and, in some circumstances, allowed to action change.*

When I discovered the concept of recovery, it represented a conceptualisation of the optimism and sense of determination that I had hung on to in my life. I *experienced* the *process of recovery* before I knew about the concept of recovery. My parents fed me messages of hope and optimism which were a contrast to the negative expectations that dominated my life when I first became unwell. The messages they fed me were a counterbalance to the presumptions of failure that seemed to surround the diagnosis of schizophrenia. Their messages of optimism were sickening and relentless – sickening because sometimes I didn't believe in my own recovery, but relentless, because I had nothing except optimism to hold on to.

Each recovery is individual. For my recovery to succeed, I used medication to help control my symptoms. Unwanted side effects blunted my thinking and my energy and sedated me. Side effects of the medication caused increased appetite and consequent weight gain. However, medication allowed me the space to live a more normal life. It allowed me to control my symptoms and not be dogged by the paranoia and suspicion that I felt as I interacted with other people. It allowed me to think without doggedly analysing each conversation for the hidden meanings that were there. It enabled me to use talking therapies to develop non-chemical strategies to beat the low self-esteem. It allowed me to function in a way that I wouldn't have been able to without it.

When I discovered the recovery concept as I started my PhD in 2007, well into my recovery, it represented the constant fight I had had with myself over 20 years of experiencing mental health symptoms, the relapses when I went back again, and the effort and energy that had to be found to move forward again. Recovery represented the journey I had travelled – without choice – the only journey open to me if I was to regain my life and live the hopes and dreams I had possessed. Recovery represented possibilities and opportunities.

Recovery must come from the individual who is ready to move to the position where they are able to experience it for themselves. It is about moving on from the suffering of the mental illness and moving to a place of greater optimism and hope – about living as well as possible with and without mental health symptoms, and living beyond that diagnosis in a fulfilling and satisfying role (Davidson, 2003). Coleman (1999) focused on the role of the self in directing an individual recovery. He stated that

*Recovery is not a gift from doctors but the responsibility of us all ... We must become confident in our own abilities to change our lives; we must give up being reliant on others doing everything for us. We need to start doing these things for ourselves. We must have the confidence to give up being ill so that we can start becoming recovered.* (p 7)

For some service users this experience of mental distress can add new meaning to their life, giving them new insights and new ideas (Roberts, 2008), although others deny it has any value, seeing it only as a source of suffering and pain in their lives. In a study on the effects of recovery and resilience in women from black and ethnic minority communities (Kalathil, 2010), one woman spoke of the importance of her mental distress in her search for her past and her identity. It reconnected her with the experience of slavery and gave her new meaning and understanding in her life.

Contrary to Kalathil's research, black and ethnic minority service users may experience institutionalised racism from many sectors of the mental health service. For example, relatively high numbers of African-Caribbean men receive a diagnosis of schizophrenia compared with white or other ethnic minority groups. In addition, they are more likely to be coerced into services against their wishes, for example, through compulsory admissions to hospital, and once in hospital, they are more likely to be physically restrained by staff and to receive particularly high doses of powerful medication (Sainsbury Centre for Mental Health, 2002). This affects their recovery and their relationship with services, resulting in them contacting services later in the duration of untreated psychosis, being less open with services, and having a suspicion and fear of being treated differently because of their cultural or ethnic background. The experience of recovery-oriented services may be something that is very alien to service users from minority communities.

In the wider community of mental health service users, some feel hesitation in using the word recovery. Mental health symptoms can be very distressing because of:

- the suffering of the mental health symptoms;

- stigma experienced by having the label of a mental health patient;

- lost potential in life;

- lost lived experiences and opportunities that other people may have had;

- lost income and poverty;

- discrimination in work.

The recovery concept does not negate this suffering but tries to define a place beyond the initial experience of mental illness. For some, the experience of mental illness is a disability/impairment that they feel they cannot get over. In reflection on recovery by the Scottish Highland Users Group (Highland Users Group (HUG), 2006) some service users felt uncomfortable with the concept of recovery at all. In this document (HUG, 2006, p 8) service users point out that:

*Many of us ... made the point that there is no cure for many of the major mental illnesses and that it was misguided to talk of recovery. We felt that a word had been adopted and given values that it didn't previously hold. We also felt that it distorted the reality of mental illness. Some of us said that if people were to say that they had recovered totally then they didn't have a mental illness in the first place. We felt that people were asking us to reach for perfection and resented this. Some of us also felt that the whole idea was wrong – we have very hard lives and to expect these to change for the better is silly and misguided.*

This suggests that for some service users, recovery is frightening and their mental ill health insurmountable. Some perceive that recovery denies the real distress of their mental health needs. Moreover, they are reluctant to use the recovery concept to move from the position of suffering as a victim to taking control of one's own life. For some, recovery can only be about freedom from symptoms and freedom from impairment. However, recovery, as developed by the service-user movement isn't necessarily about freedom from symptoms. It is about living as good a life as possible with or without the diagnosis of mental ill health (Anthony, 1993; Coleman, 1999).

Many consumers (Coleman, 1999; Deegan, 1996) define recovery as a process, a movement, or a journey. They recognise the continuing nature of mental distress, with its fluctuating moments of wellness and suffering. This notion of a process or a journey is in contrast to psychiatric outcome measurements of schizophrenia. Recovery is no longer about maintenance but is about living well with mental health problems, and living beyond the label. Through this process, the journey is absorbed and allows the service user to move from just living with the disability to living beyond the disability (Spaniol et al., 2002). I had to rebuild a positive identity, a positive sense of self-esteem and of self-value. I had to make sense of the suffering and move to a place where the suffering no longer dominated my life, but was a part of my life, absorbed into the wider picture and meaning of my life. Then I could begin to live beyond the disability.

Some service users may be limited by their social circumstances. They may be living in poverty, poor housing, or may be isolated, may not have transport to optimise their access to services to support recovery. Recovery may not just be about what is 'within' but also what is 'without'. Some service users draw upon the medical model where recovery is defined by optimal life functioning. They note recovery in the terms of Liberman and Kopelowicz (2002), in which clinical recovery is a key to personal recovery.

The service-user movement recognises the struggles with these insurmountable issues. It defines mental health recovery as leading a valued and valuable life, about accepting the self and the limitations – when they present – of that illness. Anthony (1993, p 15) sums up this process of recovery:

*Successful recovery from a catastrophe does not change the fact that the experience has occurred, that the effects are still present and that one's life has changed forever. Successful recovery does mean that the person has changed, and the meaning of these facts to the person has therefore changed. They are no longer the primary focus of one's life. The person moves on to other interests and activities.*

This means that service users recognise the restrictions of the definition of personal recovery and demand something more complex: an understanding of the necessity to achieve a level of symptom reduction and quality of life.

The meaning of recovery is full of contradictions. It is a sticky concept that cannot be pinned down to one or other meaning (Stickley and Wright, 2011). It is open to interpretation and is as yet not strongly defined. Campbell et al. (2008) argue that, while it is a worthwhile concept, it has become a social construct. Although it can respond and change to the needs of different individuals, this aspect is problematic because it can be defined by professionals, rather than by service users and carers as they apply it to their lives. Indeed, the UK study, the *Roads to Recovery* (Mind, 2002), found that the concept of recovery meant many different things to different people. The concept could mean freedom for some and an insurmountable mountain for others. The report concluded that: *These respondents highlight the very different ways people define recovery and how difficult it is to find one way of describing it* (p 4).

# The journey

How can we balance the need to quantify and measure recovery with the need to describe it? Liberman and Kopelowicz (2002) emphasise the need to *go beyond the hype, vague 'vision' and glittering generalities ... and move into the realm of empirically supported validation of an operationally defined concept of recovery*. They focus on quantifying and measuring the recovery concept rather than defining the qualitative experience and process of fighting with the diagnosis of schizophrenia. Service users describe this journey and this pathway, they describe the components that support recovery, and what promotes and hinders their recovery. There is a detailed understanding of the nature and process of recovery in the descriptions of personal recovery. How to take this further?

Recovery is described by many researchers, service users and professionals alike as a journey, a process or a pathway (Anthony, 1993; Brown and Kandirikirira, 2006; Slade, 2010). Although the recovery of service users and carers is an individual journey (Deegan, 1997;

**Figure 4.1** The stages of recovery (Spaniol et al., 2002)

Mind, 2002) that cannot be captured by a single description, it is helpful to provide an over-arching structure within which these journeys are experienced. There seems to be a general consensus on the elements that are commonly experienced on this journey, and some researchers have tried to capture this in staged models that show the progress of recovery (Andresen et al., 2003, 2006; Spaniol et al., 2002). Spaniol et al. (2002) represent the recovery journey as shown in Figure 4.1.

Andresen et al. (2003) also looked at studies examining phases in the recovery process. They suggested five stages in the recovery journey.

1    Moratorium: a time of withdrawal characterised by a profound sense of loss and hopelessness.

2    Awareness: realisation that all is not lost, and that a fulfilling life is possible.

3    Preparation: taking stock of strengths and weaknesses regarding recovery, and starting to work on developing recovery skills.

4    Rebuilding: actively working towards a positive identity, setting meaningful goals and taking control of one's life.

5    Growth: living a full and meaningful life, characterised by self-management of the illness, resilience and a positive sense of self.

These stages reflect Spaniol et al.'s (2002) model of the recovery journey describing the moments from the first occurrence of the mental ill health symptoms, along the journey of recovery, to living beyond the disability and the illness of the mental health diagnosis.

In the next section I describe this process in more detail, aligning the staged models to the service-user experience of recovery. I use my own process of recovery to represent the experiences of the wider group of service users who have been labelled with the diagnosis of schizophrenia.

## The stages of the recovery journey

Service users note that when they first become unwell they are confused, scared, frightened and anxious. They may hear voices and have little comprehension of what is happening. They, their families and those around them may not realise that mental distress is present, and there is confusion and chaos as the family and service user either begin to seek help or avoid contact with medical services. Spaniol et al. (2002) have described this point as being *overwhelmed by the disability*. It is a place of beginning and confusion after the first occurrence of mental ill health in the service user. This equates to Andresen et al.'s (2003) first stage: *moratorium*. This moment is catastrophic and is a moment of chaos and deep distress.

At this moment I had no sense of the future, or any future at all. I was overwhelmed by the enormity of the experiences and felt deeply distressed, confused, terrorised and frightened by the experiences of the symptoms. I had no control over my thinking: in a place of surrender to the paranoia and strange thoughts, unable to make sense of the world around me. I was lost in a quagmire of mental health symptoms, hospitalisation and fear of what would happen in the future.

The second stage for the service user has been described as a place of *struggling with the disability* (Spaniol et al., 2002). The service user is at a point of struggle when things are very difficult and the mind is still quite chaotic following their diagnosis. The service user may be suffering from debilitating side effects of medication, negative symptoms and feelings of anxiety and stress. They may at this point be struggling with the life-changing knowledge that they have a mental health need, may need to take medication, and may be embarking on a long journey of recovery. Andresen et al. (2003) called this moment *awareness*.

At this point, medication began to work and I began the slow and difficult journey of recovery. I had little understanding that this journey would take so long, that I would have to cope with life-long limitations, and that I would have to struggle so hard. The journey, at this point, did not reflect a realisation that all was not lost, it was rather a slow acceptance that life would be different from this point. I began to recover and began to fight to regain a normal life, struggling with medication side effects, sedation, anxiety, stress, paranoia and occasional return of auditory hallucinations. It was a time of reactive depression, low self-esteem and a realisation that there was no panacea, that recovery would be hard and difficult work.

The next point for the service user is a place of *living with the disability* (Spaniol et al., 2002). The service user may be attending education classes, training classes, or taking part in leisure activities to build their confidence. This is characterised by the service user actively working towards a positive identity, setting meaningful goals and taking control of their life. This can be a very difficult point for a service user to attain as they are stuck in a place of struggle with symptoms and side effects of medication. When they do reach this point, the illness limits and bounds what they can do, but they feel that life has some worth and they have an identity of value. Andresen et al. (2003) called this *preparation*. This moment runs concurrently with *rebuilding*: actively working towards a positive identity, setting meaningful goals and taking control of one's life.

This moment of living with the disability for me continued over 12 to 15 years following the breakdown. It incorporated many processes of relapse and regrowth. I had moments when recovery seemed to require me to break down and rebuild parts of myself. It was almost as if I had put the bits of the jigsaw of my life, mind and psyche together in a way that didn't quite match and meet at the edges. I had to take the pieces of the jigsaw out, which left huge holes in my functioning, and then re-insert them in the right way. Talking therapies such as Cognitive Behaviour Therapy helped me to put the jigsaw pieces back, helped me to work out how to manage ongoing paranoia with techniques other than medication, and how to reason that I could be a 'good enough' worker rather than having to be a perfect worker. I worked in paid work throughout my period of recovery. Many of these experiences helped me to rebuild the self and begin to start my dreams of changing practice through my experiences. I slowly began to quicken my mind and sharpen it again. A long, slow and painful journey.

The next step is *living beyond the disability* (Spaniol et al., 2002) when the service user is living a full and meaningful life, characterised by self-management of the illness, resilience and a positive sense of self. The service user is in control of their life. The illness dwindles in importance and stops dominating their lives and their interactions with the world. They are 'in recovery'. Andresen et al. (2003) conceptualise this moment as *growth*.

For many service users this is a point they cannot reach. They have a life-long struggle with living with the disability, managing the limitations of their lives and never really moving beyond the label of the illness. Their diagnosis is the main identity of their life. They are a schizophrenic, they are a depressive or they are a manic depressive. Their identity is their label and it is the way that other people see them.

At the end of a long fight of living with the disability I have finally moved to points when I am living beyond the disability. I lead a full, positive life where the labels that dominate my life are: wife, mother, senior lecturer, researcher, PhD student. People define my life through the social roles I undertake rather than through my illness label. However, at times I find myself still living with the disability when anxiety and stress recur, and I have to live with and manage symptoms, but much of my life is positive and in a place of living a full and meaningful life. There is always a danger of symptoms recurring or the illness label dominating my interactions with other people.

In the section above, I have shown how I can identify my own journey of recovery with the staged models suggested by these two research groups. Yet how can we state that recovery is an individual journey, but describe it with an overarching framework? There is indeed a fundamental tension between arguing that recovery is an individual process and presenting the experiences as staged models (Andresen et al., 2006). This staged model can, however, be used as a map to enable a service user to begin to understand their recovery. This map is a cipher to enable people to relate to their own journeys. It describes both a *process of recovery* and an *attainment of recovery*, yet it does not define recovery.

A staged model of recovery is important for service users to begin to have hope and to see a chance of recovery. Many say that it is through listening to their peers that they are able to become more hopeful and optimistic. It is through seeing recovery in others that they are able to see recovery in themselves. Indeed, the recovery concept emphasises the importance of self-management of mental health problems and with it the notion of expertise by experience. It positions the service user in a place of living with the disability and even at times living beyond the disability. It may also reflect a sense of acceptance of the mental health condition and a sense of reconciliation with the experience. Yanos et al. (2008, p 437), however, describe how a sense of acceptance of the mental health diagnosis can hinder rather than promote recovery because the service user *loses previously held or hoped for identities (self as student, self as worker, self as parent, and so on) and adopts stigmatizing views (self as dangerous, self as incompetent, and so on)*. This sense of a worthless and pathological self is referred to as *internalised stigma*. This can seriously hinder the service user's journey of recovery because they believe they can't hold responsible and valuable positions in society.

My story describes the experience of suffering, but also draws on the positive that has to be found from suffering. I had to believe that there was a reason behind the suffering. Having trained as a social worker, I dreamed of using my experiences to bring recovery to others, to counteract the stigma and discrimination of mental ill health. As a social work researcher, I drew on the concept of the Wounded Healer (Nouwen, 1979). It is from the experience of suffering that one is able to relate to others and begin to use the suffering of the self to alleviate the sufferings of another. I accepted my experience of mental ill health and absorbed it into my being. Indeed, some forms of 'acceptance' of mental ill health can lead to a positive sense of self and may not necessarily mean subscribing to a psychiatric or self-stigmatising model as Yanos et al. (2008) have suggested. The person may accept the label of schizophrenia but see it as part of their expertise by experience. In this scenario, the person confronts stigma and discrimination in their community, confronts self-stigmatisation in other service users, and demonstrates how service users can become full citizens in society to live beyond the label.

This journey of sharing is of essential importance to helping other service users in their recovery. From the experience of suffering, as in the concept of the Wounded Healer, moments of commonality and shared problems can begin to heal and give succour to another. By sharing this experience with other service users, there is potential to help others in their recovery. The notion of expertise by experience enables others to embrace their experiences and begin to live for recovery.

# Conclusion

In this chapter I have discussed the medical model of recovery and how the recovery concept has emerged to bring about new hope for those with a diagnosis of schizophrenia. I have explicated the concepts of both personal recovery and clinical recovery and described the traditions from which they emanate. I have described my own journey of recovery and reflected on how it relates to the personal concept of recovery. A staged model of recovery has been introduced and its importance has been explored in helping service users to decode the journey that they must take to return from the place of being overwhelmed by the disability to living beyond it (Spaniol et al., 2002).

In conclusion, recovery must, I believe, first belong to the individual and more widely to the service-user community. Recovery is a journey. It is about an individual's life story and how they manage it. Pathways of recovery based on staged models that describe service users' experiences have the potential to offer other service users the opportunity to understand the journey and see a map to their own recovery. Through sharing the knowledge of recovery from their own perspective, others can draw on the expertise by experience and develop their own pathway to recovery. Recovery, if owned by the service-user community, has the potential to change individuals' lives and support them in their lives.

# Part Two
# The Importance of Context in Psychiatry

# 5 The Part Can Never Be Well, Unless the Whole Is Well

## By Keverne Smith

## Introduction

Do we live in a mentally healthy society? There is a variety of ways in which this wide-ranging question might be investigated. This chapter begins the process by putting the question in historical perspective. Of course, there are diverse areas of mental health, and it would take many books to investigate all of them historically, so this contribution concentrates on society's response to one experience everyone has to endure – the experience of loss, especially after a bereavement, and of the grief which follows it. The book as a whole shows that some of the issues which arise when we explore responses to grief historically relate to other areas of mental health as well. But why should we think there is a problem with the way our society deals with grief? Here are three contemporary examples which suggest this is a question worth asking.

In 1995, the freephone Child Death Helpline became available nationally. As Jean Simons records, a large number of bereaved parents phoned, not simply to express their anguish about recent deaths, but about children who had died from the Second World War onwards. Even more significantly, parents whose children had died up to 50 years before frequently felt guilt that they still had unresolved feelings, that they still suffered from grief (Simons, 2001, pp 161–62). Two things are apparent here: firstly, some parents had not been helped by the norms of mourning in our society in coming to terms with this most discordant of deaths, the loss of a child; and secondly, that social norms had encouraged them to feel guilt about their feelings, that 'normal' people should be able to push a death aside after a decent interval and keep their upper lips stiff.

A second example is more complicated. Princess Diana was someone who captured public attention both as a royal celebrity who seemed to be the victim of an inward-looking institution and as someone who was able to connect with many who felt marginalised, not just in this country, but around the world. So, as many commentators have noted, it is no wonder that her death in a high-speed car chase drew widespread attention, and the immediate and extensive media coverage pressed the tragedy on people's attention. But what is also interesting is the way in which so many people, in many cases without consulting anyone else, felt drawn to her London residence to leave flowers, so that there was a forest of flowers which could never have been placed by a graveside. It was not enough for many people to pay their respects to her privately; they needed to set off on a kind of pilgrimage, an activity out of fashion in modern society. I do not want to suggest that this mourning for Diana was not genuine; but I do want to suggest that, in T.S. Eliot's famous comment about *Hamlet*, there was grief *in excess of the facts*.

Indeed, as Richard Johnson (1999, p 32) notes, *Many people told television interviewers or radio chat show hosts how they had cried for Diana, but also at the same time for some other loss, unmourned at the time*; thus they recognised that this communal grieving was cathartic, allowing them to access feelings 'normal' mourning had not enabled them to express. And, as Matthew Engel (1997, p 26) noticed, the crowds of mourners *seemed as near as it was possible to get to a cross-section of the country: young and old, men and women, rich and poor, black and white*. J. Mallory Wober (2000, p 133) confirms this impression in a cross-category survey he and G. Middleham conducted in 1997, in which a quarter of the 400 respondents said they had cried within ten minutes of hearing of Diana's death.

I would argue that this need for, and display of, public, rather than private, mourning, often via flowers, reflects a sense of absence, a sense of grief within ordinary people which had been deprived of a socially acceptable outlet. As Goody and Poppi (1994) show, flowers have traditionally played a much more minor part in the expression of grief in England than in countries like Italy, and when used have tended to be confined to family wreaths at a funeral and (modest) flowers on a grave. But in this case we can see a collective need to break out of the confines of traditionally acceptable mourning.

A linked instance is the development of Wootton Bassett as a shrine where respects could be paid to soldiers who had lost their lives in Afghanistan and elsewhere. The large groups of people lining the processional route were soon not just made up of local people, but included many who had travelled a considerable distance to be there. Of course, media attention and an establishment desire to promote the military contributed to the growing scale of the event. But, according to the official British Legion website, some of the most telling details in the earliest repatriations arose by chance; for instance, the ringing of the church bell *started when a bell-ringing practice was taking place just before the Repatriation was due, and as a mark of respect the one bell was tolled on that occasion. Since then it became part of the 'ceremony'*.[1]

The inverted commas around the word ceremony are telling, indicating an awareness that improvisation was feeding into a need for a commemorative ritual. At the same time, some local residents were made uneasy by the expressions of deep pain from some family mourners, so there was tension as well as harmony.

I would argue that these examples, despite their differences, demonstrate a lacuna in many people's experience of death and loss, a need for something more than society at present offers. Indeed, in some respects, death is now almost a taboo subject, usually taking place away from home, where it is managed within a specialised institutional world. The dead body is separated from the mourners, usually to be reduced to ashes on the equivalent of a conveyor belt.

But there are signs of revolt against this impersonality and lack of connection. One is the development of funeral services written in part or in whole by the person approaching death, and presenting a memorial to that person's interests and character which mourners will recognise and treasure. Coffins crafted for the individual have been developed for those who are interested and can afford them.

A need for a connection with something outside of oneself and one's own family group is reflected in, for instance, the development of woodland burial sites. The first one was set up by Carlisle City Council in 1993, and now there are more than 260 of the sites in Britain. Bodies are buried in biodegradable coffins at these sites, with or without an additional ceremony. There are no headstones to mark the burial place, but the mourners know where the coffin was laid and can return to the site, as they might to a traditional graveyard.

## Rebellion against impersonality

Another sign of rebellion against impersonality is the horrified reaction to the suggestion in the draft of the fifth revision of the *Diagnostic and Statistical Manual of Mental Disorders* (often shortened to DSM), produced by the American Psychiatric Association, that anyone suffering from more than a fortnight's sadness, loss of energy and interest in life, and sleeplessness following a bereavement may have a major depressive disorder, or MDD.[2]

Of course, there are cases where unresolved grief can lead to mental health problems; but healthy grief for a dearly loved partner or family member often lasts well beyond a fortnight, without needing any medical intervention. Indeed, it is the tendency to medicalise grief in the DSM draft that has caused such furore, both from professional bodies, such as the British Medical Association (via its journal, *The Lancet*), and in the popular press (for example, Libby Purves' article, 'Why Must Grief Be a Sign of Mental Illness?' in *The Times*, 20 February 2012). This uproar demonstrates that there is much unease at this attempt to claim heartfelt grief as a no-go area for ordinary people, a territory reserved for the professionals. A further motive for suspicion is the knowledge that similar medicalisations have led to an increasing reliance on pills and medicines, an increase fuelled in part by the pressure exerted by the billion-dollar multinational pharmaceutical industry.

How did this dehumanisation of grief develop? In an obvious way, everything develops out of something that has gone before, but there are some periods of history when decisive changes take place. Many historians locate the beginnings of a distinctively modern attitude to the world in the later fifteenth, sixteenth and seventeenth centuries, and the term 'Early Modern Period' is increasingly replacing the favoured nineteenth-century designation, the Renaissance, as a result of this perception. I would argue that this is true in terms of attitudes to death and mourning in Britain, and in much of northern Europe and North America (and to other aspects of mental health as well). The sixteenth century is the time of the Reformation, and one of the main targets of the Protestant reformers, especially those who followed John Calvin, was what they judged to be the over-elaborate Roman Catholic rituals and displays of grief following a bereavement. For them, mourning for a departed one should be moderate, since otherwise it would suggest a lamentable lack of faith in Christ's promise of resurrection. God's elect would go to Heaven, so why mourn for them? The rest would be justly dispatched to Hell to be punished for their sins, and more than perfunctory mourning for them implied a questioning of God's judgement and justice. There was no third place, as Catholics believed, no Purgatory, so those still alive were powerless to ameliorate the fate of the dead by prayer or ceremony, and the best thing they could do, as rational beings, was to get over their grief in a decent interval of time, think of the living and get on with life.

As the Protestant hold on power strengthened, many writings and speeches extolled the virtues of circumspect mourning (Houlbrooke, 1998, p 308). A particularly interesting example comes from an anonymous letter, published in 1630, 'A Handkerchief for Parents' Wet Eyes upon the Death of Children', which seeks to console bereaved parents:

*He is not clean gone, but only gone before. His mortality is ended, rather than his life. You have lost him for a time, God hath found him for ever... Rejoice and bless God, that you had such a son. Had him, did I say? You have him still. Not one child the fewer have you for his taking hence ... There [in heaven] you shall one day see him again face to face.* (Anonymous, 2009, p 221)

Mourning is not condemned in the letter; but it must be moderated. This orthodoxy sometimes finds its way into the popular entertainment of the time. For instance, in *All's Well that Ends Well* Lord Lafew states, *Moderate lamentation is the right of the dead, not excessive grief* (Act 1, scene 1, lines 55–56), and in *Hamlet*, Claudius tells Hamlet that, although it is laudable to mourn for his father, it is *unmanly* to prolong such grief (1.2.94). Claudius' wording is significant. Reforming ideas gained sustenance from medical ideas of the period, which were ultimately derived from Ancient Greece, to provide a model of grief (and many other things) which was distinctly masculine (Maclean, 2011, p 26). Men were considered 'naturally' hot-blooded, and their heat burned off moisture, while women were like sponges, and shed tears and lamentations whenever any strong emotion squeezed them. One of the charges Hamlet lays against himself is that, rather than being a man of action, as Claudius and his dead father require him to be, he unpacks his heart, like a common whore, in words and images of grief. This is one of many examples from Shakespeare's time in which self-control is seen as the most socially desirable constituent in a response to bereavement. Explicitly, this is a requirement for men, but the implication is that women too should learn manly restraint, as Hamlet's mother Gertrude demonstrates after her husband's death, and as Ophelia fails to demonstrate when her father is killed by Hamlet.

## Against the prevailing orthodoxy

But the frequent recurrence of statements asserting the value of moderation and self-control in the Early Modern Period, especially in sermons, suggests that many people were finding it difficult to rationalise their feelings in the way that the prevalent ideology required. The notebooks of Richard Napier, which Michael MacDonald (1981) has tabulated and analysed, present an early example of this. Napier was a Buckinghamshire clergyman who acted as a combination of counsellor and astrologer for those who came to him with emotions which they could not come to terms with, and he recorded these visits from 1597 to 1634. Difficulties in coping with bereavement were equal second as a cause for these consultations, suggesting a widespread problem in his locality at least.

Inevitably, detailed records of this sort are rare, but supporting evidence comes from the work of historians such as Ralph Houlbrooke, David Cressy and Linda Pollock, who have specialised in primary sources of the period. From personal papers, journals and the like, they have found a wealth of evidence suggesting that many people found that they could not conform their mourning to the official requirements. An especially interesting example involves a seventeenth-century wood turner called Nehemiah Wallington, whose daughter had died at the age of four. For one thing, there are fewer records of the responses of people of Wallington's social rank; for another, he was a man of puritanical sympathies, who in theory supported the Calvinist dismissal of protracted grief. In practice, however, he found the opposite: *The grief for this child was so great that I forgot myself so much that I did offend God in it, before I broke all my purposes, promises and covenants with my God, for I was much distracted in my mind, and could not be comforted, although my friends spoke so comfortably to me* (Pollock, 1983, p 135). A further interest is the fact that this grief is for a very young daughter, at a time when much more social importance was attached to grown-up sons and heirs; and yet Wallington is inconsolable.

In *Birth, Marriage and Death*, published in 1997, David Cressy (p 393) summarised the altered understanding brought about by such primary source research: *Historians once advanced the notion that people in the past did not love each other and were coldly unemotional in the face of a death in their family. But the bulk of the evidence indicates that love, pain, and grief were deeply and widely experienced.* In other words, for much of the twentieth century historians read people's responses to bereavement in the light of the dominant Protestant ideology, and it was only in the final decades that the evidence was looked at more comprehensively, and the extent to which feelings overflowed their orthodox bounds was properly registered.

At first sight, these historical references might seem a great distance from our modern world, but the requirement for men in particular to suppress emotion is still powerful; for instance, in this plea from a father in Nebraska, whose daughter had just died:

*Those people who would comment about Jenny's death would say how sorry they were and then ask how my wife was. This concern for Chris was appreciated, for she was terribly shaken by Jennifer's death. Along with concern for Chris' well-being came words of wisdom or advice as to my conduct on how to handle my wife in this situation.*

*When is it my turn to cry? I'm not sure society or my upbringing will allow me a time to really cry, unafraid of the reaction and repercussion that might follow. I must be strong, I must support my wife because I am a man. I must be the cornerstone of our family because society says so, my family says so and until I can reverse my learned nature, I say so.* (Taylor et al., 1986, p 172)

This father realises the importance of crying for his dead daughter, but has internalised the social constraint on such behaviour, and realises he does not have the strength necessary to fight it.

Another relevant feature accelerated by the rationalism of the Reformation was the development of modern science, which gradually led to a more secular approach to burial and mourning. As Michel Foucault in particular has explored, this was accompanied by the rise of the professional, whose specialised knowledge partially or wholly excludes ordinary people from, among other things, the process of dying. An example would be the way in which the preparation of corpses for burial has moved from the home to the funeral parlour (a euphemism which tries to create a bogus sense of domesticity and homeliness).

Public health concerns, again a result of the increasing emphasis on a scientific approach to living and dying, went hand in hand with this increasing impersonality. In the last century this process was accelerated by modern warfare, especially the two world wars, where multitudes died on the battleground and had to be removed as quickly as possible to prevent the spread of disease, as well as for reasons of morale. Often, indeed, only fragments of bodies survived, making the concept of burial even more problematic. Death and dismemberment on such an industrial scale required disposal on the same scale.

Since the Second World War, the unprecedented increase in lifespan in the Western world has accelerated the sense of impersonality at the end of life. More and more people reach a situation where they cannot manage in their own homes, and their family, even if they are within reach, cannot give them the continuous care that they need. Thus an increasing number of people die in institutions such as hospitals, hospices and old people's homes.

## Conclusion

What tentative conclusions might we draw from this necessarily brief contemporary and historical survey? One is that we need to focus more strongly on our sense of human connection, and contact, with loved ones who die. For instance, as death and grief become more commercialised and depersonalised, it is unusual nowadays to witness the corpse of a family member or neighbour being laid out at home in the front parlour, or modern equivalent, and prepared for burial there. Not so long ago it was the norm for friends, relatives and neighbours of the deceased to visit the family home to pay respects and stay there close at hand to comfort the bereaved directly and personally. Visitors would find it entirely natural to approach the coffin, look directly inside and communicate something overtly or covertly about their feelings. Yet there are no good reasons, particularly in relation to public health, why it is better if this is carried out elsewhere.

There are legal precedents for private cremation to take place, and unless there are suspicious circumstances, no requirement for any interference with the corpse by funeral companies increasingly owned by large-scale businesses using industrial-style techniques to drain the body fluids and inject chemical preservatives. As with fast food, fast communication and fast living, so it is that death and grieving have to be hastened along. In life, people have been taught to think there is a 'pill for every ill' and that modern science can find cures for diseases previously untreatable. Quick fixes can relieve an ache or pain but fail to reveal the cause of that pain and obscure the opportunity to sort out the cause for a sustainable outcome rather than repeatedly treating the symptom. All of this takes time, and modern society requires a fast pace, an immediacy that is out of synch with human need. Rethinking the balance between the familial and the professional, the personal and the commercial, requires us to challenge the status quo, to pay much more attention to our sense of human agency and natural feelings so the professional does not obliterate the human.

Further, we need a more flexible approach to the forms of grieving which are socially acceptable. This need is confirmed by much recent work on bereavement; for instance, Kenneth

Doka and Terry Martin's *Grieving beyond Gender* (2010), which emphasises that, while there are patterns in human mourning, these have often been applied too rigidly by theorists, with insufficient attention given to the varied needs of individual mourners. Their research focuses on gender, but has implications for other traditional divisions, such as race and culture, as well. Indeed, the need for this awareness will increase as Western society becomes increasingly pluralistic. Mourners who need to express their inner pain in public as well as in private should be allowed to do so without being made to feel guilty, or coming under pressure to suppress such feelings.

Finally, we must recognise that the social emphasis on grieving in private can leave people feeling isolated and unable to express their full feelings. As we saw at the beginning of this chapter, many people draw inner sustenance and strength from taking part in communal ritual. For many people, this still takes the form of a traditional religious ceremony; but, as we can see from examples such as the death of Princess Diana, and the Wootton Bassett repatriations, the catharsis of communal ritual is not limited to those with a specific religious faith. Our society has placed on a pedestal the individual who achieves, especially in the economic sphere. Again we need to rethink, and re-feel, the balance between the individual and the communal, and find new and acceptable ways for grief to be expressed in public. And it is not only in the sphere of mourning that this lack of balance needs to be corrected. Perhaps at one level we can think about mourning as another aspect of a natural reaction to a friend, relative or colleague with mental health problems. So we mourn the 'loss' of their personality, faculties, self-perception – what made them who they were and how we interacted with them. The language of psychiatry and the classification of mental illness is littered with the narrative of loss, absence, failure, incapacity or incoherence.

Common parlance includes reference to 'being away with the fairies' or 'out of their mind' when describing a suffering human being. And never far away is the concept of contagion – will we 'catch' this disease if we come too close to it, is it hereditary and thus a kind of family curse? A person is referred to as having 'lost their mind' when they do or say something out of the ordinary, provocative and maybe strange. All of this impels us to fear mental illness, to seek to control it for social reasons, to distance ourselves from it, and to hand it to professionals with their neat, clinical 'detachment', documents, pills and procedures. Because to get closer to mental illness risks exposing our own internal and psychological vulnerabilities, it risks illuminating aspects of our personality which under the right conditions could break out into mental illness or a florid breakdown. So modern psychiatry colludes with these primitive fears, denials and attempts at dehumanising the person. The person with mental health problems, like the dead or dying person, can become a diagnosis, a number, a classification and an object – all the better to make us feel different and secure, not like them.

## Key learning points

•   The need for a balanced and flexible approach to the process of grieving. Theoretical models are helpful up to a point, but mourners living in a pluralistic society should be encouraged and supported in finding a kind of grieving which is based on their individual needs.

- The dehumanisation of the process of mourning by excessive professional control should be resisted.

- Time needs to be allowed to those whose mourning is healthy, but fails to fit a preconceived pattern of how it should develop.

# 6  Being Disturbed: The Impact of Severe Personality Disorder on Professional Carers

## By R.D. Hinshelwood

*Professional men, they have no cares – Whatever happens, they get theirs.*
Ogden Nash, 1935

## Introduction

Ogden Nash's quip implies a perfectly neutral attitude on the part of a professional to the affairs of the people he deals with. Perhaps it is a familiar view of professional people. We need our accountants, lawyers and so on to give us an objective view of our affairs. Maybe that should be what is needed from the caring professions. However, I have argued that, within psychiatry, carers are particularly disconcerted by the work they do (Hinshelwood, 1999a, 2004). In this chapter, I wish to look in some closer detail at these interpersonal processes that occur between carers and those they care for, with particular emphasis on personality disordered people.

This chapter will take a critical perspective, questioning and problematising the standard approach to care provision based on the consumer model as developed since about 1990 in the UK's NHS. The critique will involve a perspective based on a relational model, in which 'users' will be recognised as in a relationship with their carers, rather than merely objects of care; and indeed 'carers' are, equally, in a relationship with their users. In other words, the critical position is to focus on 'users' *in context*, and in the relational environment of care. Increasingly, the discovery of the notion of 'compassionate care' (DH Commissioning Board, 2012) has begun to point to the human environment of relationship – the concern, feelings and generally of the psychic pain in providing and receiving care.

Diagnostic terms such as personality disorder, and role assignments such as 'user' even, will be used here *only* in their descriptive sense, and not in the labelling functions that allot persons to professional categories of abnormality or social role. The enquiry in this chapter is (a) whether such a contextualising of persons within relations may add to our understanding of care provision and its problems, and (b) if it does so add, what does it lead to in terms of doing things differently.

# The relational context of care

Consider,

*The patient was led into a quiet room for her relaxation therapy. She remained there with her nurse, who locked the door and pressed a button on a tape machine which played for 20 minutes. The nurse sat down and appeared bored from over-familiarity with the tape. At the end, the nurse switched off the machine, unlocked the door and led the patient out.*

This occurrence is by all accounts not very uncommon and not at all exaggerated. It is not bad in that it follows a care pathway for the patient, observes ethical requirements and manages health and safety risks. But, what, as the tutor might ask a class of trainee nurses, is wrong?

The answer depends on the point of view. In formal terms, the nurse could not really be seriously faulted; the patient got her relaxation therapy. From another point of view, criticism might be strong: the context of the patient was assumed to be a machine playing a tape, while the relationship with the carer (the nurse in this incident) appeared to be relegated to non-existence. The role of care was interpreted as merely semi-custodial; keeping the door shut, switching the machine on and being on hand for possible crises. Any personal quality to this care functioning was pre-empted by a point of view that interpreted care in the strictly formal sense. What is demonstrated, hopefully, is that there are first of all different points of view about what care is.

Most people, if they were not a nurse on duty, would find themselves rather averse to the formal, semi-custodial and mechanical interpretation of the care depicted here. What makes a nurse adopt that interpretation when she comes on duty? She may have just dropped her child off at nursery, said goodbye to her husband with a kiss, rung mother about the visit at the coming weekend. I make this construction to emphasise that nurses providing care are actually emotionally sensitive and normally related people. Only in the context of the relations at work do they switch into another mode in which they interpret care in another way, a depersonalised and mechanical one.

Of course, my construction may be wrong. The nurse may not have the ordinary relations of life. That may be common across the board of nurses. They may all be unfeeling battleaxes, at home and at work alike. Is it the case that somehow this unit into which we glimpsed above has gathered into its recruitment net a highly selective set of such battleaxes, who practise their profession in this way? No doubt this is a research question which could be settled by the appropriate research design with data from the personality profiles of the nurses staffing the unit.

I am not going to report such a research project, though it would have been quite feasible to do so. Instead, I want to explore another possibility. This is based on the hypothesis that staff, such as the nurse depicted, do in fact change their interpretive point of view in different contexts. This pressure of the human, relational and group-dynamic context is in fact well researched, going back to the early social psychology experiments of Asch (1952), Sherif and Sherif (1956) and Milgram (1964) from the mid-twentieth century, and the Stanford Prison Experiment (Haney et al., 1973).

*A note on method*: The method of investigation here is to develop a working hypothesis – that is, a hypothesis that does work in explaining the occurrences of events. There is not an attempt to test the hypothesis through its therapeutic outcomes. Rather it is tested in an alternative way. It is customary to make the assumption that a therapeutic approach is *only* testable by virtue of its yield of successful outcomes for users. This assumption is restrictive, and it would require the space of another chapter to address this. It is sufficient, hopefully, to say that another method is appropriate for more subjective fields of study; this is a method which assesses the explanatory power of a hypothesis. In other words, a theory that can explain more than a rival theory has a claim to be a better theory (see, for instance, Edelson, 1984). This does not supplant the method-of-outcome study, but outcome evaluation needs to come *after* evaluation of explanatory scope.

In assessing theories, there are various characteristics to be considered; added to the two here – explanatory power and outcome success – there is also a criterion of plausibility; a theory that depended on the phases of the moon as determining of mood is less plausible before its explanatory scope and outcome success are addressed. These issues relevant to the methodology of therapeutics cannot be further detailed in this chapter, but lie behind the choice of method.

## The search for explanation

Instead of re-doing such experiments, I want to develop a hypothesis about how such a thing can happen. In other words, what the hypothesis has to cover is the fact that nurses, who on the whole are highly caring people (in fact, probably the most caring that could be found), end up bored, impersonal and unfeeling.

Dubbing it 'the Lucifer effect', Zimbardo (2008) could speak as an authority on this process of corruption, having organised the experiment at Stanford. There, volunteers simulated guards and prisoners. The shock was that quite ordinary people became alienated brutalising guards, not simulating at all. This, he said, was a process connected to the Abu Graib atrocities. Inhumane behaviour occurred in Iraq when allied soldiers attacked and tortured civilians they were supposed to be protecting. Zimbardo tracked the cause to the anonymity of the guards, the de-individuating impact of uniforms, routines and so on. However, such depersonalisation and the bleaching of humanity from human relations had been well recognised throughout history. And in fact, 50 years previously, Menzies Lyth (1959) had described the depersonalisation that crept in and dominated the practice of nursing. She pointed to a very similar phenomenon but apparent in a very different institution. That kind of institutional pathology was then of great interest at the time, in the period following the Second World War, and gave rise to the term 'institutionalisation' (Barton, 1959; Martin, 1955), with the classic account given by the anthropologist Irving Goffman in his book *Asylums* (Goffman, 1961), in which he drew parallels between various 'total institutions', including prisons and mental hospitals.

Many processes in mental health services have negative results that go against the good intentions of the staff and hinder them in spite of themselves. Those with good intentions find themselves in organisational settings that they could not condone if they had a more objective view. In a way, this is the saddest aspect, and yet, at the same time, it is the most human aspect of psychiatric care. In an original study, Hardcastle et al. (2007) addressed not just the reactions of the users to the service and its achievements, but those of the caring professionals as well. A number of individual cases were taken, at random, and personal stories of the *experience* of care in this case were gathered from the patient, doctor, nurses, relatives, social workers and so on. It presents a seriously disheartening account of the misperceptions and unread messages that appear to be endemic within a psychiatric unit.

Despite the prevalence of these descriptions of whole-institution phenomena, the problem has been to understand how this antithesis of care occurs even among those most committed to caring. Explanatory hypotheses have been difficult to generate, and until they exist, the what-to-do paragraph is difficult to write.

I shall now develop such a hypothesis for consideration, but first we need to understand what it is that we need to explain. I shall draw attention to the following characteristics that appear resistant to explanation:

- the essentially self-defeating loss of compassion in humane work;

- the inability to bring the awfulness of one's own impersonal reactions to conscious awareness;

- the difficulty in reflecting on that loss;

- the observation that a depersonalisation and loss of identity is involved; and

- the observation that this is not merely an individual aberration but is collective within a specific institutional context.

This catalogue of features oversteps purely behavioural categories, and points to experiential ones, those of identity and a moral imperviousness, in particular, and also a severe restriction of awareness and self-awareness. Elementary features, the wearing of uniforms, seem shallow to explain the deep distortions of persons, work and the care relationship.

The problem can be graphically illustrated in the following vignette. It points to certain relational issues that obtrude in the care setting. The example (Davies, 1996) is a team of carers involved in the rehabilitation of a serial offender. The professionals display their personal relatedness, which fails to deliver effective care, but instead becomes an involvement that riskcd potentially disastrous results. The following is my précis of the original account.

*A disturbed man, Bill X, had a harsh mother as a child. She was violent and humiliated him. When released from prison where he had finished a sentence for brutal sexual crimes, he asked to be kept inside. The request was naturally refused. He subsequently engaged with the helping network in a specific way.*

*He was dangerous and a specific plan had been set out at the hostel he was to go to, to ensure that only male staff dealt with him. However, the arrangements quickly broke down for extraneous reasons. He was taken into intensive counselling by a female worker; and a female prison visitor who had visited him in prison continued to see him, including taking him to her home, where he assaulted her. Another female worker offered counselling, sometimes in evening sessions, and afterwards said she had forgotten he was a rapist! The female staff had been drawn into taking up powerful professional roles with him, to be inviting, and then to withdraw from him, giving him that intolerable feeling of powerlessness again.*

*So, the care network responded disastrously to his continuing disturbance. The staff did not seem to realise that the arrangements had broken down.*

*What went wrong could be traced very specifically to a repetition of the experience of care the man had as a child. His mother was very powerful and controlling and continually made him feel powerless; he had effectively no father with whom to identify. His sense of male power was unpractised and uncontrolled. In the hostel, the male staff disappeared – changed job, or went on courses, like the ineffective father, and the female staff did their best to take over, as mother had.*

*The staff seemed unable any longer to think about the client realistically, or even to remember his case fully. The fairly simple professional insight that his violent and humiliating criminal activity was connected with violence and humiliation he received from his mother seems never to have been usable.*

Davies' presentation arouses concern that the man's evident wish to receive some sort of help for his internal state was not 'read' by the helpers, and he progressed to further violent crimes, one of which was the assault on the female helper. There is commonly a problem 'reading' the plea for help from such troubled people. Instead, the carers, in this case, became caught up in the intra-psychic 'drama' of the person they cared for. There is a very specific concurrence between the man's own sought-after parent and the actual carers he came across. His action of requesting to stay in prison, for instance, was outside the remit of the prison authorities, and no doubt felt bizarre even to the man himself. He was helplessly rejected. The attack on the 'caring' visitor lacked any conscious significance, but unconsciously spoke to his humiliation by women and the revenge he sought.

The deeply personal past in which Bill X was trapped came to be represented in actual terms by the present selection of people. The women in the team became embodiments of the mother who caused such humiliation. This was predicted, consciously, and a plan made, but, because of the obscure social forces, professional prediction changed to unconscious enactment without the staff realising that they had forgotten the prediction, or their professional task and work. The man's demand was treated with a 'care' response, but not a reflective one. It was a sentimentalised sympathy, which passed as maternal caring, but in the event became his experience of maternal humiliation. Neither the man nor the carers were able to articulate what was happening. No proper symbolisation, conscious representation or thought survived. They unconsciously played out the man's powerful issues, in the care context, and this interfered with the minds and work of trained professionals. They carried out their *conscious* tasks, apparently unaware of how this man's conflicts were determining the care network. Such dramatisation, by staff, of the inner worlds of those in the institution, is a very common (but unrecognised) phenomenon (Hinshelwood,

1987). Thus the work of the team and of a whole service can be said to be affected by this process.

This vignette illustrates the main characteristics listed above. The staff succumbed to very odd identity issues, as if they were playing out roles for the index client, abandoned the capacity for important professional thinking, and lost awareness of what was happening to them. The context is relational. The team, and, it should be noted, the client himself, operated *in relation to* each other.

In the next section, I shall therefore pose a hypothesis on the basis of this account, which can be investigated for its ability to explain the phenomenon. It will take a critical position vis-à-vis the labelling function of the phenomena and the behaviour of individual personality traits that appear to be corrupted. It is not character traits that 'behave', but persons. And, in the present account, persons behave in the context of relations with other persons. The hypothesis adopts the view that much happens outside the awareness of people, in the gaps, as it were, within the relations between them, and creates what can be called an implicit culture, composed of shared and hidden (or unconscious) attitudes towards the work, and towards the subjects of care.

## Subjective experience and the social defence system

The deeply internal impact of the work on the team collective is striking and demands that we turn to a psychology that is not driven by objectivity but has its focus on the inner world of experience. There is only one direction in which we can turn. As Glen Gabbard said of psychoanalysis:

*In an era of quick-fix managed care approaches and rampant biological reductionism, we can derive a great deal of gratification from the fact that we still see value in the unique subjectivity of the person who comes to us for help. We seem to be entering a new version of the Dark Ages, an era when treating others with understanding, compassion, and patience is viewed as cost-ineffective and too time-consuming. We can all take a measure of gratification from the fact that in this darkest of times, we are the bearers of the flame.* (Gabbard, 2000, pp 713–14)

Disregarding the bitterness of the sentiment, Gabbard's import is that the bearer of the flame that enlightens the subjectivity of persons is the psychoanalyst's approach. Moreover, the critique implied is that cost effectiveness is not so easily glossed over. Indeed, the risks in Davies' case suggest that an insight into the subjectivity of the team, as it evolves together, is highly important, and is worthy of question, investigation, of the time involved, and of the costs should risks become actual.

## What can the theory of anxiety and defence explain?

The single message is that there are hidden processes in individuals which emerge in relations with others (and therefore within groups) and which players may often be unaware of. Psychoanalysis does not supplant the psychology of conscious experience or of personal behaviour. But when mysterious things cannot be explained, it may be as well to check if the hidden world of the psychoanalyst has any explanatory leverage to complement the conscious psychology.

The psychoanalyst's focus is on psychic pain, and the way the human mind renders it subterranean. This is surely, on the face of it, worth looking into when considering such high-stress occupations as mental health care, general nursing, custodial prison work and the endangering career of a soldier in the army.

Against such assaults on the personality, the person takes cover. So the hypothesis I am proposing to test is the following:

*The stress of the task leads to processes largely outside of awareness that tend to distance carers from the stress, but in the process distort the task, the forms of practice and the nature of care.*

This is not pathology, this is humanity. Moreover, the individual member of staff, the carer, is an individual in a context. And the context of the carer has multiple dimensions; it includes the impact of the user, plus the presence of other carers also working under similar impacts. Individually, and also collectively, carers take action to protect themselves from too much stress.

The hypothesis being developed is that the emotional impact on the individuals who provide care for people spreads into effects on the organisation as a whole, on its sets of cultural attitudes, often implicit, and on the work practices which are determined by these attitudes. These are insidious processes that occur *outside* of awareness and push attitudes and practices into forms that will alleviate some of the stress of the working activity.

Studies of the kind of impact the emotional stress of its members has on an organisation have appeared regularly since Elliott Jaques' psychoanalytic understanding of the unconscious process in a factory, and Isabel Menzies Lyth's (1959) classic study of a nursing service. Organisational attitudes, working practices, and even the overall task of the organisation, become adapted to this secondary goal of implicitly relieving stress. Menzies showed that the stress of nurses on long shifts with patients who are frightened, dying, mutilated and in physical pain can be relieved by the implicit attitude and practical requirement that the nurse keeps an emotional and relational distance from her patients.

A long series of similar studies have been reported showing similar ways in which cultural attitudes and practices defend the individually stressed carers from the impact of the stress: see also Miller and Gwynne (1972), and the numerous papers in Obholzer and Roberts (1994). These unconscious collective processes that Menzies Lyth found in general hospitals (Menzies Lyth, 1959; Skogstad, 2000) have been found in psychiatric hospitals (Chiesa, 2000; Donati, 1989; Rees, 2000), and in community care (Morris, 2000). The upshot of these empirical findings is the sad recognition that those of whom most tenderness in care might be expected may become the most corrupted into depersonalising those they care for.

## The objective approach

Psychiatric services deal with difficult people, those with whom society in general cannot cope. Forensic services deal with the most difficult of those difficult people (Gordon and Kirtchuk, 2008). Then public opinion and government are surprised that it is such difficult work. My argument here is that such people are difficult because they make a difficult emotional impact on their carers. Then carers have to deal with themselves as well as their patients/clients. How we deal with ourselves in these services may not always be to the benefit of the patients, and I shall try to show how this hypothesis explains the sometimes detrimental deterioration of our services.

A while ago (Hinshelwood, 1999a), I wrote about the effect of the scientific turn in psychiatry – with the question whether its specific culture is influenced by the emotional impact of the work. The culture within psychiatry has become increasingly objective (in Britain, at least) over the last 30–40 years, and this derives from a number of obvious factors that come together.

One of the factors is the harvest of humane care that comes from accurate diagnosis and scientific treatment.

However, that is only one of the factors. There are others, which do not, of course, discount the importance of scientific work in clinical practice, but enhance it for other purposes. Such factors include the following.

•    There is a large overlay of professional pride and competitiveness with other medical specialities that comes from being especially scientific.

•    Marketing techniques are powerful, even when selling to professionally trained people, and drug companies have considerable financial resources to buy effective branding and marketing, which understandably they use to their best advantage when possible.

•    There are issues not at all as open and available to view as the two above, but which arise from the problems of stress, demoralisation, and quite relentlessly constant challenge to the guilt and repair impulses of caring professionals. These espouse a scientific attitude because of the objectivity and emotional distancing inherent in science.

The increasing emphasis on an objective scientific approach is very striking in recent decades, and the success of pharmacology in creating highly psychoactive substances has alleviated a great deal of suffering in many of our patients; however, that success has also gone along with side effects that arise from scientific objectivity. The hypothesis of this paper is that the emotional distance between staff and patients of the objective scientific approach can serve to protect mental health workers from the noxious and difficult emotional impact on themselves. For instance, people with schizophrenia are difficult because of their strange and meaningless behaviour and utterances. Psychiatric services can use scientific explanations to provide meanings which are lacking in their patients. However, the meanings that are substituted for their patients' personal experiences are those of the material process of brain physiology and neuronal biochemistry. The person of the patient is left on one side. In other words, they become depersonalised. The tendency is to exonerate the schizophrenic from responsibility for their behaviour and symptoms. Instead, it is the illness that is responsible, and psychiatric carers relate in the first instance to the illness and not to the person's experience (see Barratt, 1996, for careful observation and description of these processes).

This is somewhat unfortunate since the patient's actual experience is significantly confirmed by this approach. A central feature of schizophrenia is an existential one in which the person loses a sense of his own identity and self. Winnicott called it an interruption in the sense 'of the continuity being' (Winnicott, 1960, p 594). So I am indicating a kind of fit between the sets of attitudes in scientific psychiatry and a specific feature of the schizophrenic experience. From both directions, the patient feels less of a person, because of (a) the disorder itself, and also (b) the culture of professional carers. This unfortunate fit contributes to an enduring cycle of interaction, a factor promoting the well-known tendency for schizophrenia to become chronic.

In summary, cultural attitudes in psychiatry can be employed to help staff deal with the impact of their patients, while at the same time those attitudes make the task of caring harder and so have a self-defeating influence. Somewhat similar interactions occur in working with severe personality disordered (SPD) people – with a similar combination of self-protection and self-defeat. Such a perverse result is another challenge for the hypothesis to explain.

## Why are SPD patients difficult?

SPD patients confront staff with another challenge. Not one of meaninglessness. Severe personality disordered patients offer the opposite, a relationship *too* intensely suffused with human feelings – usually very unpleasant ones. These patients operate predominantly within a world of feelings. Characteristically, 'personality disordered' or 'severe personality disordered' patients directly and deliberately (though unconsciously) interfere with our feelings. We *feel* intruded upon and manipulated. And indeed we are. As Malcolm Pines wrote, we feel

*impelled to conform to a pattern imposed by the patient, so that we begin to feel provoked, hostile, persecuted and [have] to behave exactly as the patients need us to, becoming rejecting and hostile.* (Pines, 1978, p 115)

We are impelled in ways we are hardly aware of, yet follow. Our roles as professionals can become seriously distorted. One example is the Richard Davies (1996) vignette I started with. His example is not necessarily usual in that the team tried very hard to accommodate this man, despite their emotional blindfolds. More frequently, the experience is disagreeable, and the obvious manipulative intrusions feel like a kind of abuse of us, of our time and our help. As I wrote in a joint paper with Kingsley Norton:

*The trademark of SPD patients is an impairment of their interpersonal and social functioning. This makes it difficult to engage many of them in treatment since the clinical encounter with them is frequently marked by negative feelings, both in them but also in the staff involved in treatment. Intense and controlling feelings in the latter serve to perpetuate or aggravate an aggressive, or passive-aggressive, response from patients.* (Norton and Hinshelwood, 1996, p 723)

Given the mounting negativity – on both sides – it is not surprising that mental health professionals may indeed suffer their own painful mental disturbance. As a result, abrupt resignations, illness, anxiety, sudden and unexpected anger, inability to continue working with a patient, massive guilt feelings, despair, envy of patients' acting out, helplessness and exhaustion faced with patients' devaluation have all been described (Drum and Lavigne,

1987; Greben, 1983; Miller, 1989). In this way, the care role fails, and the mental health professional, despite their training, is in danger of being overwhelmed.

Professionals react very differently with people with this kind of impaired relating compared with their reactions to patients with schizophrenia (or with the interpersonal dynamics of other patients). With severe personality disorder, the patient is not depersonalised into an object, but instead strongly retains moral qualities, expressed in a series of condemnatory labels – 'bad' rather than 'mad'. Diagnostic categories such as psychopath or hysteric mean more usually, *The patient is not ill at all and is wasting our time*. The use of diagnostic categories betrays again the attempt to climb into a scientific attitude immune from the emotional turmoil. But here it is a thin disguise for a psychiatrist who has lost his role, and finds himself an 'abuser'. His barely concealed angry rejection often confirms the life experience of such patients whose carers have in fact proved rejecting or worse. A very large number of these patients have a personal history of childhood abuse from the people who are supposed to care. It may not be physical abuse, but psychologically and emotionally inappropriate handling that displays a lack of empathic response. The outcome for such children is an adulthood in which they persist in equating care with abuse. Confronted in this emotional way by a new carer, the SPD patient may frequently proceed with considerable suspicion and unresponsiveness. This has disastrous effects.

The carer expects and assumes his patient will acknowledge the care, and will show due appreciation. When his care is treated with suspicion and as if it were abuse, he can feel affronted, offended and condemned. In short he feels his care is abused by his patient. As a result, he is in difficulty with this patient, feeling angry at someone for whom he is supposed to remain caring. At this point, it appears the carer may go in one of two possible directions. One is that his professional super-ego and guilt lead him to bend over backwards to accommodate, as in Richard Davies' vignette, trying ever more desperately to get his care acknowledged for what it is. By pursuing confirmation of his caring capacities, he risks losing his professional judgement. The other reaction is to become actually rejecting, as if the patient has indeed become a harsh and judgemental super-ego. Then he may discharge the patient from the service – or perhaps refer him on to another service. In either case, he ceases to see the patient as in fact a patient – he has become an abuser of the carer.

Here is another instance in which the reaction of carers to the difficulties they suffer through looking after the most difficult people has side effects. With SPD patients it is a little more complicated, and a lot more emotionally disturbing, than with schizophrenic patients. Caring for SPD people leads to being invaded and taken over, while his charge regards him as an abuser of someone already traumatised.

In these various ways, the staff of services caring for SPD people may become similarly caught up in psychodynamics that act out the impact or avoid the pain of the impact of working with difficult patients who, having been abused, tend to pass on the experience to their carers. In many ways, staff deal with the guilt and pressure by going along with ways of relating that are determined by their patients. Partly to appease the apparent need, and partly to reduce the stress that presses in on the workers, they take the easy way out. What is difficult is to protect the capacity to think about these experiences – as illustrated in the

Davies example – and, specifically, to think about the pressures that mould the experiences. That capacity to reflect and even know themselves as professionals can be inhibited and lost, as we saw.

# Results

It is possible to claim that the hypothesis we developed does have an explanatory value vis-à-vis these apparently self-defeating processes that can be found in high-stress caring institutions.

Most staff are extremely dedicated and well intentioned and do a great deal of good for their patients. What we need to explain are certain unacceptable and hitherto unexplained negative developments that go on in the culture of these high-stress institutions, and in the individual persons working there as carers. And it is now possible to understand and explain these more negative developments as unfortunate, collective and seemingly hidden modes of trying to cope.

# What to do?

The hypothesis that the particular tensions described in this paper result in damaging consequences for the team may be tested in various ways. First, as I have shown, the hypothesis has a wider explanatory scope, but a further test is its practical application. The test is whether it leads to ways of working with better results – better outcomes. The kinds of outcome that count as 'better' is itself a research question, and cannot be dealt with here (but see Hinshelwood, 2002). Instead, here I shall give an illustration which has features in common with the earlier vignette of the ex-prisoner who put out of action the professionals' ability to think about the case, Bill X in the Davies example.

The problem of managing these processes is that they are not apparent to the objective eye. They creep up surreptitiously from behind. As in all instances of the effects of the unconscious life of individuals, it is difficult to manage them consciously. Thus, those minds that are impacted upon need the opportunity to think through their experiences in a setting that is not exposed to the impact. They need to find a state of mind that can take the entrusted experiences from those patients and recast them in some therapeutic way – avoiding as far as possible those defensive means of dealing with the projected experiences.

Because the unconscious effects are so strong, SPD patients were for a long time regarded as untreatable. Interestingly, however, they have recently been deemed amenable to treatment. They are no longer *a diagnosis of exclusion* (NIMHE, 2003). Can, therefore, the loss of objective thinking be compensated for by a designed and managed input? – that is, to institute a reflective space.

There is, in fact, a long history of treating personality disorders, known since 1946 (Main, 1946) as the therapeutic community method. This is of considerable relevance to what I have been saying about the potential for major enactments in the relations made by SPD people. Although in residential care of any kind, SPD patients do create enactments among their colleague patients, in the therapeutic community these incidents are kept especially under review, reflected upon and subjected to therapeutic commentary. In other words, the staff have a new field of observation available for them. Though reflective thought is severely inhibited, the therapeutic community can offer a crucially different opportunity in this respect. Staff can gain a reflective distance from enactments in the community *as a whole*, and they are not confronted with them on a face-to-face individual basis. Staff need to think together about how the community (including themselves) may be caught up in the unconscious dramatisations. There are a number of ways in which this is important, which I would like to list, but first I shall give an example from a therapeutic community. The community was organised for this kind of thoughtful reflection. In this instance, the unwittingly playing-out roles *were* brought into professional thinking. In this example, two key workers were able to discuss their particular dramatisation for a patient, Joe. Here is how it happened:

Joe, an adolescent, was transferred from a private service where he had been an inpatient for over a year. He had been admitted because of depression, self-harm and suicide risk. The therapeutic relationship had broken down. The admitting consultant psychiatrist then made a referral to the adolescent department of the Cassel Hospital, a tertiary SPD service run as a therapeutic community, to which he was subsequently admitted.

Once there, similar patterns of non-communication were soon replicated at different levels of the community, that is, he would remain silent during his individual therapy sessions and would isolate himself in his room for long periods. The relationships with his primary workers (the key nurse and the therapist) developed a deep split.

He experienced his therapist (a man) as insensitive, threatening and unable to offer any understanding or help. In the counter-transference, the therapist felt frustrated, useless and jealous of the closer and more constructive relationship Joe had with his female nurse. These two divided as a working couple. They were only able to discuss Joe's situation in a joking manner, seemingly as an avoidance of the feelings that a more meaningful discussion might evoke. Joe's efforts to split the 'couple' of nurse–therapist reached a climax when he wrote to the Consultant of the unit asking for his therapist to be changed.

The tension around Joe's care was manifested as a difficulty that his primary workers had in having a professional discussion. This was explored in a joint session with senior members of the team during the nurse–therapist supervision. Significantly, it was noted that in a recent family meeting, the lack of communication in Joe's family, particularly between his parents, had been highlighted. The family was dominated by the ineffectual parental relationship, which somehow had been re-created in the roles of the staff in the hospital.

In the course of this discussion, the therapist and nurse could start a more open exchange of feeling and this continued in other more informal settings. Joe's despair and failure – felt in this instance by the therapist – met, in a new way, a much more helpful and encouraging side (carried by his nurse). A plan was made with the nurse to encourage and support Joe's attendance at his therapy sessions. In the thinking space provided by the nurse–therapist supervision, the omnipotent and destructive fantasies behind Joe's request for a change in therapist, something he had managed to enact in other care settings, were understood and challenged. The therapist became more aware of the origin of his counter-transference feelings. The internal conflict in Joe between despair and hope was recognised as dominating both family and community.

With the greater integration within the staff team, Joe could begin to reconcile the divisions he had made within his relationships and in himself. He successfully attended his therapy sessions during the rest of his time at the Cassel Hospital and was able to express and work through his feelings towards the therapist in a new way and to move on to think about his discharge plans. Nurse and therapist, too, were able to communicate more efficiently in this important phase around Joe's follow-up plans. (Santos and Hinshelwood, 1998, pp 34–35)

Admittedly, this is not as grave a form of acting out as is frequently encountered, but it enables us to observe in slow motion, as it were, the important features of the reflection. There are several features which contribute to this being a successful piece of reflection:

- The individual carers were able to feel they could work something out and to increase the scope of their awareness, and thus to feel less helpless.

- With this sense of awareness, they were enabled to resist playing a part in the way that the carers in Davies' example did succumb.

- To reflect on the occurrences is not to reject, as so often happens. Instead, a recognition developed in the key workers so they could be with, or remain with, the disturbance, without being overwhelmed by it.

- Perhaps most significant of all, the two members of staff were able to speak together in a constructive and fruitful way, in fact in a manner that did not replicate the implicit divorce that existed between Joe's parents.

- In consequence, Joe was, shall we say, better held in the hospital's parental embrace, and able to resume a therapy process.

In connection with the last of these factors, the fruitful interaction of the staff together in a way that contrasted with Joe's experience of carers, I have in mind a short quote from Elliott Jaques:

*Individuals may put their internal conflicts into persons in the external world, unconsciously follow the course of the conflict by means of projective identification, and re-internalise the course and outcome of the externally perceived conflict by means of introjective identification.* (Jaques, 1955, p 497)

In Joe's case he was able to insert his problematic 'parents' into the persons around him in the external world, and there to witness them at variance with each other. However, in this instance, the parental roles adopted by the carers created a situation in which Joe could witness the course of this parental conflict and as a result offered him a model for greater integration in himself.

The outcome of the use of this hypothesis/theory was indeed the possibility of a continuing therapeutic relationship and a treatment success, at least in terms of the patient's return to a normal life. This is one success only but it indicates that the hypothesis does not just have explanatory power but promises at least some outcome success.

# Conclusions

The speculative hypothesis developed has been investigated in various ways. It postulates unconscious collaboration in developing cultural attitudes which distort the work, the practice and the effectiveness of treatment in psychiatry, especially with difficult patients. First, the hypothesis appears to be explanatory of occurrences which can only be weakly addressed by other hypotheses drawn from social psychology and from the criticisms about the limitations of training. And second, at least one case shows that the explanatory power follows through as a treatment success in this category of notoriously difficult and frequently rejected kinds of people.

We started by applying a critical leverage to the current over-emphasis on objectivity and the social construction by care organisations of an isolated individualism, in contrast to the context of the client plus their carers. The outcome of an objective approach fails to touch the *subjective* aspect of the care culture. Instead, using the example especially of severe personality disorder, a simple relational hypothesis was based on 'inner' subjective aspects of reacting to each other. The simplicity is, however, belied by non-awareness of the threatening impact that this dimension of care work has on workers (and even perhaps on the readers of research papers on care work!).

The testing of the hypothesis offered has led to explanations of largely unexplained occurrences which dishearten and demoralise carers and lead to less good provision for users. The result of the success of this hypothesis is not to advocate a technical role, a mechanical or scientific technology. Carers find they need to seek each other out for support and personal involvement, and to participate in reflection. In the end, it is not just what carers do, nor even what they think and express, it is how they are and how they relate, which counts. It is because they are living, acting, relating beings that they *can* care, and provide the specific attention. And moreover, an approach restricted to simple *objective* evaluation is just that, it is over-simple and simplistic (Hinshelwood, 1999a, 2010).

The importance of *being in* a relational context is not something that can be taught; it is merely being human. Instead, what may be teachable is the capacity to reflect on relational contexts. For instance, a series of workshops has been conducted over a number of years, set up with the aim of learning from action within relationships (as opposed to words), and reported by Hinshelwood et al. (2010).

Even limited successes in this direction are of great importance; the capacity to participate in a living situation is enormously heartening, to users and carers alike. It is the wish to engage with those who suffer that takes us into the business in the first place, and the ability to retain a real engagement with that suffering is the core of the job satisfaction we seek. The widely offered means and attitudes for escaping to a distance from the impact of the suffering, and towards scientific objectification, is one of the saddest things about our work, since it takes us away from the satisfactions we most seek.

Finally, it has to be left to a later communication to discuss the choice of method. Here, a hypothesis is tested by estimating its explanatory value, not in the first instance its outcome achievements. This method, known in the language of logic as 'inference to best explanation' (see, for instance, Hacking, 2001), may be as indicative as empirical outcome studies, but is neglected. The importance of understanding that we have more than one kind of method for testing our hypotheses is great, as we need to address the phenomena a hypothesis explains – such as, in the present instance, the demoralisation of those working in psychiatry with SPD patients. It is not, in fact, very useful to test by outcome theories for which there is no explanatory scope, or even those for which there is unknown scope.

Once we have hypotheses with explanatory scope, we can then point to new 'action paragraphs' to be tested by outcome. The evidence of this chapter is that our hypothesis can find specific ways of thinking and working that are informed by proper explanation.

# 7 The Psychiatric Stockholm Syndrome: The Emergence of Traumatic Bonding in Mental Health In-Patient Settings

By Tim French

## Introduction

In this chapter I am trying to sketch out some of the processes which have led to the development of psychiatric in-patient services, where the treatment of people with personal mental health difficulties is deemed by others to require hospital intervention. After drawing a historical outline that traces around military themes, I will try to blend a sociological and psychodynamic approach to produce an impression of the therapeutic relationship that exists despite, rather than because of, the best intentions of the hospital clinician.

The point of deciding on psychiatric in-patient admission is often contentious. How much power do individuals have in determining, for themselves, their own access to hospital care and treatment – especially when mental health problems are such notoriously difficult 'things' to accurately, objectively and definitively pinpoint and measure? In the final analysis, such decisions are made by the professionals, who open themselves up to criticism for the possible misdiagnosis and/or pathologisation of life's difficulties which impose themselves on the psychological and emotional well-being of the individual. Where a decision for in-patient admission is made (either imposed against the person's will under the Mental Health Act or agreed with the person, with or without some form of duress, as an informal admission), the power dynamic is fundamentally shifted when the person arrives for admission. From this point onwards, he or she is required to conform to the rules and regulations of the unit (if only for the obvious health and safety routines), and there are psychosocial boundary changes at the point which the person becomes the 'patient'.

With this artificially imposed shift in the social role in mind, it has been my intention in writing this chapter to set out some ways in which routine forms of care and treatment can affect the relationship between person(s) in need of help and person(s) tasked with providing a suitable service within the hospital ward setting. People who are in this social role – hospital patients – can change themselves in subtle ways from within, and are changed in more obvious ways from without by the system's social structures; sociological and psychoanalytic perspectives have illuminated some of the ways in which this can happen. I want to use this chapter to take another look at the relationship between the two sets of people – cared-for and carer – in a way that acknowledges the healing that can occur not only despite, but perhaps even because of, the very inequalities of power that are inevitably and inescapably thrown up by the experience of being together in the same intensive location.

I am therefore focusing particularly on those members of staff who remain within the hospital ward perimeters, occupying the same physical space with the patients at all times throughout day and night (ie nursing staff). However, the same issues and relational themes arguably hold true for psychiatrists, social workers and occupational therapists. Those who are busy providing this continuum of care-giving may not be provided with (or have room to create for themselves) enough time and psychological space to reflect on this: is the therapeutic relationship necessarily formed through a type of bonding that can be traumatic for the patient, but without either party knowing it? Is it helpful to recognise and appreciate that, however toxic the in-patient environment, the person who is a patient will benefit and experience improved mental health – in fact, is there an inevitability about this process? Does healing occur regardless of the model of care and mode of treatment?

Although therapeutic approaches in this area have become more formalised in the past couple of decades, professionalised mental health care and treatment is relatively recent; its roots can be found entwined with the development of psychiatry as it formed a distinct strand of medicine in the latter part of the nineteenth century. It is this historical perspective that I hope will serve to illuminate the idea of traumatic bonding that occurs when people are thrown together in close proximity under stressful situations.

## Trauma, conflict and care

Formalised general hospital treatment can be traced back to international conflict which occurred at a time of significant technological advance: the arrival of railway transportation and telegraphic communications in the mid-nineteenth century. At this time, organised care and treatment of physical trauma was transformed within orderly, structured routines in prefabricated medical units exported to Istanbul during the Crimean War. Paradoxically, it seems, out of the midst of human conflict and enmity came the creation of new forms of compassionate response. We can see, too, how creating the spaces and structures necessary for organisational forms of care was impossible at a domiciliary level, because the pragmatics involved looking after active combatants many hundreds of miles from home.

The concept of caring for those who were psychologically and emotionally damaged during military conflict was brought into the psychiatric hospital setting during the First World War. The male patients comprised military personnel who had been sent back home from the field of horrendous overseas conflict. Senior military clinical staff were unable to encourage or command those who had lost the power of speech to talk to them. They had witnessed unspeakable events and were now mutely facing doctors who tried to force them to talk by applying electrodes to their throats. Other, humane, forms of treatment existed for the traumatised psychiatric patients, too – at Craiglockhart Hospital near Edinburgh, for instance, these included the poets Wilfred Owen and Siegfried Sassoon, the latter treated by the psychiatrist Dr W.H.R. Rivers. His psychoanalytic approach provided a compassionate form of recovery for those combatants who had experienced not only the horrors of the battlefield, but also the brutal militaristic processes that purported to be curative. Those who were able to find the words to form poetic creative expression left, of course, a lasting testimony.

Obviously, one doesn't have to be in a battlefield to know what brutal conflict feels like, neither is everyone who encounters trauma themselves traumatised to the point of developing psychological and emotional difficulties. Perhaps it isn't difficult to understand why psychiatry has tended to create a pathology out of immensely adverse and extreme human experience. What was originally termed 'shell shock', initially conceived as a neurological lesion – a new neurological disorder – and 'war neurosis' morphed into 'post-traumatic stress disorder', becoming today's equivalent mental disorder. Thus has the biomedical psychiatric institution resulted in a blurring of organic disease and functional disorder to produce a mental illness; an oxymoron which – as we see later in this chapter – produces conflict and confusion for those experiencing psychological and emotional difficulties that can debilitate their lives.

The institutions that were set up to provide the basis of care and treatment for people with such disorders became like any large structured system, and it wasn't long before the iatrogenic aspects of asylums and hospitals became all too apparent (iatrogenesis is inadvertent adverse reaction to the treatment itself). That the side effects of the institution – institutionalisation – attacked the patient's social system long before the development of the psychoactive drugs that further attacked the nervous system has been well known. (Articulate accounts from psychological and sociological perspectives on the problems of classification of mental illness are offered by Bentall, 2003 and Busfield, 2011.)

Dichotomously, it seems, both conflict and trauma have played a significant part in opening up therapeutic approaches to a wider access of mental health services generally. For instance, during the Second World War, a military psychiatric experiment was developed at the British Army's Northfield Hospital in Birmingham; this had a significant impact on shifting the treatment of mental health care, taking it outside the hospital ward setting. The Northfield experiment featured two consecutive pioneers in group analytic psychotherapy, Wilfred Bion and Siegfried Foulkes (for instance, Bion, 1961, 1997 and Foulkes, 1946, 1983), whose work laid the innovative foundation of British group psychotherapy, as well as the therapeutic community (eg as described by Hinshelwood, 1999b). Consequently, the first psychiatric day treatment centre in the United Kingdom was created in 1946, directly after the war.

In the United States, mental health out-patient settings expanded in the early 1960s where legislation led to the forming of Community Mental Health Centers (CMHCs). This approach travelled across to the UK, where we have seen rapid incorporation of the elements of community care over the past two decades or so, particularly accelerating since the NHS and Community Care Act (1990). Consequently, late-twentieth-century mental health services in this country – as elsewhere in the Western world – saw the replacement of brick-built, large-scale, typically Victorian/Edwardian-era psychiatric establishments spaciously situated within landscaped grounds; instead there rose postmodern, compact mental health in-patient units located within the concrete grounds of local district and regional general hospitals. Emerging in the early twenty-first century, the development of Crisis Resolution and Home Treatment teams has contributed to enhanced support and treatment opportunities in what is, for many, a preferred locality – their own (individual) home. This ostensibly offers care, support and treatment in the environment of least restriction.

## The need for in-patient admission: to heal and be healed

However, for the person whose crisis exceeds (and who lack means of immediate support) the level of distress and risk – often when it is experienced outside so-called 'normal' working hours – then in-patient admission to psychiatric services remains a necessity, whether by volition or enforcement. Such admissions may be of just a few days' duration. Apart from these emergency admissions, however, are the majority of individuals on the inside of the mental health in-patient system, whether remaining voluntarily or detained under the Mental Health Act. For these disparate patients (I'm settling on this term now, since the person is necessarily expected to be patient and follow the hospital unit norms, rules, procedures and boundaries), we can observe a new pattern emerging within the interpersonal relationship between patient and staff. This involves a quite unique, dynamic tension inside the modern psychiatric unit, because of the dichotomous nature of the role of the nurse in this clinical in-patient setting.

Since a mental health nurse is the professional discipline which patients will most often routinely encounter in this environment, and to *nurse* is to *care*, I want to say something about the nature of the 'transpersonal'. The therapeutic relationship can be defined by a coming-together (this is sometimes referred to within the psychoanalytic literature as a 'rapprochement'); this means an interpersonal, external attitude which is able to mirror the internal reconciliation necessary to allow the patient's disturbed psyche – for the person whose psychological and/or emotional self is troubled – to find some reorganisation and equilibrium. This psychotherapeutic method is necessary in addition to (and sometimes, perhaps, beyond) the competence of the nurse in performing the skills and proficiencies required of that profession's techniques. Some authors describe mental health nursing as combining art and science (Norman and Ryrie, 2009). This seems to resonate harmonically with the approaches found in psychoanalysis and analytical psychology (pioneered by Freud and Jung, respectively).

To extend Freud's description of one of the roles of the mental health professional into the nursing analogy, it might be necessary to clean a wound that the patient cannot bear to touch or manage themselves. In the painful process of cleansing, with the patient's safety paramount, the carer has a valid and sufficient reason to probe, help locate and remove the unwanted, unhealthy and possibly infectious material. In psychodynamic terms, this is psychic content – a psychological process, of which the patient is both conscious and (largely) unconscious, having heavily significant emotional valence. Provided with the right type of psychological support and given favourable conditions, Freud sees the person as inherently capable of recovery; in common with the humanistic approach, the patient can experience growth which works towards a healing of the wound and a return journey to health.

As with Freud, and perhaps developed to a somewhat greater extent in his own work, Jung recognised the importance of mythology, and realised the direct mythological influence on the human psyche transpersonally, through collectively unconscious means. He likened this process to a tuberous plant that grows by reaching and spreading far and wide but submerged beneath the surface of the ground, to emerge and flower as if a dislocated separate entity. Jung realised that myths represented archetypes – processes from the shared (ie collective) experiences in humankind's far, far distant past. He was impressed by the *mythologue* of the Wounded Healer, believing that this forms the basis of an unconscious relationship between patient and clinician. There is often a duplex, or two-fold mirroring aspect of material that unfolds between the two in the relationship. Jung referred to what he called 'psychological facts', which may be considered in more circumspect manner in our age of science (where empiricism has taken on a different meaning in relation to objective, controlled studies – as opposed to sensory subjective experiences), that the person may well be unaware of their own psychic wound, and yet this can be the source of the healing for others.

Jung was one of the world's first psychiatrists – he entered the medical profession towards the latter part of the nineteenth century, at a time when psychiatry was establishing itself as a separate branch of medicine: dismembering the body and mind (literally with the medical school cadaver, conceptually and symbolically with the concept of the part that the psyche plays in the existence of the person), and studying the organic and functional mental disorders for signs and symptoms of pathology. (Foucault (1965) has noted the territorial staking of psychiatry's claims to map the geography of the body with the 'clinical gaze' – turned from the neurologist's squint of brain tissue under the microscope, to the structural conceptual models of the unlocatable mind, and now seemingly turning back again by twenty-first-century neuroscientists to the functioning brain with magnetic resonance imaging.)

Jung believed that the doctor – or therapist/clinician – unconsciously activates his or her own wounds as a source of the power to help others to heal. For mental health nurses (as well as doctors, social workers, occupational therapists and others), the pain of their personal 'psychic' wound may be resolved during the process of delivering compassionate care. This experience can be the foundation for empathy, which can be enhanced further through various processes, such as choosing the challenging upward path of personal psychotherapy. Jung, however, recognises the danger of the clinician's psychic wound being conflated with the patient's, thus exacerbating the healer's own personal difficulties. Being a psychiatric doctor or nurse is not without its psychological and emotional risks, clearly; interpersonal relationships need safe and appropriate boundaries.

If we consider the history of interpersonal relations between mental health nurses and the person(s) in care over, say, the life of the National Health Service, then we can trace back and forth between Hilda Peplau (1952) and Phil Barker (Barker and Buchanan-Barker, 2005; Barker, 2008). We could summarise the quality of the relationship as equal to, if not more important than, the physical care environment. But in juxtaposition to this, staff in mental health hospital units recognise that their patients are increasingly high risk, and often pose unexpected difficulties that threaten their professional attitude. For instance,

Hinshelwood (1999c) has described how some people with diagnoses such as schizo-phrenia or personality disorder present particular challenges to the professional attitudes of staff who provide care in hospital settings, within an increasingly technical psychiatric context.

One can argue that this approach purporting to be 'scientific method' diminishes the thera-peutic milieu, not necessarily because of the level of disturbance, illness or distress arising from the patients, but because the physical and cultural environment has changed within the increasingly bureaucratic demands of the nurse as clerk – official civil servant, rather than caring minister to the fellow citizen. Of course, the origins of these ideas have been notably proposed by observers from social anthropology (for instance, Goffman, 1961), philosophy (Foucault, 1965) and critical psychiatry on both sides of the Atlantic (Laing, 1965; Szasz, 1961, 1970).

We could reconsider, then, whether therapeutic interpersonal relationships are important in in-patient mental health establishments. For some people (especially those entering the in-patient system for the first time), these psychiatric facilities don't seem like hospitals; these units (clinical misnomers to replace the word 'ward') are covered with care 24 hours a day, and such facilities are increasingly in demand. The pathological requirements to access these resources have risen significantly; in other words, the needs of individuals to warrant admission must now be dramatically severe. Given the reality of these circumstances, why should interpersonal relationships have a high priority when the work is now about man-aging the risk and covering your back, and 'care' is a mere acronym for 'cover arse, retain employment'?

# The personal in interpersonal

All the same, we can sense that something works for people with profound mental health difficulties; we can point to beneficial effects of medication, if actually taken 'properly' (as it were – ie ingested rather than secreted; and taken for a duration that outlasts the undesir-able side effects to reach the therapeutic benefit); or perhaps we could indeed recognise the improvement that electroconvulsive therapy (ECT) can bring in certain specific cases. Beyond these approaches, however, what is there for the hospitalised person but rest and confinement (compared with the traditional psychiatric asylum model of rest and work)? It seems that whatever model, paradigm or therapeutic approach is used in practice, it is the interpersonal dimension between helper and person in care that somehow works. A safe space, the forming of relationships with care-givers and between peers, and the re-forming of relationships with important people in the patient's life – these seem to be the important factors.

We may know how this operates: the clinician may work within a clear structure, with explicit objectives, towards an agreed outcome (often loosely referred to as the 'Care Plan', or the 'Care Programme Approach' – how many of our patients have heard this acronym with no appreciation of its meaning?). Or perhaps we may only 'know' how a therapeutic relationship works through sensing intuitively that something seems to be effecting a positive change somehow … something 'feels right'. So long as a therapeutic impact is occurring, does it really matter?

In in-patient settings, a desired outcome is almost certainly brought about through a helpful, positive, therapeutic relationship; but perhaps this relationship is in itself a consequence – an effect rather than a cause – where nurses and patients are drawn together in close, often tense and sometimes dramatic circumstances. In other words, I suggest that acute mental health in-patient nurses don't necessarily (and perhaps, on occasions, they rarely) set out to consciously form healthy, healing relationships – but that they happen anyway; that they even surface for the wrong reasons, but that they are helpful and healing nevertheless. Without guidance and supervision, however, these relationships have the power to transform both parties in dysfunctional and damaging ways.

In hospital, something dynamic occurs within the clinical space where people are together; a new and tangible force is generated. Even if the patient is informal (and voluntary admission in this country has only been possible since the 1930s), their carers are their captors, and so are dynamic tensions captured. Of course, the professional nursing role is necessarily custodial where people are at significant and serious risk in the presence of mental disorder, and the Mental Health Act may be enforced. The individual will then either be in a physically secure location – that is, locked inside a building – or else sufficient staff will necessarily ensure that person remains under surveillance (and will, if deemed necessary, be physically prevented from leaving the unlocked building). Increasingly, on 'open' units, however, the doors are usually locked with an electromagnet, and only knowledge of a multi-digit security code or possession of an official staff photo ID card read by electronic sensor will effect an entrance or exit. And yet we see relationships building despite – or perhaps, more accurately, because of – the person being in close proximity of staff (ie nurses) who share common spaces.

## The 'Stockholm syndrome'

This is essentially what happened in a notorious event (which happened to be an armed robbery), which occurred in the Swedish capital Stockholm in 1973, when gunmen burst into a bank and held the staff hostage. The analogies between this incident and contemporary psychiatric in-patient care are not immediately obvious, but consider the dynamic relationships that unfolded in the siege. Within a confined location, in what was supposed to be a place of utmost safety and security, a well-organised and dedicated team of focused individuals wielding power and control (albeit unauthorised) dictated the terms and living conditions of vulnerable others, over a period of time. A sort of perverted role change occurred; the people in control were not customers, and therefore the role of the bank employees – which they remained – necessarily changed in relation to their captors. They were no longer to be considered as 'staff', working to serve the needs of the customers (or 'service users'); they were captive detainees, with a growing level of dependence on others within and outside the building.

The insight gained from arbitrarily grouping people together as either detainers or detainees is not unknown and has been graphically demonstrated in the Stanford Prison Experiment (Haney et al., 1973). Those in power roles quickly develop rules and group norms that dominate, subdue and ultimately suppress their fellow man, as Zimbardo (2008) has elaborated more recently. Interestingly, however, the psychologically close and emotionally binding relationships that developed inside the highly stressful situation in Stockholm were between the detainees (the hostages) and their captors – not with their rescuers; these relationships were so powerful that they endured far beyond the detention period. The resulting so-called 'Stockholm Syndrome' is well documented, and in a mental health context has been related to the type of traumatic bonding which may be perceived between victim and perpetuator of abuse.

Within psychiatry as a whole, somewhat similar themes can be traced back to Thomas Szasz, the critical psychiatrist who considered mid–late-twentieth-century mental health care from within the dominant biomedical perspective, and found analogies with the Spanish Inquisition on the occasions when the patient expresses his or her evidently erroneous beliefs (notably the so-called psychotic delusions found in schizophrenia, but perhaps, we could add, the 'faulty thinking' found in the negative automatic thoughts associated with depression and anxiety) and has to 'confess' these to the authority of the psychiatrist. While the medical model still predominates within much of twenty-first-century mental health in-patient care, we are witnessing the role of the care manager gradually superseding the consultant psychiatrist. For instance, the recently amended Mental Health Act (1983/2007) sees the term *Responsible Clinician* replacing *Responsible Medical Officer*. Cognitive Behavioural Therapy treatment was given a significant boost with the UK government's Improving Access to Psychological Therapies (IAPT) project funding high- and low-intensity treatment by psychologists, nurses and other associated practitioners, respectively. Many clinicians and mental health service users would argue that increasing the availability of psychosocial interventions can only be a good thing, thereby reducing mainstream psychiatry's reliance on medication for mental disorders that may equate to 'problems with living'.

However, I suggest that two things are occurring. One is that the management of care is producing a new order of authority figure, with non-medical clinicians – even those who are working within the social model in a recovery context – dealing exclusively with the functions of consciousness, and minimising or indeed neglecting the elements which lie submerged below the surface. Even experts by experience may not see what lies beneath. I mention the importance of unconscious processes here, not necessarily from a psychoanalytic perspective, but because the nurse's fundamental role of developing interpersonal attitudes first and last is being eroded by clerical and managerial risk reduction. Second, we are witnessing traumatic bonding taking place in our psychiatric in-patient units, where the detainees (patients) find themselves, in conditions of heightened psychological conflict and emotional arousal or dysfunction, increasingly drawn to those staff responsible for their detainment. In contradistinction to Szasz (1970), the balance of power is shifting away from the psychiatric consultant (who used to determine which patients got admitted to what beds); with no other professional discipline to fill the void yet (until, for instance, the nurse becomes the *Responsible Clinician*), this has caused something of a vacuum on the psychiatric ward, into which the patient is getting sucked.

Detainment here is not used in the same sense as containment, which was examined by Menzies Lyth (1959) in a study of nurses in a general hospital setting. Arguably, her research remains just as accurate and valid more than half a century later, in the psychiatric care setting: energies which could have been used to attend to patients' needs are dispersed at both individual and group (ward team) levels. The defences of unguarded nurses – by which I mean those who work without the necessary psychodynamic (and perhaps psychoanalytic) attitude – become institutionalised in the social systems that have evolved at departmental and organisational levels. This will occur wherever individuals work without giving sufficient regard to unconscious processes which directly influence cognitions and emotions, and thereby, indirectly, behaviour. This serves to work against patient care in the 'here and now', and is evidence in support of regular clinical psychodynamic supervision – preferably for both the individual and the group. The absence of these forms of support will be seen in increasing attention directed towards the bureaucratic requirements of care, and will be measured in the increasing amount of time nurses spend in the ward office. This was noted by David Rosenhan's researchers, who posed as pseudo-patients in the classic study of the pathologising of normal behaviour in psychiatric in-patient settings (Rosenhan, 1973), many years before the introduction in the UK of the Care Programme Approach and the associated paperwork requirements.

## Conclusion

Human relationships will inevitably flourish and give support for those able to provide and receive care wherever the need exists, so long as we can perceive the mutual benefits that are available to both parties. This is inevitable in the same way that a vacuum creates movements of energies; helpful responses are necessary reactions between helpful care-givers and people in trouble. Forms of detainment will not change any time soon in mental health in-patient units. However, without a psychodynamic approach informing mental health nurses' – and others' – care in this setting, and without good systems of clinical support and psychodynamic (rather than, or perhaps one should say supplementary to) caseload management supervision, then detainment will inevitably result in emotionally and psychologically charged relationships.

Instead of having reciprocal healing properties that professionally help the patient and enlighten the nurse (or other disciplinary carer), traumatic bonds will form; roles will be confused, boundaries will be broken and confusion and anxiety will abound. In such circumstances, detained people may be perceived as physically safe, and agreeable interpersonal relationships may form nevertheless. However, because bonding can occur under anti-therapeutic circumstances, when the time comes to separate at the occasion of discharge, I suggest the Stockholm Syndrome is activated at an unconscious level, causing dependency and difficulty in observable processes such as discharge and attitudes of antipathy at the point of re-entry into the system (or even at the future mention of that person's name).

In the context of economic crisis, budget cuts and reductions in service provision, it is inevitable that those working within in-patient settings are going to be subjected to increased workloads and less time to reflect and experience a containing psychodynamic supervision and support. Recent press headlines record the way older people within hospitals or care homes have been abused, neglected and mistreated. The Royal College of Psychiatrists recently reported a lack of compassion and care among nurses and doctors in mental health services. These are all symptoms of the Stockholm Syndrome manifesting itself from the collective and individual unconscious, provoked by neo-liberal policies that fail to take cognisance of the intense personal relationship dynamics unleashed within in-patient care. Indeed, the orthodox reaction when confronted by this phenomenon is to become even more distancing, controlling and defensive by erecting procedures and protocols – as if these mechanistic measures are the solution, when they are really the problem. Doctors, nurses and social workers have professional associations, trades unions and other forums where they can advocate for something different with the power of a collective voice. Line management structures and patient representative bodies can be utilised to challenge orthodox, defensive practices and remind the remote, distanced managers that in the long run staff and patients can all benefit from personal insight and the power of psychodynamic, reflective care and support.

# Part Three
# Contemporary Developments and Reflections

# 8 Culture and Meaning in Child and Adolescent Mental Health

## By Steven Walker

## Introduction

If adult mental health is the Cinderella of health service provision, in terms of the amount of taxpayers' money spent as a proportion of overall health care, then child and adolescent mental health must be one of the mice pulling the crystal coach. In the UK after several years of real increases in services, a survey in 2012 by the charity Young Minds found a reduction in budgets being reported.

UNICEF (2011) described worldwide progress towards improving the welfare of children and young people since the 1991 World Summit for Children as poor and highlighted concerns about the well-being of children in the UK. Huge challenges exist in many South American, African and Asian countries to improve diagnosis and identification of troubled children, while in the industrialised countries of North America and Europe unprecedented levels of child and adolescent mental health problems are being reported (Lidchi, 2003; Walker, 2003). Islamophobia, anti-semitism, ethnic cleansing, genocide and increasing human rights abuses characterised the end of the twentieth and beginning of the twenty-first century. Child trafficking is another ugly feature of modern life and the source of degrading experiences leading to mental health problems.

Appalling and distressing imagery of the ability of humankind to violate and destroy each other in acts of uncontrolled rage or planned systematic torture and mass murder have become imprinted on our collective consciousness. What must children and young people make of the world around them and the behaviour of adults towards each other? What overt or covert messages are they picking up about the value of human life and how to relate to other people? And what meaning do children and young people attach to behaviour rooted in a lack of respect for others' culture?

This is the global backdrop to this chapter which seeks to challenge orthodox thinking within child and adolescent mental health services by exploring and understanding how, by employing cultural competence in our therapeutic practice, we can reach out to children and young people from any religious, ethnic or social background and engage them in work that makes sense and is relevant to them personally. Fine words appear in abundance in policies, procedures and legislation relating to racism, discrimination and children's rights but they do not translate easily into practice. By adopting a culturally competent framework we may play no small part in contributing to the essential task of restoring fundamental professional and societal values of respect, acceptance and concern for every young person. If we demonstrate confidence and a willingness to acknowledge the importance of cultural differences and how they impact on a troubled young person's self-concept, then we are making a positive statement both socially and therapeutically.

This chapter cannot in the space available address the historical, political and economic contexts that have brought us to this stage in the evolution of humanity, essential as they are to embed the text in the intellectual topography. Instead it will start from where we are and offer a resource combined with practical guidance for counsellors, psychotherapists and all those working in caring contexts with children and young people, seeking to improve and extend their therapeutic repertoire and manoeuvrability.

The last 20 years has witnessed the gradual relaxation of barriers previously preventing the movement of people within an enlarging European Union and increasing levels of global transnational migration, together with the exponential increase in air travel between continents. Combined with mass movements of refugees and asylum seekers either fleeing persecution or poverty, countries are experiencing rapid sociological changes affecting the cultural and ethnic constitution of previously homogeneous societies. The notion of multicultural societies is not new and laws have been passed to protect ethnic minority communities against prejudice and discrimination for many years. Yet the outcomes for black children and young people are still always lower than for comparable white children and young people, whether we examine the data on exam results, occupational status, income levels or the negative numbers in juvenile justice, state accommodation and lone parenthood.

Not many years ago the term global village (McLuhan, 1964) was coined to describe how the world was shrinking metaphorically, through technological developments and mass communication, resulting in the bringing together of different peoples and cultures. The optimists felt that this would enable greater understanding and sharing of values and mutual respect and tolerance. The pessimists felt that the closer we got, the more the differences between peoples would be magnified and result in conflict based on fear and rejection of alternative beliefs and customs. Economic disparity would then cause envy and anger leading to discontent and hostility between peoples. History teaches us that nationalism – the political expression of a country's culture – can easily translate into expansionism, leading to imperialism and colonialism, with dire long-term consequences after short-term benefits have been exhausted.

Until relatively recently, you would have been hard pushed to find culture mentioned in therapeutic textbooks other than in a chapter on ethnicity or anti-discriminatory practice. Even then, these chapters seemed to be, at worst, tokenistic and, at best, a belated attempt to provide some help to practitioners seeking knowledge and skills in working with a diverse community of clients whose needs had been traditionally neglected. Anti-racist texts especially in the more progressive social work, nursing and psychology fields were not uncommon in the 1970s and 1980s, but their often hectoring tone and limited therapeutic utility left many feeling berated, criticised, emotionally bruised and intellectually unsatisfied.

The concept of cultural competence can take away the anxiety and fear from exploring different ways of engaging children and adolescents, many of whom (from whatever background) would find it hard to access help for their psychological problems. Cultural competence can be considered as a staging post along the road of self-discovery and improvements in theoretical and practical therapeutic concepts that are necessary to respond to the changing socio-cultural landscape. As we as a human race evolve, so must our therapeutic techniques and methods and models of practice so that no young person is neglected, overlooked or denied access to the help of another human being because they are different.

This chapter will define a culturally competent practice by illuminating the synergies between culture and meaning as they are applied in practice. This will help construct a framework for a coherent practical basis for modern students or qualified staff seeking to advance their skills in counselling, psychology or psychotherapy. In addition, sociological material is used to provide an important and often overlooked element that affects the prospects for successful therapeutic engagement. Thus, by demonstrating how seemingly different paradigms can be employed in a synchronised pursuit of improved process and outcomes, the chapter will mirror the capacity for practitioners to feel more at ease in working with cultural difference.

There is a need to fill a gap in the available literature that fails to fully address the needs of the changing demographics and ethnic tapestry of contemporary multicultural societies. It is necessary to develop the dated concepts of anti-racist and anti-discriminatory practices that were necessary to challenge Western ethnocentric practices embodied in the classical textbooks, but which have often succeeded in paralysing practitioners and have raised anxieties about potentially harmful practices. Cultural competence therefore moves into a different intellectual and emotional realm from the either/or, punishment/guilt paradigm affecting therapeutic work with children and young people. Doing this will liberate and empower practitioners seeking to meet the needs of all the troubled children and young people who come to them for help (Walker, 2010).

## Cultural diversity

Religion and spirituality are very important dimensions of cultural diversity which must be actively considered in order to practise in child and adolescent mental health services in a culturally competent way. Until recently these subjects were neglected in orthodox texts and psychiatric practice. Yet the principles underpinning the counselling and psychotherapeutic helping relationship offer a complementary model to build on the capacity for healing that is associated with religious and spiritual experience. They also fit with the concept of personal growth and social justice enshrined in psychosocial practice. It is suggested that religion and spirituality can be equated or seen as quite distinct concepts. Spirituality, it is argued, refers to one's basic nature and the process of finding meaning and purpose, whereas religion involves a set of organised, institutionalised beliefs and social functions as a means of spiritual expression and experience (Carroll, 1998).

Religion and spirituality have traditionally been separated in their application to an understanding of the human condition employed by counsellors and psychotherapists. It is as if our desperate need for recognition and importance has to be privileged over all other influences – particularly those that impinge on the realm of the unconscious and psychological. Some go further and suggest that religions typically act to increase anxiety rather than reduce it, or they are an instrument of oppression and control over women and the poor (Sinha, 1998). The complexities and subtleties of different cultural manifestations of relationship dynamics are lost on those relying on media stereotypes. The central features of spirituality have been described as:

- **Meaning** – the significance of life and deriving purpose in existence;

- **Transcendence** – experience of a dimension beyond the self that opens the mind;

- **Value** – standards and beliefs such as value truth, beauty, worth, often discussed as ultimate value;

- **Connecting** – relationships with others, God or a higher power and the environment;

- **Becoming** – a life that requires reflection and experience including a sense of who one is and how one knows (Martslof and Mickley, 1998).

These spiritual needs can be explained in psychological terms as well. The conventional literature available to counsellors and psychotherapists can be used to explain these ideas in many ways using evidence from orthodox science and theories that have stood the test of time and served professionals well. Yet there is a lingering doubt, perhaps, that on deeper reflection the concepts of faith, purpose and the search for meaning are inadequately quantified in the language of scientific certainty that asserts they are just thought processes or embroidered survival needs. Even in this age of evidence-based practice, we know that to ignore our intuitions and gut feelings risks denying us and the children and young people we aspire to help a most valuable tool (Walker, 2012).

It cannot be coincidental that the further the human race moves towards scientific and rational certainty, aided by the bewildering power of computers and technology able to explore and manipulate the biological foundations of life using genetic research, the more people seem more determined than ever to seek answers to fundamental questions about existence, whether from organised religions or alternative forms of spirituality. Jung believed that therapists needed to recognise the relevance of spirituality and religious practice to the needs and workings of the human psyche. He suggested that a psychological problem was in essence the suffering of a soul which had not discovered its meaning – that the cause of such suffering was spiritual stagnation or psychic sterility.

*Religions are psychotherapeutic systems in the truest sense of the word, and on the grandest scale. They express the whole range of the psychic problem in mighty images; they are the avowal and recognition of the soul, and at the same time the revelation of the soul's nature.* (Jung, 1978)

Jung's concept of archetypes suggests that unconscious components of the psyche are revealed through dreams and fantasies at critical points of internal conflict. This transcendent process mediates between oppositional archetypes in order to produce a reconciling symbol. This experience enables children and young people to achieve gradual individuation and the revelation of the self. Some of the central experiences of individuation, such as the hero's journey, the metaphor of death and rebirth or the image of the divine child, are paradigms of religious experience (Nash and Stewart, 2002). They migrate into myths, fairy stories and legends as we saw in Chapter 7 and are therefore accessible for work with troubled children and adolescents.

A sense of religion or spirituality has the capacity to inhibit or enhance culturally competent therapeutic work with children or young people. You may feel that an over-reliance on beliefs of this nature is symptomatic of a denial defence and a fatalistic outlook in your clients. On the other hand, you may believe that having faith in something outside of themselves permits a child or young person to experience a sense of purpose and greater good that can enhance a therapeutic intervention. As a counsellor or psychotherapist you may also have religious beliefs or a sense of spirituality that helps you in your therapeutic work. It might also hinder your work if you encounter an atheistic belief system in a young person or a religious affiliation that contradicts your own. Although still to be fully developed, the evidence does suggest that spirituality has a protective function against developing psychological problems. Children and young people who possess such a sense of spirituality are considered more resilient in the face of traumas, including sexual abuse, and less prone to mental health and adjustment problems in adolescence (Resnik et al., 1993; Valentine and Feinauer, 1993).

# Religion and belief

The relevance to counselling and psychotherapy of religion and spirituality cannot be under-estimated as they form a part of the covert or overt belief systems of children and young people that will to a larger or lesser extent impact on the work at hand. This is not to say that only those who have a religious faith or a belief in spirituality will have their therapy affected. The impact of not believing or of having firm ideas about the absence of spiritual feelings can be just as important. What is relevant is the existence of the ideas of religion, gods and spirituality in society and how individuals and families orientate to them – or not. Most cultures can trace back into deep history evidence of their ancestral heritage and the ways early civilisations sought to explain the world around them. These tend to involve the intervention of a supreme being or power with the capacity to control the natural elements vital for the survival of the species.

We can understand how, without the tools to predict the climate and manipulate food production methods, primitive people thousands of years ago felt vulnerable and frightened by natural phenomena. Seeking explanations for unpredictable events – good or bad – was perfectly natural. These ancient understandings echo throughout history. They form part of the fabric of world heritage. They have evolved, changed, and in some cases stayed more or less the same. Settlers in developed countries embrace unorthodox and ancient customs, while some native cultures in developing regions absorb modern theological concepts and spiritual practices. There are pockets of Christianity in strict Islamic states and places where minority religious beliefs are persecuted. Thus, for many children and young people, these frightening experiences will already have become part of their psychological lives (Walker, 2005).

The age of enlightenment and the scientific paradigm provided an alternative set of explanations for why things happened as they did. Thus began a perennial tension between rationalism and religious divinity symbolised in the creationist versus evolutionist debate about the origins of humanity. The polarisation of these two ideas should intrigue the inquisitive therapist – the need to find extreme opposites to charge an argument or debate might mask deeper ambivalence that is too uncomfortable to bear. Similarly, the way that certain religions seek to claim a single truth or denounce others as heretical should serve as useful material for engaging with particular children and young people. What meaning does this have for the child's temperament of problem-solving skills? What are the advantages and disadvantages of holding such profound beliefs? The certainty of a person's belief could be measured by the depth of their mixed feelings or their absolute terror of the other point of view.

Here again we encounter the concept of the other – the opposite which is not part of us and must be avoided, rejected or overwhelmed. In earlier centuries, countries went to war and mass murders took place with official sanction on the strength of one's religious beliefs. The history of modern societies has been shaped as much by the religious struggles of previous stages of development as by the economic and political forces motivating people to embark upon social change or revolution. To try to better understand these processes theorists would look for the interactive nature of religious development and political and economic movements – how one influences the other and vice versa. Psychodynamic theorists might formulate an explanation based on the primitive insecurities driving those individuals leading these mass movements and ideologies. Either way, a combination of the two offers us a therapeutic understanding of these powerfully important contexts within which individual children and young people evolve their own psychic road map.

Today, the world is said to be constructed into geo-political blocks based on economic power and geographical position. But there are also the equivalent and much more complex theo-political blocks which have the capacity to invoke strong feelings and mass change in whole nations or significant sections of them. There are about 40 contemporary known religions and sects throughout the world. This offers evidence of the incredibly rich tapestry of religious material available to incorporate within our comprehension of the enormous culturally diverse world our clients inhabit. It also demonstrates the potential for interfaith rivalries and offers a fertile seed bed for those charismatic figures seeking to influence young people towards a religious and spiritual certainty that claims priority over all others. As with any strong belief, when it turns into obsession it has the potential for great destructiveness.

## Culture and spirituality

The decline of organised religious expression in the Western world has been documented in recent years and to some extent is blamed for the increasing prevalence of emotional and behavioural problems in children and young people who are a generation supposedly without moral guidance or social values, according to reactionary pundits. But what is less well documented is the evidence that experiences of the sacred or spiritual remain widespread, especially among children (Cobb and Robshaw, 1998). Evidence suggests a strong underlying belief system in young people in the concept of spirituality – even by those avowed atheists. Spirituality goes beyond the narrow definition of religion and offers a different and arguably more difficult paradigm within which to understand the troubles of children and young people. There are identifying characteristics that can help us in our therapeutic work, but with such diverse meanings and interpretations it becomes harder to be certain about what spirituality is, how it can be defined and whether there are universally accepted categories (Swinton, 2003).

We are in effect entering an aspect of children's experience that transcends description and is difficult to express adequately in words. The very nature of the spiritual is inexpressible because it springs from the innermost depths of the human experience. If we are to engage with the religious and spiritual aspects of children and young people's culture then we need to find a way of accessing this rich reservoir of material within which important therapeutic work is ready to be done. The orthodox medical model, whether employed by clinicians or adhered to by parents and carers, may frame a child's psychological difficulties in a bio-psychosocial formulation that encapsulates all the intrinsic and extrinsic variables thought to explain the problem. But when working in a culturally competent manner we need to consider the various ways different cultures conceptualise psychological problems. If that means using a spiritual explanatory framework, then so be it.

The recent ban on girls wearing the hijab at school in France has served to illustrate the potential destructiveness in the underlying tensions between the former colonial countries and their legacies of immigration and cultural diversity. The French state education system reflects the secular model of society created in the aftermath of the revolution. The strict separation of religion from the state has provided the context in which the wearing of the hijab is perceived as a religious symbol and therefore disallowed in school. Following the French example, some schools in the UK have also banned the wearing of the hijab. For some girls, this may represent an attack upon their religion and result in considerable anxiety and depression. Evidence suggests that the wearing of the hijab in Western societies is a complex act involving a desire to remain within their tradition and at the same time to challenge it, while also seeking to create a space for equality (Ghuman, 2004).

If the child or young person, from whatever culture, has a belief system that accepts and takes account of a spiritual dimension then, rather than pathologising this, a counsellor or psychotherapist needs to reflect on how this meaning may be affecting the problem concerned. It might be part of the problem, or it might be maintaining the problem, or it might be stopping matters getting worse, or it might offer a way out of the problem. Resisting the impulse to make untested and unfounded assumptions may be hard but bearing uncertainty and keeping open all possibilities will be more helpful in the long run.

Spirituality therefore can be seen as an intra, inter and transpersonal experience that is shaped and directed by the experiences of individuals and of the communities within which they live out their lives (Swinton, 2003). An example to illustrate this is provided by the development of the Family Group Conference approach to child welfare in New Zealand, which is based on a cultural–religious indigenous concept among Maori people that emphasises the relationship between Celestial and Terrestrial knowledge. The origin of the Family Group Conference was, according to Maori belief, a rebellious initiative by the children of Ranginui, the great Sky Father, and Papatuanuku, the matriarch Earth Mother. Protected in a darkened cocoon by their parents, the children desired freedom to explore the outer limits of the universe. The family conference that was convened included close and distant relatives and grandparents, who were all regarded as part of a single spiritual and economic unity (Fulcher, 1999). Thus each Maori child's cultural identity is explicitly connected to their genealogy or *whakapapa*. The Family Group Conference is now being incorporated into mainstream child protection and adult mental health services in the United Kingdom, where extended family members are invited to participate in care planning.

# Diverse child development

Is there a point at which a child develops a sense of spirituality? Can we relate this to Western orthodox developmental instruments? One of the central tenets of religious belief is that of death and a belief in an afterlife. Jung considered that belief in an afterlife was important for mental health, whereas Freud suggests it was an unhealthy denial. In the context of the rise in self-harming behaviours and suicide rates among young men and the life-threatening risks in anorexia nervosa, it is clear that the subject of death and its connection with belief or lack of belief in an afterlife must be an important variable. The terms intrinsic and extrinsic religiousness have been coined in order to more closely define the complexities behind religious belief. Intrinsic religiousness is characterised by a young person extending their beliefs beyond acts of worship into every aspect and behaviour in their life. It is foundational to their concept of self. However, a young person with extrinsic religiousness is motivated by a self-serving instrumental approach to life that uses religion to provide status and social support. It has been compared to a neurosis in the sense that it is a defence against anxiety, whereas intrinsic religiousness makes for positive mental health (Paloutzian, 1996).

Until about the age of ten, children are generally understood to be unable to grasp abstract concepts. If we accept the more abstract and non-literal aspects of religion then it follows that before that age religious education in schools is failing to connect with children. This has been acknowledged to some extent in studies examining difficulties in establishing in-school educational programmes aimed at tackling social exclusion and using religious studies as a means to enhance cultural respect (Jackson, 2004; Larsen and Plesner, 2002). Recent evidence suggests that religious education in schools is now a focus for policy makers seeking to increase understanding and respect between children of different religions or world views that fosters knowledge about and respect for freedom of religion or belief as a human right (Jackson, 2004). It is argued that older schoolchildren can demonstrate meta-cultural competence in classroom discussion about different religions by developing their ability to handle new and unfamiliar cultural material with skill and sensitivity (Leganger-Krogstad, 2000).

However, this relies on a narrow definition of religious development and cognitive capacity. Perhaps the concept of spiritual development enables us to begin to understand that such a process begins at a much earlier stage of development, at a point when children are trying to make sense of the multiplicity of sensations and experiences bombarding them. The cognitive complexity in religious language is more a barrier to children's spiritual expression, and in order for us to better understand it, we need to learn how to listen to the language of children and young people, within which is ample spiritual expression. Studies of children's spirituality using cross-cultural and multi-faith samples confirm the profound nature of spirituality and that spirituality is not only about what children talk about but also how they talk, act or feel about all sorts of things (Coles, 1990; Hay, 1990). It is important to bear the following points in mind when seeking to assess whether religion and spirituality are relevant to your work with a child or young person.

•    Don't initiate discussion about religion – this will invariably elicit learned facts rather than the natural associated images and metaphors actually used by children.

•    Accept that children may spontaneously introduce religious or spiritual concepts consistent with heightened states of awareness similar to meditational experiences.

•    Create accepting conditions and an open environment to encourage the child to speak freely without censure or dismissal.

•    It is important to respect and value the child's religious beliefs and statements in order to reinforce the validity of expressing a personal point of view.

•    In some situations you can initiate discussion about spirituality as a way of demonstrating that the conventional secular taboo which suppresses these matters can be challenged. This may encourage the child to share their most private and confusing thoughts in other areas of life.

# Psychology and meaning

The Western model of psychological illness tends to ignore the religious or spiritual aspects of the culture in which it is based. However, Eastern, African and Native American cultures tend to integrate them (Fernando, 2002). Spirituality and religion as topics in general do not feature often in the therapeutic literature, yet they can be critical components of a child's and young person's psychological well-being, offering a source of strength and hope in trying circumstances. Children for whom family and faith backgrounds are inseparable may need encouragement to feel comfortable in multi-faith settings. You need to address this dimension as part of the constellation of factors affecting children and adolescents, bearing in mind the positive and sometimes negative impact spiritual or religious beliefs might have on their mental health. It is well understood that children communicate about feelings and experiences more easily through responses to stories. Direct work that allows them to use their imaginations and access their own spirituality through stories can be liberating.

The therapeutic value of Western individualistic concepts is incomplete in attempting to alleviate suffering and alienation for collectivist and land-based cultural groups. In their work with aboriginal communities in the Canadian Arctic, Beatch and Stewart (2002) show how significant problems related to depression, addiction and family violence are linked with cultural loss through colonisation, environmental destruction and assimilation by Western influences. Aboriginal healing includes strengthening cultural belonging, identity and community-based self-determination. Indigenous outlooks indicate a preference for ecological systems, holistic processes, belonging at the community level and reliance on traditional beliefs and values. A culturally competent approach embracing this context requires practitioners using counselling and psychotherapeutic skills to adapt and synthesise their work with prevailing indigenous ideas in order to maximise effectiveness.

Multiple care-giving of young children in Australian Aboriginal culture has attracted concerns based on Western notions of attachment theory and the need for secure attachment relationships with primary carers. However, this concept is inappropriate when we consider that research has demonstrated that Aboriginal children can sustain and thrive with multiple attachment figures that are wholly consistent with societal norms (Yeo, 2003). Indeed, there are sometimes lengthy absences from parents related to important sacred initiations or religious ceremonies necessary for the child or young person's spiritual development. These findings resonate with research in the UK and elsewhere studying the developmental progress of black children raised in single-parent households with multiple attachment figures (Daycare Trust, 2000).

In South American countries, the influence of the Catholic church and family planning, combined with poverty, a history of military dictatorships and a culture of machismo, has produced a culture of extreme social inequality where children can easily drift into prostitution, child labour or become homeless. In these conditions authoritarian family structures create a climate where domestic violence thrives (Ravazzola, 1997). Here liberation theology translates Christian concepts into activity that challenges the prevailing order and offers hope of better circumstances and prospects through revolutionary struggle. Children and young people can thus link religion with empowerment and liberation from inequitable and socially unjust conditions.

Children and young people may well wonder about religion and spirituality, either directly or indirectly. They may encounter friends, family members or others for whom such beliefs are an intrinsic part of their lives. In our work as counsellors or psychotherapists, these people may well enter into the conversations and reflections ventilated by clients. This could trigger an interesting exploration by the child or adolescent about the meaning of life or a search for the answer to the question: what is religion? Your own perspective and theoretical orientation will guide you in considering how to respond. Do you take this literally or metaphorically? Do you enable the client to speculate, describe their hidden fears about such matters or suggest an interpretation that seeks to address underlying dilemmas or conflicts around the issue? The following list attempts to bring forward a definition or to describe the common characteristics of religions around the world (Whiting, 1999).

- They look for the something else or somebody beyond the world of senses and scientific measurement. This something or somebody controls all.

- They have great figures, men of vision who seem to perceive the something else more than other people.

- They all express themselves in the written word, trying to encapsulate what they believe in.

- Each religion gives to its own people advice on how to behave and what to do to draw close to the something else or somebody.

- Religions are often practised by people coming together in common worship at special places.

- Religions often bring people together at special times for particular celebrations.

- All religions hold special funeral ceremonies and grapple with the problem of whether there is life after death.

# The inner world of the child

Research findings that explored the concept of spirituality with several groups of school-age children, some of whom held deep religious convictions and others who belonged to no formal religion, discovered that it is rare to come across a child who does not have at least an implicit spirituality. Even in the most resolutely secular boy evidences of spiritual sensitivity emerge, sometimes through self-contradiction, or allusive metaphor, or through Freudian slips of the tongue. Our task is not to detect the presence of spirituality, but to understand how it becomes suppressed or repressed during the process of growing up (Hay, 1990).

Four core qualities of spiritual experience have been identified – awareness, mystery, value and meaningfulness/insight. They are often assumed to be consistent with positive life-affirming experiences. However, children who experience wonder, awe and mystery can quickly become distressed and fearful – even terrified – if a secure and stable main carer is not available to contain those negative feelings. Many religions contain concepts of hell and punishment which could trigger profound feelings of despair that are experienced as completely overwhelming, physically and psychologically.

Sin is defined variously in many religions and for a child or young person comes with the sense of failing to be satisfactory – for example, from early toileting experiences through to exam performance or adolescent sexuality. The sense of sin and failure is quickly transformed into guilt and shame, resulting in feelings of depression, distress and despair, unless there is some balancing influence. Children and young people without this balancing experience and with deficits in their environment and personal temperament are likely to develop mental health problems at the time or later on in life. It is easy for children to feel that they are failing or cannot fit easily into the world. This is the opposite of spiritual experiences of value, insight and relatedness. A persistent sense of sinfulness or failure prevents the development of healthy relationships (Crompton, 1996).

This is illustrated in the story of the Hindu god Krishna, who was very naughty as a small boy. When he was accused of eating dirt, his foster mother Yasoda ordered him to open his mouth. When he did so she became terrified at the sight she beheld, revealing as it did the eternal universe. Krishna understood that such knowledge would be harmful to Yasoda so he erased her memory of all she had witnessed. This tale illustrates how awareness and closeness to the divine can be potentially overpowering or harmful. A sense of connection to the supreme being in religion can be mediated through a connection with nature and the environment. However, if children witness the harm being done to the environment or the threat of war, they can become very anxious. What do children and young people make of the increasing deterioration of their environment and lurid tabloid tales about the greenhouse effect and extreme weather events? Do they see this as the retribution of a powerful god punishing humanity for spoiling a once pristine planet offered to us as a habitat? And are those teachers and parents lecturing them about the virtues of conservation and recycling instilling a sense of guilt masquerading as virtue?

Children involved in war as victims or combatants are deprived of the enjoyment of spiritual rights. Research demonstrates the severe and enduring mental health problems experienced by refugees and asylum seekers from areas of conflict (Hodes, 2000). Psychotherapists and counsellors can utilise spiritual beliefs in helping children recover from dehumanising and traumatising atrocities by enabling the expression of terror and fearfulness through reconnecting them with their prevailing religious constructs that have been abandoned. Some of these children will perhaps have a strong sense of guilt inherited from a religious belief system that blamed humanity for the death of Jesus. The death of parents, siblings or close relatives will probably have resonated with these inherent guilt feelings, compounding them into a persecutory frame of mind. Therapists would need to be careful with evoking a religious construct that could inadvertently exaggerate already troubling feelings.

The link between spirituality and cultural competence is emphasised if we enlist an understanding of spirituality that suggests it is the outward expression of the inner workings of the human spirit. In other words, it is a personal and social process that refers to the ideas, concepts, attitudes and behaviours that derive from a child or young person's or a community's interpretation of their experiences of the spirit. It is intrapersonal in that it refers to the quest for inner connectivity, and it is interpersonal in that it relates to the relationships between people and within communities. And it is transpersonal in so far as it reaches beyond self and others into the transcendent realms of experience that move beyond that which is available at a mundane level (Swinton, 2003).

## Therapy and cultural belief

Therapeutic work with children and young people from whatever theoretical or pragmatic model or perspective will, among other things, address the belief system of the individual and/or their family. Belief in this sense usually means exploring the client's beliefs about their problem as the start of establishing a helping relationship. The client may believe that their problem/s are the result of divine intervention – a punishment for a sin or misdemeanour of some kind. Among some cultures there is a potent belief system that spirits can possess people and make them unwell or be invoked to help them with a problem. In the case of a child or young person who is causing concern among teachers, social workers or health professionals, there may be a simple diagnosis or assessment of the cause of the problem but this may not fit with the family's beliefs about the cause. However, belief also relates to religion and spirituality. If the therapist is unable or unwilling to explore this aspect of belief then they may be missing a vital component of the individual or family's overall belief system about how the world works and how problems arise and, more importantly, what is likely to be effective treatment.

There is potential for a rich and sophisticated understanding of the interplay between counselling and psychotherapeutic principles and a more explicit acknowledgement of a spiritual dimension to child and adolescent psychological health. Epidemiological studies provide a raft of orthodox explanations for emotional and behavioural problems encountered by children and young people, but they neglect the possibility that difficulties may occur from responses to their spiritual environment. The previous version of the diagnostic manual of mental illnesses included the category of spiritual disorder for the first time (APA, 1994).

However, the implication was that this area represented a threat to a young person's psychological health – overlooking the positive effects of spiritual health. In terms of culturally competent practice, this ought to provoke our curiosity at the very least.

The notion of a special place has been identified in research with children, and this signifies a potent context for reflection. The association children and young people have with this special place can be interpreted as an actual physical place (like a church, mosque, synagogue, temple or even a tree or gang den) or a desirable place within themselves seeking peace and contentment. Using this concept therapeutically opens up another avenue for practitioners who seek to explore the inner world of children and young people. It may relate to the notion of the secure attachment base or even a fantasy of returning to the womb and an infantile state. Older children may feel this concept is beneath them and will be most resistant to exploring this special place, but younger children who maintain a more active sense of imagination and magic may be more open to working in this psychic space.

A recurring theme associated with relationship issues as the source of some problems is that of trust. Children learn the benefits of developing trusting relationships but also the hurt and pain of a betrayal of trust. These can be related to parental abuse or neglect or a school friend's disclosure of a promised secret. Thus trust contains an element of hope in something intangible beyond a reassurance or schoolyard bargain. If children can connect with a sense of trust in some kind of transcendent benevolent power such as a god, then this, too, can be a fruitful area for exploration of their own vulnerability, limitations and dependence (Crompton, 1996).

The importance of spirituality is illustrated when we appreciate, for example, that spirituality is the cornerstone of the Aboriginal identity. Australian Aboriginal spiritual tradition places the origin of each Aboriginal clan in its own land. These clans hold deep spiritual links with their lands, which were formed in Dreamtime. The ancestral creative beings that travelled across the continent at the beginning of time established land boundaries between different Aboriginal clans and the sacred sites. Ritual obligations and religious ceremonies are carried out at these sites in order to reinforce the bond Aboriginal people feel with their lands. If they move from the land or it is taken from them, they lose their cultural identity and self-esteem (Yeo, 2003). For example, psychological problems have been linked with the Australian government's policy of forced removal of people from Aboriginal lands (Human Rights Commission, 1997).

A powerful argument is advanced by several authors who recommend incorporating a more explicit acknowledgement of the role that religion and spirituality can play in our work as therapists. The concept of postmodernism and its reductionist thesis for deconstruction of scientific or non-empirical certainties is challenged by an appeal to that which is ignored or rendered silent. In essence it is argued that because postmodernism emphasises separation and groundlessness in a context whereby every prevailing orthodoxy is questioned, people are paradoxically developing an appetite for community and connection. Moules (2000) suggests that we exist beyond our cultural creation and interpretations and learn from diversity connection through variety – to learn from the uncertainty of knowledge but not to deny any knowledge. In order to respond to this dilemma and enable counsellors and psychotherapists to harness positive aspects of religion and spirituality in their work, a theory of multicultural therapy has been advanced that offers a multidimensional paradigm to guide practice (Raval, 1996; Sue et al., 1996). The authors suggest that:

- it is necessary to have a meta-theory of counselling and psychotherapy to allow different theoretical models to be applied and integrated where possible;

- both counsellor and client identities are formed and embedded in multiple levels of life experiences and contexts, therefore treatment should take greater account of the child or young person's experience in relation to their context;

- the cultural identity development of the counsellor and client, and the wider power differentials associated with this, play an important role in the therapeutic relationship;

- multicultural counselling and therapy effectiveness is enhanced when the counsellor uses modalities and defines goals consistent with the life experiences and cultural values of the client.

The theory stresses the importance of multiple helping roles developed by many cultural groups and societies. Apart from the one-to-one encounter aimed at remediation in the individual, those roles often involve larger social units, system intervention and prevention. Multicultural counselling and therapy helps the child or young person develop a greater awareness about themselves in relation to their different contexts. This results in therapy that is contextual in orientation and which is able to respectfully draw on traditional methods of healing with a spiritual or religious dimension from many cultures. Paul Tillich (1963) alluded to this when he described something called *theonomy*, meaning the pursuit of culture under the impact of spiritual presence – a liberal humanism with an underlying spiritual depth.

It is perhaps a paradox that the decline of organised religion in white Western societies, combined with the consequences of previous imperialist expansion throughout the world, has produced a growing culturally diverse population, among whom are large numbers of devout religious communities with highly developed spiritual belief systems that organise social behaviour. While pundits, politicians and policy makers observe increases in antisocial behaviour among disaffected and disadvantaged young white people and blame the absence of religious values and thus moral standards, they are at the same time witnessing a growth in ethnic minority religious and spiritual affiliation, resulting in social, psychological and educational attainment. Culturally competent practice aspires to understand and support both groups of children and young people to help them make sense of their beliefs or lack of them in terms of vulnerability or resistance to psychological problems.

## Conclusion

The relevance to modern child and adolescent mental health services of culture, religion and spirituality cannot be overestimated as they form a part of the covert or overt belief systems of children and young people that will to a larger or lesser extent impact on work in psychological intervention. Their absence from mainstream psychiatry is a serious deficit. Most cultures can trace deep evidence of their ancestral heritage and the ways early civilisations sought to explain the world around them. These tend to involve the intervention of a supreme being or power with the capacity to control the natural elements vital for the survival of the species. Psychiatrists, counsellors, psychotherapists and psychologists underestimate at their peril the importance of these concepts to children and young people.

The history of modern societies has been shaped as much by the religious struggles of previous stages of development as by the economic and political forces motivating people to embark upon social change or revolution. Any practitioner who can embrace these ideas or, at the very least, accept their relevance to a young person's existence will be empowered. If workers are empowered then it follows that children and young people have the chance to feel empowered. And this offers us an interpersonal and intra-psychic therapeutic understanding of these powerfully important contexts within which individual children and young people evolve their own psychic road map.

The Western model of psychological illness tends to ignore the religious or spiritual aspects of the culture in which it is based. However, Eastern, African and Native American cultures tend to integrate them. Culture, spirituality and religion can be critical components of a child and young person's psychological well-being, offering a source of strength and hope in trying circumstances. We need to address this dimension as part of the constellation of factors affecting children and adolescents, bearing in mind the impact, positive or negative, spiritual or religious beliefs might have on their mental health.

Although the core qualities of spiritual experience are often assumed to be consistent with positive life-affirming experiences, they also contain concepts – such as awe and mystery, hell and punishment, sin and guilt – that can trigger profound and overwhelming feelings of terror and despair. Tread carefully when venturing down this path.

There is thus the potential for a rich and sophisticated understanding of the interplay between counselling and psychotherapeutic principles and a more explicit acknowledgement of a spiritual dimension to child and adolescent psychological health. The notion of a special place, either physical or spiritual, that has been identified in research with children is a potent context for reflection. You can create this special place in your work with troubled children and young people by demonstrating explicitly or implicitly that you are open to their perceptions of the world around them, that you will not dismiss or ignore their belief systems or privilege any cultural norms or attributes. At least begin with an acceptance of who they define themselves as, then a journey of recovery and the foundations of resilience can begin.

# 9 Racism and Mental Health

By Lena Robinson

## Introduction

This chapter examines the part played by racism in the development of Western psychology and psychiatry. It argues that Eurocentric standards of mental health are often inappropriate for ethnic minorities because they are based on the philosophies, values and mores of Euro-American culture, and these variables are used to develop normative standards of mental health. What constitutes mental health or mental illness is, therefore, always in relation to a Euro-American normative standard.

The dangers of cultural and Eurocentric bias are just as great in research on ethnicity and mental health as in the practice of psychiatry. There is a long history of research comparing European and non-European behaviour and mental processes which has often come to conclusions that now seem blatantly racist (Fernando, 2010; Sashidharan, 2001), but were accepted as valid at the time. Although crude racist conclusions are no longer apparent in cross-cultural mental health research, implicit or subtle racism still pervades the discipline.

## Racism

Racism results from *the transformation of 'race' prejudice and/or ethnocentrism through the exercise of power against a 'racial' group defined as inferior, by individuals and institutions with the intentional or unintentional support of the entire culture* (Jones, 1981, p 28). Dominelli (2008) specifies three main forms of racism. Individual racism is conceptualised as a person's 'race' prejudice based on biological considerations and involving actual behaviour that is discriminatory in nature. Without institutional backing, individual racism remains at the level of prejudice. Institutional racism includes the intentional or unintentional manipulation or toleration of institutional policies that unfairly restrict the opportunities of targeted groups. Institutional racist practices relate to the exclusion of ethnic minority groups – for example, African-Caribbean and Asian groups – from having access to employment, housing, education, health and social services.

Institutional racism lies at the heart of a pattern in British society whereby:

*there are three interconnected happenings: a) disproportionate numbers of black men being compulsorily detained and diagnosed as 'schizophrenic' by the mental health system; b) disproportionate numbers of black youngsters being subject to stop and search, arrest and then being charged, leading to magistrates and judges sending them to prison; c) disproportionate numbers of black children being excluded from school. All this adds up to the failures in three social systems, mental health, criminal justice and education, reflecting institutional racism in society as a whole.* (Sashidharan, 2001, p 125)

In addressing institutional racism, *mental health services cannot afford to ignore racism within its own structures and within the systems of psychiatry and psychology ... psychiatry will always need to address the cultural diversity of society and racism in all its forms* (Fernando, 2003, p 217).

The third type of racism is cultural racism. The root of cultural racism is in a continuing Eurocentric philosophy that values mainstream (dominant culture) beliefs and attitudes more highly than culturally diverse belief systems. It refers to the beliefs, feelings and behaviours of members of a cultural group that assert the superiority of that group's accomplishments, achievements and creativity, and attribute this claimed cultural superiority to inherent racial differences. In cultural racism the 'in-group/out-group' division is based on the supposed superiority of culture and racial background of one group over another (Axelson, 1985).

According to Fernando (2002, p 18), *racism affects our perceptions of culture and these assumptions are incorporated into the training of professionals.* In British society, there is a hierarchy of cultures and those of 'racial' minority groups are ranked very low (Ahmed, 1996). Western European religion, music, philosophy, law, politics, economics, morality, science and medicine are all considered to be the best in the world. References to black clients' cultures frequently reflect negative valuations rather than sensitivity (Ahmed, 1996; Fernando, 2010). The white majority value system summarised by Katz (1985) and elaborated upon in more recent texts (Pedersen, 2003) serves as a foundation for cultural racism when it is perceived as the 'model' system, and when those individuals who possess alternative value systems are thought of by the white majority as being deficient in some way.

Racism has an adverse influence on the mental health of ethnic minority populations in Britain and the United States. It is embedded in psychiatry and in the way service provision systematically puts ethnic minority people at a disadvantage (Fernando, 2009; Littlewood, 1992a). The roots of racism within psychiatric care can be traced to the conceptual and theoretical framework of what constitutes modern psychiatry (Fernando, 1988). The theories that inform current practice in assessing, diagnosing and treating ethnic minority people contain inherent negative stereotypes, beliefs and fears. These in turn play a significant part in the type of service black and ethnic minorities receive (Fernando, 2009).

In any discussion of incidence and prevalence of mental illness rates among black and minority groups, we need to recognise that racism influences those factors that contribute to mental disorder, as well as those that affect the duration and severity of an illness (Sashidharan, 2001). If one attempts to gain an overview of mental illness as it relates to black populations (both in Britain and the United States), an examination of the literature will readily reveal that black people are perceived to be more prone to psychological disorders than white people, and characteristically to have higher rates of mental illness (Fernando, 2010). Thomas and Sillen point out that: *investigators have made generalizations about epidemiology of black psychiatric disorders based on very little evidence ... and often these speculations were used to reinforce racist concepts* (1972, p 215).

Fernando (2010, p 109) argues that *although there is some concern in Britain about racism in psychiatry, this has not led to the adoption of any particular strategies to counteract it.* Everyday psychiatric service is characterised by:

the failure by most professionals in the mental health field, whatever their ethnicity, to allow for racial bias in practice and institutional racism in the delivery of services; institutional practices, such as mental health assessments and risk assessments, that are inherently institutionally racist being put through in a colour blind fashion that does not allow for bias. (Fernando, 2010)

## Deficiencies in the Eurocentric perspective

The question one must ask is whether psychological theories which have originated in Euro-American, white middle-class-dominated clinical settings have relevance in working with ethnic minority clients. The *albatross of racism and oppression has overshadowed thinking in Western-Eurocentric psychology and all of Social Science since its inception in the nineteenth century* (Jackson-Lowman, 2004, p 599).

Many psychologists (eg Jones, 2004; Owusu-Bempah and Howitt, 2000; Robinson, 2009) have noted the inadequacies of Western psychology. The failure of Western psychology is found in both its approach to and conception of the study of people.

Psychology is premised on the belief that the Western model is not only universal but is good. Throughout the history of Eurocentric psychology and psychiatry, the diagnosis of personality functioning in black people has been objectionable. This is especially true of the diagnosis of personality disorder where early Eurocentric practice advanced diagnoses like drapetomania, in which escape behaviour by an enslaved African was considered a disease of the mind, and dysaethesia Aethiopica, in which an African's resistance to enslavement was seen as a hebetude of mind (Thomas and Sillen, 1972). It was argued that *freed slaves showed a much greater proneness to mental disorder because by nature the Negro required a master* (Thomas and Sillen, 1972, p 61). This kind of pernicious misrepresentation of black people's psychological functioning continued as Eurocentric psychology matured (see Guthrie, 2003), and has been immensely damaging to the health and welfare of black and ethnic minority people.

The conventionally accepted paradigms and discoveries of Western psychology do not provide an understanding of black and ethnic minority people. Even a casual observation of the history of psychology will demonstrate that psychological literature from the last hundred years has been based on observations primarily on Europeans, predominantly male and overwhelmingly middle class. General psychology has failed to provide a full and accurate understanding of black reality. In fact, its utilisation has, in many instances, resulted in the pathologisation of black and ethnic minority groups.

Guthrie, in his book *Even the Rat was White* (2003), provides us with an overview of the problems and inadequacies of Western psychology. For example, in regard to psychology and race, Guthrie points out that Western psychologists not only provided inaccurate data that led to racist conclusions, but that their behaviour and conduct also call into question the intentions of psychological research. The latter point is important. Has the covert and, in some instances, overt 'intention' of Western psychology been to accept as true the inferiority of black people? Guthrie argues that, in regard to African people, Western psychology in general accepted as a basic a priori assumption that African people were inferior.

Those thinkers who have shaped the thought of Euro-American psychology have all directly or indirectly asserted the superiority of European races over non-European races. Despite the diversity of the various schools of Western psychology, they seem to merge unequivocally in their assumption of the Eurocentric point of view and the superiority of people of European descent. It is not surprising, therefore, that the conclusions reached from the application of their concepts and methods are invariably of the inferiority of non-European peoples.

In 1869, Francis Galton published his major work on *Hereditary Genius* and argued that, based on his 'scientific scale of racial values', he was able to conclude that the average intellectual standard of the Negro was at least two grades below that of whites. He proposed that a new science should start up, called eugenics, by which intelligent individuals would have children together and less intelligent people would be prevented from having children, through compulsory sterilisation, in an attempt to improve the quality of the human race.

Edward Thorndike, who was thought by many to be America's greatest psychologist, wrote, in his book *Human Nature and the Social Order*, that *the principle of eliminating bad genes is so thoroughly sound that almost any practice based on it is likely to do more good than harm* (1940, p 44). Thorndike, who also helped to develop the army intelligence test in the USA, believed and stated that *the institution of slavery existed because the black man's original nature was conducive to exploitation* (Thorndike, 1940). William McDougall, who has been called the 'Father of Social Psychology', also advanced the position that all people of African descent were innately intellectually inferior to whites (McDougall, 1921). The assumption that black people have 'intellectual deficits' still persists (for example, Hernstein and Murray, 1996).

# Models of Western psychological research on black and ethnic minority people

Various models can be traced in Western (Eurocentric) psychological research of black and minority groups (Sue and Sue, 2008; Thomas and Sillen, 1972). These models include the inferiority and the deficit (deprivations) model.

The inferiority model maintains that black people are intellectually, physically and mentally inferior to white people due to genetics/heredity. It focuses on the role of genes in explaining differences between black and white people. The model apparently gave some authors a scientific basis for regarding black people as inferior (Hernstein and Murray, 1996; Jensen, 1969, 1987; Rushton, 1988a, 1988b).

The deficit/deficiency model – which can be traced in Western-Eurocentric social science research of black and minority groups – contends that black people are deficient with respect to intelligence, cognitive styles and family structure due to lack of proper environmental stimulation, racism and oppressive conditions. From this deficit model came such hypotheses as 'cultural deprivation' (Valentine, 1971), which presumed that, due to inadequate exposure to Eurocentric values, norms, customs and lifestyles, blacks were 'culturally deprived' and required cultural enrichment. Fernando (2002, p 18) notes that *the ideals of mental health implicit in the thinking that underlies training [for psychiatrists] would naturally adhere to the values which are derived from Western culture, because cultures are seen hierarchically on the basis of racist assumptions about where they 'come' from*. Within psychiatric practice, *minority ethnic groups continue to be deemed as deviant from the white norms one way or another, either as requiring or receiving too much or too little psychiatry* (Sashidharan, 2001).

Some psychologists express little interest in trying to understand any culture other than their own. For many Euro-American social scientists the word 'different', when applied to black and ethnic minority people, became synonymous with 'deficient'. For example, many psychological tests, standardised on white people, are inappropriately applied to black people, causing them to appear less intelligent or deficient. Van de Vijver and Poortinga (1997) have discussed the problems of culturally biased psychologists who administer and interpret culturally biased psychological tests.

A main feature of Eurocentric psychology is the assumption among psychologists that people are alike in all important respects. In order to explain 'universal human phenomena', white psychologists established a normative standard of behaviour against which all other cultural groups were to be measured. What appeared as normal or abnormal was always in comparison to how closely a specific thought or behaviour corresponded to that of white people. Hence, normality is established on a model of the middle class of the Caucasian male of European descent. The more one approximates this model in appearance, values and behaviour, the more 'normal' one is considered to be. The obvious advantage for Europeans (whites) is that such norms confirm their reality as the reality. But the major problem with such normative assumptions for non-European people is the inevitable categorisation of anyone unlike this model 'as deviant'. In fact, the more distinct or distant you are from this model, the more pathological you are considered to be (Fernando, 2002).

Western psychology's attempt at establishing a normative standard for human cognition, emotion and behaviour is questionable. Psychological theories of personality, intelligence, motivation, learning, language development, self-concept, etc., were standardised on whites and applied to black and ethnic minority people. A model of white middle-class personality has been *utilized as a measuring stick against which all other psychological development is assessed'* (Sinha, 1983, p 7); *the standard against which others must measure up* (Segall et al., 1990, p 93).

Any diagnostic scheme dealing with ethnic minority people which fails to recognise the truth of ethnic minority experiences and does not adequately provide for their inclusion in interpretative data is not only inadequate but profoundly unfair (Bhui et al., 2003; Fernando, 2002). In Britain, mental health practitioners who have little understanding of Asian and African-Caribbean cultures tend to look upon the minority client's values and cultures as inherently inferior to their own (Fernando, 2002). It is often assumed that distinctive racial, cultural and linguistic features are deviant, inferior or embarrassing.

# Biased diagnostic instruments

The central issue underlying the problem of racial bias in psychiatric diagnosis is the dominance of a white, Western viewpoint in psychiatry. One of the most well-known diagnostic approaches is the American system known as DSM-III (DSM is short for the Diagnostic and Statistical Manual of Mental Disorder, and III refers to the third edition, published in 1980). Traditional assessment frameworks such as the DSM-III-R (third edition revised) use a European worldview and behaviour as the standard of normality.

*Even the inclusion of a list of so-called 'culture-bound syndromes' in an appendix of the DSM perpetuates this biased viewpoint, because a clinician applying such culture-bound labels is nevertheless expected to adhere to the DSM authors' approach to diagnostic formulation.* (Ali, 2004, p 74)

This results in increased rates of misdiagnosis among black and ethnic minority people. Loring and Powell (1988) found in a sample of US psychiatrists that diagnosis, using DSM-III (APA, 1980), was influenced by the 'race' (and sex) of case vignettes. Bhugra and Bhui (2007) also point out that

*psychiatric diagnostic systems deal with categories which have been developed with Western nosological categories in mind. This means that individual differences get lost in the diagnostic encounter. Although DSM-IV has started to take the impact of culture into account, day-to-day interactions may not be affected at all.* (p 119)

The Association of Black Psychologists is concerned about the DSM-V manual. The Association notes that '*lowering the diagnostic threshold for several disorders will lead to unwarranted and potentially detrimental diagnosis among African Americans. The possible inclusion of so-called 'Attenuated Psychosis Syndrome' is a major concern as related to African Americans, who already experience mis- and over-diagnosis, especially with disorders such as schizophrenia.*

The use of 'objective' psychological inventories as indicators of maladjustment places black and minority people at a disadvantage. The diagnostic tools used to define personality deviance, such as the projective methods of personality assessment, the Rorschach and the Thematic Apperception Test, are based on the accumulation of certain signs (inferred from verbal responses) in proper proportion to reflect normality. The projective method of personality assessment rests on the assumption that the more unstructured methods of assessment, those that present the individual with highly ambiguous or inherently meaningless stimuli, obtain a qualitatively richer yield of the unique aspects of the individual personality. Careful interpretation of the data presumably allows clinicians to make inferences about the deep rather than surface structure of personality: the individual's needs, fears, conflicts and defensive mechanisms and other dynamic aspects of personality. Cultural differences are not acknowledged in the determination of deviance. It is important to note that psychometric projective techniques such as the Rorschach Ink Blot Test (Rorschach, 1942) and Thematic Apperception Test (Murray, 1938) depend heavily upon psychoanalytical theoretical underpinnings for their interpretations. Psychoanalysis has been *branded racist on the grounds that some analysts have adapted it blindly for application to other cultures and groups* (Bhugra and Bhui, 2007, p 122).

Jones and Korchin state that: *Until more is known about the influence of ethnic cultures on responses to the Rorschach, it is only reasonable that standard scoring categories be applied with caution. [Furthermore], inferences about the meaning of responses to projective techniques are particularly vulnerable to cultural bias'* (Jones and Korchin, 1982, p 22).

## Racial bias

There is considerable American literature on the likelihood of racial bias intrinsic to the Minnesota Multiphasic Personality Inventory (MMPI) – a personality test that is widely used in the USA and Britain. Numerous studies document that black and minorities receive more severe diagnoses and tend to score higher on, for example, the MMPI paranoia and schizophrenia scales than their white counterparts (Jones, 2004). If a group of black people were administered a personality test and it was found that they were more suspicious than their white counterparts, what would this mean? Some psychologists have used such findings to label black people as paranoid. In Britain, there is considerable evidence of an excess of paranoia among black people (Bhugra and Bhui, 2007). This pathological interpretation of paranoia has been challenged by many black psychologists as being inaccurate (eg Whaley, 2001a). These authors argue that, in order to survive in a white racist society, black people have developed a highly functional survival mechanism to protect them against possible physical and psychological harm. Whaley (2001a) perceives this 'cultural paranoia' as adaptive and healthy rather than dysfunctional and pathological. This model of black coping was reiterated and expanded upon by Whaley (2001b). The personality test that reveals black people as being suspicious, mistrustful and 'paranoid' needs to be understood from a larger socio-political perspective. Black people who have been victims of discrimination and oppression in a culture that is full of racism have good reason to be suspicious and mistrustful of white society.

Jones and Korchin maintain that *ethnic differences on measures of psychopathology like the MMPI are less likely due to differences in actual level of adjustment than to differences in the meaning of items from one group to another. This ... implies that a different set of validation studies must be established for minority subjects* (1982, p 22). A number of other authors, for example, Adebimpe (1994, p 100) argue that *despite major advances in diagnostic technique, there is good evidence that problems in the recognition of specific psychiatric illnesses [in black patients] persist.*

## Negative stereotypes

Some of the other factors that are likely to increase the likelihood of misdiagnosis among black people are socio-cultural disparities between the clinician and patient and negative stereotypes of black people (Jones, 2004). It is important to note that the vast majority of black people who have been labelled psychologically disturbed, mentally ill or abnormal have been evaluated and labelled by white diagnosticians. From initial contact through every stage of treatment to discharge, black patients are less likely to encounter black decision makers compared to the size and strength of the white majority. A number of stereotypes operate in the encounter between black people and the welfare agencies of the state. African Caribbeans are stereotyped as aggressive, excitable and defiant, and Asian people are seen as meek, passive and docile. Analysis of these culturalist stereotypes suggests a *pathologization of cultural differences*. Other prevalent stereotypes are that Asians are not *psychologically minded*; Asians somatise mental distress and present only physical symptoms; Asians *look after their own* within their extended family networks (Dominelli, 2008).

We need to question the implicit Eurocentric bias in psychiatrists' diagnosis of mental illness. Mental health, more than any other health field, depends on communication for diagnosis and therapy (Bains, 2005). Attention must be paid not only to what a patient says and does but also to the cultural context of the client's communication (Ridley, 2005). Some studies have found that a diagnosis of schizophrenia may be made solely on the basis of the client's belief in supernatural phenomena, a belief that was generally unacceptable to the interviewing clinician. This example of misdiagnosis based on a Eurocentric bias and nosology system cannot be considered unique. An early US study (Baskin et al., 1981), using both black and white psychiatrists as diagnosticians, examined the influences of client–therapist differences on diagnosis. The results indicated that white psychiatrists were more likely than their black counterparts to diagnose black patients as schizophrenic. In fact, the black psychiatrists, who were assigned a total of 271 patients (141 black and 130 non-black), diagnosed only two patients (both non-black) as schizophrenic, while white psychiatrists diagnosed 15 per cent of their total case load and 20 per cent of the blacks as schizophrenic. Baskin et al. (1981) concluded that diagnosis was not an objective assessment, but was in fact an assessment of observable behaviour compared to the cultural standards of the psychiatrist.

Doctors in Britain will have been trained *to recognize a classical picture of disease which has arisen in European culture and has therefore been described in European terms. It is too often assumed that this is the normal pattern for other people from other lands* (Tewfik and Okasha, 1965, p 603). Some black authors (for example, Thomas and Sillen, 1972) have argued that indicators of positive mental health among black people – such as a willingness to challenge the conditions of racism, an awareness of society's hostility towards black people and a strong identity with one's own culture – could be perceived negatively by a psychiatrist unfamiliar with the black norm. British psychiatrists are likely to misinterpret black people's expressions such as grief, distress and anger as signs of schizophrenia (Fernando, 2003; Littlewood and Lipsedge, 1997). Furthermore, British psychiatrists, trained in the conventional manner, fail to correctly recognise the true medical significance of black patients' symptoms because they lack an adequate knowledge of the black person's culture and how it influences the manifestation of mental illness (Fernando, 2009).

## Diagnostic errors

The lack of relevant knowledge of African-Caribbean history, belief systems and so on, and of the influence such a cultural background could have on the manifestations of psychological distress in African Caribbeans, has led to errors in diagnosis. Consequently, inappropriate use of such categories as schizophrenia is being made (Fernando, 2003; 2010). It therefore *appears likely that the observed rates of classical schizophrenia reported among the West Indian born are exaggerated* (Littlewood and Lipsedge, 1997, p 318). Adebimpe (1981) has also found that in the USA black patients run a higher risk of being misdiagnosed as schizophrenics, whereas white patients showing identical behaviours are more likely to receive diagnoses of depression. It has repeatedly been stated in the Eurocentric literature that depression is rarely found among blacks in the USA and Britain. Black people are viewed as having a primitive character structure, and as being too jovial to be depressed and too impoverished to experience objective loss (Adebimpe, 1981). Symptoms of depression are more accurately perceived by white psychiatrists when the patient is white than when the patient is black (Bhugra and Bhui, 2007).

Psychiatric misdiagnosis is a serious problem, as diagnosis serves as the basis of treatment, referral and subsequent discharge. The relationship between type of diagnosis, type of treatment and ethnicity of patient has been documented in the literature (Cox, 1977). Regardless of the psychiatric diagnosis, black people in the USA and Britain receive harsher treatment (eg drug therapy, seclusion and restraint) than their white counterparts, because blacks are typically perceived as more violent than whites. More recent reviews of the psychiatric literature continue to show that black people are often stereotyped as not being psychologically minded, and as lacking the psychological sophistication and motivation necessary for successful therapy. The over-representation of black people in British psychiatric hospitals is attributed *either to 'cultural' factors which quintessentially distinguish black people from white people or to notions of black pathology* (McKenzie and Bhui, 2007).

## Perception of patients

Although Eurocentric psychology is mature at 133 years of age in 2012, its diagnosis of mental disorder in black people remains detrimental in contemporary times. Lewis et al. (1990) present evidence that, for psychiatrists, the factor of race will substantially alter their perception of patients and will influence the type and severity of diagnosis as well as the mode of treatment. According to Fernando (2002, p 108), *psychiatric diagnoses continue to carry racist undertones ... racism in Western culture continues to permeate the disciplines of psychology and psychiatry in research, theory and practice*. Over the years, a number of crude diagnostic pseudo-categories such as 'West Indian psychosis' and 'Caribbean psychosis' have come into operation. These categories have not been coined as a result of theory, and there is no research to legitimise their practical use. Littlewood (1992b) also noted that the diagnosis of cannabis psychosis is applied more frequently in the African-Caribbean population despite the lack of convincing evidence supporting a major aetiological role for cannabis in severe psychosis (Onyango, 1986). It has been argued that mentally ill British African Caribbeans are treated more punitively and are more likely to be 'labelled' with diagnoses of schizophrenia or cannabis psychosis because of racist attitudes among psychiatrists (Littlewood and Lipsedge, 1997). The reality of racism as a major force within psychiatric decision making and treatment, though often denied, is central to any understanding of black people's experience of psychiatry. Black people who come into contact with the mental health services are more likely to receive medication than 'talking therapies' such as psychotherapy or counselling. Sashidharan (2003) reported that *mentally distressed black people are more likely to be locked away, that rates of compulsory admission are markedly higher and that black and minority patients are more likely than white people to be assessed as requiring greater degrees of supervision, control and security. The evidence, which attests to the discriminatory nature of psychiatric care in Britain, is incontestable ... until we begin to address racism within psychiatry, in its knowledge base, its historical and cultural roots and within its practices and procedures, we are unlikely to achieve significant progress in improving services for minority ethnic groups* (Sashidharan, 2001, p 245).

Although there is some concern in Britain about racism in psychiatry, this has not led to the adoption of any particular strategies to counteract it. However, *the challenges to both psychiatry and psychology are increasing, particularly from users of psychiatric services and from organizations run by black and Asian people* (Fernando, 2002, p 109).

## Conclusions

I would like to conclude this chapter with a quote from Fernando:

*The universalist psychiatric/psychological doctrine, ie that Western concepts of the mind, of illness models and treatments have global relevance, subsumes within it a distinct racist judgement of cultures and peoples – often only partially concealed. And psychiatric diagnoses continue to carry racist undertones. Current practitioners tend to ignore the racist dimension of their disciplines and therefore little, if any, action is usually taken to counteract the effects of racism in practice. Consequently, not only are racist traditions perpetuated, but also, racism in Western culture continues to permeate the discipline of psychology and psychiatry in research, theory and practice* (2002, p 108).

# 10 The Mirage of Mental Health Law Reform

## By James Trueman

## Introduction

Mental health legislation is a rare and powerful weapon. It provides the means to deprive an individual of their liberty, perhaps indefinitely, when they have not committed a crime against society or any civilian. It allows certain groups within society (ie health and social care professionals) to enforce compliance with chemical (and other) treatment regimes, and being subject to detention under it places a mark against an individual for life. Given the potential of this area of law, one might expect that its reform would be a considered affair, undertaken to ensure that the best legal vehicle exists for the treatment of those in need of mental health care, and informed by the finest expert evidence of senior professionals and legal academics. Indeed, one might assume that the objective is to ensure that the most appropriate and least restrictive statute is enacted.

However, in contrast to what we might desire, reform of mental health legislation in the UK is not generally a process stimulated by measured, objective discussion. It tends to occur when compelled by periods of crisis, largely fuelled by public or media outcry, which propel society and then parliamentarians out of the relative calm of dormancy. Indeed, the UK's history of legislative reform is scattered with the ebb and flow between these two states, between the apparent (if not effective) hive of activity during crisis and the disinterested lull of dormancy.

Consequently, the recent Labour Government's attempt to reform the Mental Health Act 1983 was similarly viewed as an aggressive risk management policy initiative, generated by limited, but well-publicised cases of violence, committed by people who were known to mental health services (eg P. Brown, 2006; Hewitt, 2008; Prins, 2008). Moreover, despite earlier Thatcherite attention to public opinion and aggressive media management (Hennessy, 2001, pp 425–26; Oborne, 2005, pp 14ff), Blair's Labour administration was singled out for diligently monitoring the voice of the public through focus groups, opinion polls, etc., principally under the influence of political strategist Philip Gould (Seldon, 2005, pp 130–31; Wolff, 2002). Tony Blair, in particular, was portrayed as a 'preference-accommodator' in relation to public opinion – enslaved to the focus groups and unwilling to take risks with government popularity (Rawnsley, 2000, p 13; Theakston, 2003, p 119).

These two discourses became enmeshed to negatively frame the reform of the Mental Health Act 1983 as a hasty response to perceptions of public outcry, enacted by a government willing to erode civil liberties, in its attempt to protect its own public image. The difficulties in progressing the reform process were largely laid at the feet of an obstinate and unlistening political administration, intent on getting its own way, while all other stakeholders were generally framed as the virtuous protectors of what is good and right.

Given the historical pattern of political response to public pressure, it is understandable that Labour's approach was framed as nothing more than an unbalanced 'moral panic' (Cohen, 1972; Hewitt, 2008; Paterson, 2006; Pilgrim, 2007). Perhaps the government did man the 'moral barricades' in an attempt to resolve the perceptions of risk that existed. Yet, the perceptions of their actions are not wholly consistent with the internal events that shaped the reform management. Moreover, they were not the only instrumental stakeholder in the reform process, with the power to influence both opinion and events. The media presented a formidable image of the drivers for reform, although this was often neither accurate nor comprehensive. Lastly, both professional and political lobbying affected the reform process. This identified one particular professional group as having a dominant influence on the reform of the Mental Health Act 1983, and the detrimental consequences of the traditional adversarial politics within the halls of Westminster.

While an exhaustive analysis of the entire reform process is outwith the practical scope of this text, this chapter examines the one-sided, 'moral panic', view of the reform. In contrast, it argues that the reform process was the product of an interconnected and historically embedded matrix of influences and relationships.

## The mirage of mental health law reform

The issue of mental health legislative reform came to prominence early in New Labour's first year in office (from May 1997), with the presentation of various amending Private Members Bills to the Houses of Parliament from June 1997 onwards.[1] Meetings concerning the reform of the Mental Health Act 1983 took place between government officers and stakeholders during 1997 and proposals circulated the Department of Health from early February 1998 (Brown, 1998a, 1998b). However, Paul Boateng did not publicly reveal any plans to undertake such a review of the legislation when he was asked directly by Members of Parliament.[2] Subsequently, within months of Mr Boateng's inconclusive responses to the House during March 1998, various announcements were made concerning review processes and government policies, which highlighted that the reform of mental health legislation was very much an active and ongoing target.

Amid pronouncements that 'care in the community' had failed, and that a small but significant minority of patients had become a danger to the public, as well as themselves, Frank Dobson announced in July 1998 the need for a new 'Third Way' for mental health and that he was setting up a review of the Mental Health Act 1983 (Dobson, 1998). He identified that as the *first step in this process*, he would appoint a small team of experts to advise him on the areas of current legislation which needed revising or supplementing.[3] Subsequently, on 22 September 1998, Paul Boateng announced that Professor Genevra Richardson had been appointed to commence a *root and branch* review of the Mental Health Act 1983 (Boateng, 1998).

While the wholesale review of mental health legislation commenced, the management of dangerous, mentally disordered individuals was also subject to consideration. This first became common knowledge on 26 October 1998, when Jack Straw publicly indicated that he believed there needed to be changes in the law and practice concerning violent people with mental disorder who had been diagnosed as not likely to respond to treatment.[4] Subsequent announcements within Westminster clarified Labour's intention for proposals concerning people with severe personality disorder who were considered dangerous.[5] However, because of the lack of agreement throughout the reform process, from Frank Dobson's announcement in July 1998, to the Royal Assent of the Mental Health Act 2007 on 19 July 2007, the English legislative reform process took nine years.

# Government influence

While the reform of the Mental Health Act 1983 occurred between 1998 and 2007, events in the first nine months of this process set the tone of how the Labour government appeared to engage with the reform process, and the stakeholders involved. Pivotal in this early phase was the constitution and activities of the scoping committee, chaired by Professor Genevra Richardson (and therefore referred to as the Richardson Committee). Various issues existed surrounding this committee; these centred on the composition, purpose and timescale for the group.

How members of the Committee were chosen is not entirely clear, although these decisions would appear to have had an impact on the process. We know that the government sought an *eminent academic or lawyer* to chair the Committee, although we do not know why. Professor Richardson matches this limited description of a potential appointee, although this description also relates to other (albeit inconclusive) general comments in proposal documents, concerning the technical legal amendments that were required to the Mental Health Act 1983 (Brown, 1998a, para. 9(viii), para. 26, 1998b, para. 8(viii), para. 25).

Professor Richardson's comments when chairing the Darren Carr Inquiry are likely to have made her an attractive appointee for the government. This is because she noted that while Mr Carr was considered dangerous, *neither his disorder nor his symptoms were immediately amenable to treatment*, and this fact *appropriately* limited the relevance of mental health legislation powers (Richardson et al., 1997, para. 17.6.2). Her report consequently noted that if society wanted to impose controls on people such as Mr Carr, *irrespective of the presence of a treatable mental disorder*, then it should give *psychiatric services (or indeed any agency ... the powers necessary ... expressly in legislation* (para. 17.6.2–17.6.3). This proposition (particularly surrounding the psychopathically disordered), matched the government's focus on risk and the mentally disordered as a danger to society (Boateng, 1998; Dobson, 1998). It would therefore be logical for the government to assume Professor Richardson would recommend explicit legal powers to achieve greater public protection. However, the Committee's final report did not mirror the government's apparent desire to place risk before capacity.

The effectiveness of the Richardson Committee would be affected by the clarity of its purpose, although the government did not express that consistently. Frequently Professor Richardson was described as leading a scoping study to *kick-start* the review process, to *accelerate the thinking* around what the new legislative framework should look like (eg Boateng, 1998; Department of Health, 1999, p 142, para. 14). The Committee's written terms of reference underpinned this, detailing that ministers were seeking advice on the degree to which the Act needed updating and required advice on the *scope of the issues to be considered* (Department of Health, 1999, p 127). As such, the purpose of the Committee was framed as stimulating the review process, rather than actually completing it.

However, despite this framing of a preliminary and limited role, at the first meeting of the Richardson Committee, Paul Boateng then stated that the Committee was *being asked to undertake a root and branch review which will consider all the major issues that must be addressed and to make clear recommendations on how to deal with them in legislative terms* (Department of Health, 1999, p 143: para. 16). Contrary to Mr Boateng's earlier press release in which he stated that the government was looking *for clear advice on how to take forward a root and branch reform of the law* (Boateng, 1998), and the embryonic phrases he used elsewhere (eg *kick-start*). Mr Boateng indicated that he was charging the Richardson Committee with completing this endeavour, and that he expected a thorough job to be done.

## Contradiction and confusion

This contradiction led to a confused ongoing interpretation of the Committee's role. The continued framing within political discourse and official documents was that Richardson had been appointed to review (or undertake a *major review* of) the Mental Health Act 1983,[6] with writers such as Houlihan (2000, p 870) referring to Richardson's work as the *recent root and branch review of the current legislation*, and in doing so, using Mr Boateng's representation of the process rather than Mr Dobson's *first step* framing.[7] In contrast, the Richardson Committee was described elsewhere as having a more preliminary role, such as taking *forward the first phase of a review*, being appointed to *start the review* or as a *study group set up to identify the main issues to be addressed in the review of the legislation* (Thorp and Wright, 1999, p 25; O'Keeffe and Scott-Moncrieff, 2000, p 667; POST, 2003, p 2).

Four options were considered for the review of the Mental Health Act 1983, including (1) a full Royal Commission; (2) an External Expert Team carrying out the whole review (as in Scotland); (3) a Department of Health Review Team carrying out the whole review; and (4) an Expert Scoping Team, with a second-stage process by a Department of Health Team, to develop specific policies. A full Royal Commission was not considered necessary, and it was felt in particular that it would be difficult to limit the scope of the Commission's deliberations to ensure fit with the direction of the government's strategy for mental health and their wider policies, including criminal justice. The last of these options (4) was considered to offer most of the advantages of (2) and (3), as (a) it would be one of the cheapest options; (b) the Scoping Team would confer independence while the terms of reference could be tightly focused, and the Department Team could manage the second-stage process and therefore control the final output; and (c) it could be completed within the very tight time schedule the Department of Health was hoping to achieve (Brown, 1998b, para. 23–28). Consequently, in addition to the terms of reference and political boundaries, a range of limitations and requirements were imposed on the Richardson Committee in terms of time.

The Committee was expected to report progress on their work to the government on a monthly basis. Furthermore, despite being tasked with undertaking a *root and branch* review, they were to provide a final report back to ministers by April 1999 (within six months of commencing their scoping review) (Department of Health, 1999, p 128). It was only as a consequence of Professor Richardson's desire to submit a draft version of their report for consultation that John Hutton extended the timetable until the end of June 1999, and this was again extended to 15 July 1999 (therefore being nine months in total from the first meeting) (Hutton, 1998; Department of Health, 1999, para. 1.17).

The restricted time available for the Richardson Committee's work is marked in Appendix B of the Report, with a disclaimer that the scoping review was undertaken around their regular jobs, and that *the work should be read and understood in this light* (Department of Health, 1999, p 129). Richardson also commented that, since the timetable had not allowed the Committee to reflect on the results of the programme of research supporting the reform, the government should ensure they did so in determining its eventual legislative strategy (Department of Health, 1999, p 16, para. 1.24). However, it is questionable whether they actually did.

## Lack of scrutiny

A consequence of this situation was that neither the issues concerning mentally disordered offenders, nor the policy concerning dangerous people with severe personality disorder, were subject to detailed scrutiny by the Richardson Committee. They thus did not become integrated elements of the reform (ie in so far as they fell outside of the scope of the Richardson Committee proposals), and remained separate processes effectively solely managed by or associated with the Home Office. Accordingly, the Richardson Report, and the subsequent discourse reflected the lack of cohesion between the different government departments and their policies.

This lack of cohesion contributed to confusion over who 'the government' was. The uncertainty focused on who was in control of the reform, as expressed by Genevra Richardson:

*the Government, and I am not quite sure whether I should be talking about the Department of Health or the Home Office here, has focussed on the prevention of harm or the reduction of risk.* (JCDMHB, 2005a, Ev 2)

Nonetheless, an overarching opinion was that the Home Office was driving the reform process. This view was probably most prominent concerning the dangerous and severe personality disorder (DSPD) policy proposals. The concept for these was first signalled when a reviewable detention order for those with *severe personality disorder*, who posed a grave threat to the public was proposed (Department of Health, 1998, para. 4.31–4.34). Jack Straw's reference to *the indeterminate but reviewable detention of … dangerous, severely personality disordered individuals* underscored this,[8] and prepared the way for the policy document 'Managing Dangerous People with Severe Personality Disorder: Proposals for Policy Development' (Home Office and Department of Health, 1999).

The DSPD proposals faced overwhelming opposition (eg Chiswick, 1999; Eastman, 1999b; Gunn, 2000; Health Select Committee, 2000b, pp lviii–lxi). Much of this opposition was centred on the collocation of 'dangerousness' with 'mental disorder' (and the perceived stigma this created), and on a claimed false expectation that dangerousness could be accurately predicted, and therefore prevented (eg Dolan and Doyle, 2000, p 309; Home Affairs Committee, 2000c, para. 73, App. 6: part 2, para. 1; JCDMHB, 2005a, Ev 74; Royal College of Psychiatrists and Law Society, 2002, para. 7; Szmukler, 2001, p 85).

In contrast, commentators outside of the government, including, most notably, Professor Tony Maden, resisted these concerns. He argued that any drug or medical intervention that caused 25 deaths a year would be banned without a thought. Yet, in mental health, he contended that psychiatrists were *dismissing as occasional*, the deaths of 50 [sic] innocent bystanders at the hands of individuals with mental health problems, and that the true level of homicides was higher than that being cited (particularly by Crichton and Darjee, 2007), as quoted figures only included those in recent contact with mental health services, and not all homicides committed by individuals with mental illness (eg Public Bill Committee Debate, 2007 Mental Health Bill [Lords], MH 68; Maden, 2007a).

Maden also challenged the position being presented about the reliability of risk assessment (or lack of it) – as illustrated by Dr Tony Zigmond in his evidence to the Joint Committee scrutinising the draft Mental Health Bill 2004:

*the notion of predicting that somebody is a clear danger either to themselves or, indeed, anybody else ... is rather a fallacious one. My colleagues and I are not good at it.* (JCDMHB, 2005a, Ev 81: 81)

Professor Maden believed that risk assessment had *improved tremendously over the last 10 or 15 years ... and that ... general psychiatric services probably have too much concern*. Specifically, he was critical of writers such as Szmukler (2001), who took a pessimistic view of risk assessment, arguing that psychiatry *must not persist in assuming that violence, an uncommon complication of mental disorder, is unimportant because of its rarity* (Maden, 2001, p 479). Maden asserted that as there was evidence linking mental illness with violence, attempts to argue that violence had nothing to do with psychiatrists served *only to cause further damage to the profession's public image* (2005, p 121).

## Negative attitudes

Resistance to DSPD was enhanced by a view that personality disorder was not treatable (eg *the whole point about personality disorder is that it cannot be treated*),[9] and therefore should not be included within mental health legislation. Arguments cited limitations in research evidence concerning treatment to reject DSPD. However, negative attitudes towards personality disorder had inhibited research into the disorder ever taking place, limited the provision of specific services and training, and the diagnosis was not applied (nor patients admitted), as it was seen as 'unacceptable' (Fallon et al., 1999b, pp 5, 143, 146, 225, 322, 464, 494; Moran, 1999, pp 3–4; Royal College of Psychiatrists, 1999, p 13). Although, conversely, patients of a particular 'sort' (of interest to senior psychiatrists), or with personality disorder and circumstances of an *unusual, horrific, or bizarre* nature, were admitted, irrespective of their identified need or treatability status (Fallon et al., 1999b, pp 164, 464).

Despite a lack of clear consensus regarding the diagnostic term severe personality disorder (Duggan, 2005, p 26), in contrast to the criticisms above, it has been used widely enough to suggest that it is accepted by a broad selection within the mental health community (eg Francis et al., 2006, p 32; JCDMHB, 2005c, Ev 854, Ev 1136, Ev 1333; Kisely, 1999; Moran, 1999; Royal College of Psychiatrists, 1999, p 11). Specifically, the Fallon Inquiry explored the concept of severe personality disorder at some length, suggesting it as an alternative for psychopathic personality (disorder), and also as a definition for a group of individuals who both experienced personality disorder and posed a risk of causing serious harm to others (Fallon et al., 1999a, para. 1.17.1, 1999b, p 93).

The idea of abandoning the term 'psychopathic disorder' was supported by some (eg Fallon et al., 1999b, pp 58, 491–92, Royal College of Psychiatrists, 1999, p 11), while others argued that all it would achieve would be to switch the pejorative labelling, that it would change the words, but would not alter the debate (Fallon et al., 1999b, pp 142, 188). However, evidence to the Fallon Inquiry clearly illustrated that there was significant support for the concept of severe personality disorder, with witnesses contending that it was a *legitimate generalisation*, *valid diagnosis* or *valid clinical diagnosis* (eg Fallon et al., 1999b, pp 83, 139, 263, 345, 526). Moreover, witnesses to the Inquiry either specifically collocated dangerousness with severe personality disorder, or argued that, while dangerousness did not equate to severe personality disorder, dangerousness would be seen in the combination of a condition such as severe personality disorder and the commission of an act that would be seen as dangerous (Fallon et al., 1999b, pp 40, 57–58, 93, 395). In other words, there was a natural tendency in some witnesses to create a term that described individuals as presenting with dangerous severe personality disorder, before the government's working group had introduced the term.

Critically, we may never know how the DSPD policy was formulated, as government officials have admitted they are unable to locate the records related to the DSPD working group – acknowledging this represents a *serious deficiency* or *serious failings* in the *Department's record creation and keeping practice* (Doole, 2009; McDonald, 2009). Interviews with those we can identify as being involved may bear some fruit. However, it must be borne in mind the information they could offer would be mediated by their own interpretations of the proceedings, and by their variable memory of past events (Hall, 2008, p 124–25).

## Media: the fourth estate

Representations of mental illness and the mentally ill in the media can have an extremely powerful effect (Cutcliffe and Hannigan, 2001). They have the power to construct the perceived reality that affects how we view the world, but they also constitute our knowledge of that world (van Dijk, 1993, p 258). Various representational elements contributed to the process and outcomes of this legislative reform experience, and these will be examined here.

Despite extensive opposition, fewer than 350 newspaper articles were published between January 1997 and December 2007 concerning the general reform of the Mental Health Act 1983. Three interconnected themes of public protection, dangerous and severe personality disorder and community treatment orders saturated the media on this subject, predominantly reflecting the government's attempt to secure improved public protection. Three broadsheet newspapers, *The Independent*, *The Times* and *The Guardian*, dominated the reporting. Over

46 per cent of the reporting presented a purely negative view of the reform, 26 per cent expressed no or a balanced view, 22 per cent mentioned the reform process during a human interest or other story, and only 6 per cent discussed the reform from a positive perspective.

However, one media story in particular was presented as having a specific influence on the reform of the Mental Health Act 1983, that of Michael Stone. He was accused of attacking Dr Lin Russell and her two daughters, Megan and Josie, as they walked home on 9 July 1996. He was convicted on 23 October 1998 and again following a retrial on 5 September 2001. Among other presentations, he had been diagnosed as personality disordered and engaged in the behaviour that illustrated the 'dangerousness' the government referred to through their DSPD policy. The diagnosis of personality disorder specifically led to a publicised view that he was 'untreatable' and therefore not detainable, although the actual care he received appears to have been of a reasonably high standard (Francis et al., 2006).

Michael Stone was cited throughout the reform discourse, particularly in the context as a driver for the reform proposals (eg Allen, 2005; Butcher, 2007, p 117; HL Hansard 10 January 2007 col.299; JCDMHB, 2005a, Ev 341: 463, JCDMHB, 2005d, para. 19, 21; Law Society, 2002, pp 14–15; Mullen, 2007, s.6). However, in contrast to limited articles about the reform in general, between July 1996 and December 2007, nearly 800 newspaper articles were published about Michael Stone and the attack on the three members of the Russell family. The reporting on Michael Stone was overwhelmingly dominated by *The Times* and by *The Sun*, both part of Rupert Murdoch's News International Group (which at this time was pro-Blair: Seldon, 2005, p 307), and constituting together 44 per cent of the coverage. Largely due to the *sub judice* rule, 57 per cent of the reporting discussed only the Russell or Stone/Russell case, without any reference to mental illness or the mentally ill. However, the intensity of sensationalist reporting in the rest of the articles created an extremely powerful body of influence.

Members of the media frequently suggested that Michael Stone was the case which exposed the existence of a loophole in the Mental Health Act 1983, centred around the treatability test for psychopathy (eg Chittenden and Sheehan, 1998, p 6; Johnston, 2002, p 5; Wooding, 2006, p 32), and that he was the grounds for the introduction of specific legislative and policy changes to 'close' the loophole (eg Brindle, 1998, p 14; Carvel and Ward, 2002, p 9). More broadly, some journalists suggested that the reform of the Mental Health Act 1983 was instigated after Michael Stone's conviction in October 1998 (eg Burrell, 1999, p 2; Laurance, 2004, p 15; Martin, 2007, p 19).

It is worth noting that many of the assertions concerning Michael Stone (eg 'untreatability' or dangerousness) were published before the report of the Independent Inquiry into his care (Francis et al., 2006) was released into the public domain. Yet, the overarching conclusion from the Inquiry was that services in Kent should be commended for the care that Michael Stone had received, and that this was emphatically not a case of a man with a dangerous personality disorder being generally ignored by agencies or left at large without supervision (Francis et al., 2006, p 5, para. 4). Nonetheless, the dominant media discourse after the publication of the Inquiry report remained consistent with that prior to the report being made public.

The primary message still presented the imagery of a damning, highly critical report, detailing a long catalogue of failings which had left Michael Stone at liberty in the community to carry out the murders he was subsequently convicted of (D. Brown, 2006; Edwards, 2006; Sapsted, 2006). Reporting overall gave the impression that service providers knew of the risk he posed and did nothing to prevent his actions (eg Carroll, 2006; Clements, 2006). Therefore, even when the media had the opportunity to 'set things right', it continued to offer a largely inaccurate and sensationalist presentation of the case, and to detrimentally affect the process of the reform.

# Adversarial politics and professional dominance

The English reform process was influenced by two primary sources of resistance. Members of Parliament, and lobbyist groups (eg Mental Health Alliance), who generally varied between those elected to represent a particular group (eg Royal College of Psychiatrists), and unelected issues-based organisations (eg SANE). Resistance to the reform from within (and without) Westminster drew on two principal approaches: the first was to present the Scottish reform process as completely and unequivocally better, which polarised this as good and the attempts in Westminster as bad; and the second was a 'combative' style of adversarial engagement, which was also a defining feature of the dominant lobbyist groups.

## Adversarial politics

Scotland was held up as a positive example for adhering to the recommendations of the Millan Committee, and the Mental Health (Care and Treatment) (Scotland) Act 2003 was identified as serving *as an excellent model for the range and specificity of principles that must be set on the face of a new Mental Health Act for England and Wales* (JCDMHB, 2005d, para. 66). For example, claims were made in Westminster that the Scottish legislation had included all of the Millan principles from the start, providing the *certainty that the Scottish Parliament found.*[10]

These claims were not, however, true, although they presented a picture of perfection which denigrated the Labour Government's attempts and highlighted any disagreements being experienced in England. This is because the draft Mental Health (Scotland) Bill 2002 did not contain any of the principles recommended by the Millan Committee, and the Mental Health (Scotland) Bill 2002 only included four of the ten Millan principles (which attracted significant criticism in Scotland, eg Mental Welfare Commission for Scotland, 2002, p 1; SPCB, 2002, pp 7, 13, 72, col. 3076, 3081, 3155, 3244).

Another criticism of the English reform focused on the drafting of the legislation in Westminster. Among other things, the English attempts were repeatedly condemned as complex, ambiguous, confusing and difficult to read,[11] with numerous calls for these to be scrapped in favour of the Scottish model (both in terms of content and presentation). Indeed, reference to the Scottish reform disregarded any difficulties being experienced north of the border, in favour of emphasising the perceived 'better' nature of the Scottish process.[12]

However, concerns about the quality of the legislative drafting and process were not unique to the English reform experience. The Law Society of Scotland condemned the Mental Health (Scotland) Bill 2002, as their best mental health specialists struggled to follow it (SPCB, 2002, col. 3245). This view was shared by Scottish politicians and lobbyists (eg SPCB, 2002, col: 3246, 3261, 3299). Despite anxieties being expressed about the poor quality of the Scottish Bill (as it had been drafted too quickly), and the significant number of amendments required, it was not withdrawn.[13]

Consequently, concerns were expressed that the compressed time available to consider the extensive number of amendments to the Bill might result in the passing of *flawed legislation*, which *would reflect badly on the [Scottish] Executive*.[14] Scottish MSPs hoped they had passed a good Bill, as they had taken *decisions ... when in our hearts we did not know whether we had done the right thing*, leading to fears being expressed that *there might be problems with the legislation that will come back to haunt us*.[15]

## Professional resistance

Reflecting the general opposition to DSPD above, opponents of the government's proposals referred to the separation of mental health and criminal justice objectives in Scotland, through the Maclean Committee, arguing that this should be undertaken in England (eg Coid and Maden, 2003, p 406; Darjee and Crichton, 2002, p 7, 2004, p 634; Feeney, 2003, p 351; Health Select Committee, 2000b, para. 156; JCDMHB, 2005a, Ev 420: 699). This was based on the historical professional reluctance of Scottish psychiatrists to support admissions with a diagnosis of personality disorder, which was itself rooted in the Dunlop Committee's rejection of the legal term psychopathic patient, because it was considered meaningless and stigmatising, and because most people with primarily severe antisocial behavioural problems were not deemed suitable for hospital care (Department of Health for Scotland, 1958). Consequently, while 26 per cent of patients in English special hospitals were diagnosed with personality disorder alone, only 5 per cent were diagnosed as such in Carstairs, the Scottish special hospital, and most of these had been admitted prior to the psychiatric cultural shift in Scotland (Darjee and Crichton, 2003; Fallon et al., 1999b, pp 82–83, 120; SPCB, 2002, pp 3084, 3100, 3351; Taylor et al., 1998; Thomson et al., 1997).

## Joint Committee on the draft Mental Health Bill

The Joint Committee scrutinising the draft Mental Health Bill 2004 (JCDMHB, 2005d) broadly rejected the government's proposals. The Chair, Lord Carlile, summarised their conclusions, stating that the Bill was *fundamentally flawed ... too heavily focused on compulsion and currently there are neither the financial resources nor the workforce to implement it* (JCDMHB, 2005b). However, this was really to be expected. Not because the draft Bill was so bad, rather, it was inevitable given the membership of the Committee.

At any one time there were 24 members on the Committee. Despite Zigmond's (2005b) claim that there was a majority of Labour Party members on the Committee (which would suggest that the Labour Party had a greater hand in criticising its own draft Bill), 12 were always Labour MPs or peers, and the other 12 were constituted by other members from either the House of Commons or House of Lords.

However, while this appears to suggest a balanced membership in terms of political affiliations, this is simply not the case. Even though a strong contingent of the Labour Party was present, this included Dr Howard Stoate MP and David Hinchliffe MP, who were both members of the Health Select Committee in 2000 which rejected the government's early proposals for legislative reform, including specifically the Managing Dangerous People with Severe Personality Disorder policy document (Health Select Committee, 2000b). Mr Hinchliffe was also among three Labour Members of the House of Commons on the Joint Committee, whose voting record indicates a history of rebelling against the government.

Lord Carlile, the Chair of the Joint Committee, was himself involved with the mental health charity Rekindle, and had a family experience of mental illness. In addition to these personal drivers, Lord Carlile was also a long-time personal friend of Professor Genevra Richardson (JCDMHB, 2005a, Ev 1), who expressed her distinct unhappiness with the way the government had used the report from her Committee (JCDMHB, 2005a, Ev 2–9). The close and accommodating nature of their relationship is evident to the observer. For example, Professor Richardson was courteously and freely given time to make an opening statement. However, almost every other witness to the Joint Committee was advised that this was an option, but was firmly steered away from making any opening remarks (eg JCDMHB, 2005a, Ev 1–2: 1, Ev 79: 71, Ev 107: 109, Ev 155: 141):

*We are discouraging opening statements but if you feel absolutely driven to make one, please do. That is a question expecting the answer no.* (JCDMHB, 2005a, Ev 182: 176)

Consequently, the Joint Committee was dominated by parliamentarians who were likely to oppose the government's proposals. The majority had a pre-existing bias against the government's proposals and the Chair had an affiliation with witnesses who were also opposed to the direction the reform was taking. The Committee's recommended 'radical overhaul' (JCDMHB, 2005b) is therefore hardly surprising.

## Public Bill Committee

Possibly one of the best illustrations of damaging partisan and adversarial politics in Westminster can be found in the Public Bill Committee. For example, Tim Loughton had organised an impromptu evidence-gathering session after the second reading of the Bill in the House of Commons. There were concerns within the Committee about the official framing of this, with invitations being distributed by him claiming it was a 'special all-party' session. The Committee spent half an hour debating the official nature of this impromptu session, with government members arguing that it *smacks of undermining the work of this [Public Bill] Committee* or that it *struck me almost as a political game to try and trip up Labour Committee members.*

This early exchange within the Committee illustrates the tone and style of the rest of the proceedings. Opposition members largely utilised whatever adversarial tactics they could to challenge or undermine the government's position, and in reply, government members undertook likewise. This included possibly some of the most aggressive exchanges within the Parliamentary discourse concerning the English reform, with Conservative MP Charles Walker being sternly rebuked by the Committee Chairman. In quick succession, he called Rosie Winterton *fatuous*, said to her *Oh, shut up* and immediately after, interrupted her again, stating *This is really boring now* (Public Bill Committee Debate, 2007 Mental Health Bill [Lords], col.183–185).

This adversarial style of engagement was an overarching detrimental feature affecting the reform of the Mental Health Act 1983. Use of combative metaphors was common, with conflict framed between opposition forces and the government, but also between professional groups (eg Eastman, 1999a, p 206; Fallon et al., 1999b, p 69; Goodchild, 2006, p 22; *Independent on Sunday*, 2005, p 37, 2006, p 16; JCDMHB, 2005a, Ev 213: para. 3.1; Rayner, 2007; White, 2002, p 97).

Such language became apparent early on, significantly emanating from the medical profession. Zigmond (1999, p 705) illustrates this with a metaphorical call to arms following a failure of the psychiatric community to provide feedback on the Richardson Committee's draft proposals. He used a similar approach a few years later, in the third issue of the series of correspondence from the Royal College of Psychiatrists, entitled 'Draft Mental Health Bill, Letter from Campaign Headquarters'. This might appear to be limited to a political campaign, and the correspondence title 'Letter from Campaign Headquarters' indicative of a politically orientated operation. However, frequent metaphorical representations from the College contextualised their actions within a military conflict (eg *The battle is on*, *We have won the battle*, *The battle is won. As for the war?* or *The government's recent climb down is not a victory: the real battle is about to begin*; Doyle, 2002, p 16; Eastman, 2006, p 737; Home Affairs Committee, 2000c, para. 172; Zigmond, 2005a). Consequently, the Royal College of Psychiatrists', or its members', framing of opposition to the government's reform proposals, was commonly collocated with a combative struggle.

## Professional dominance

While a range of professional groups lobbied against the reform of the Mental Health Act 1983, the Royal College of Psychiatrists (and the medical profession in general) dominated this process from early on. From the Health Select Committee in 2000, through to the enactment of the Mental Health Bill 2006, the College's voice and opinion overshadowed any other lobbyist. In particular, it is clear that by the publication of the draft Mental Health Bill 2002, the College's approach to lobbying had evolved from the naïve and inexperienced political lobbyists when the Act was first drafted (Bluglass, 1984, p 131).

By this time, they were proactive, politically focused and comprehensive in method. Exposure and influence was sought through a range of channels, including direct contact with MPs and peers, the news media and professional and internal titles (eg *pH7*, the Parliamentary Health magazine), and through attendance at party political annual conferences (eg Bloomfield, 2002, p 13; Bosseley, 2002, p 6; Carvel, 2004, p 8; Daw and Zigmond, 2004; Royal College of Psychiatrists, 2004; Zigmond, 2002, 2003c, 2004a, 2005a; Zigmond et al., 2003). The direct lobbying of politicians by College members was encouraged through their letters from 'Campaign Headquarters', and as soon as the draft Bill 2002 had been published, the College was promised opposition support from Peers in the House of Lords (Zigmond, 2002, 2005b).

While the College was active throughout the reform, significantly, it successfully influenced the two primary processes that dominated the events, the Joint Scrutiny Committee that reviewed the draft Mental Health Bill 2004, and the debates of the Mental Health Bill 2006. Once the membership of the Joint Committee was announced, Tony Zigmond wrote to each

MP and Peer asking if the College could assist them. Consequently, both before and after the College gave their official recorded oral evidence, a range of Committee members held private meetings with the College, or requested additional information outside of the Committee process (Zigmond, 2004a, 2005a). As with the Health Select Committee above, the College was referenced frequently in the report of the Joint Committee scrutinising the draft Bill 2004. Indeed, Zigmond (2005a) noted that the College had been *cited over 100 times – more than any other source*. The College was repeatedly referenced in support of fundamental propositions opposing the government's reform proposals (eg JCDMHB, 2005d, Ev 15: para. 31, Ev 23–24: para. 62, Ev 37: para. 91, Ev 44: para 120). Generally, nearly all of the Joint Committee's recommendations reflected the evidence submitted by the College or the Mental Health Alliance.

The level of attention paid to the medical profession became more acute as the 2006 Bill made its way through the Committee stage of the Lords. Numerous citations were made again to the College, but also to related references such as the *General Medical Council*, the *medical profession* or *psychiatric circles*. Briefings from medical sources were referred to as coming from *the professionals*, illustrating further use of euphemistic terminology, and de-emphasising any variance between the professional groups and absorbing all under the dominant medical banner.[16]

A typical example of the sway afforded to the College can be seen in the language of Lord Owen, himself a former medical practitioner and opposition MP of 26 years. His words almost appear to represent a warning to the government (van Dijk, 2006, p 56). Do as the doctors ask, or risk losing your legislation again:

*It will not distress me tremendously to see this Bill lost again. The Government should recognise that they have already lost Bills in this area and they could well lose this Bill. They will have to show a good deal of feeling and understanding for expert opinion. The Royal College of Psychiatrists deserves a serious hearing on this Bill. Where it has doubts and where it wants amendments, it should be listened to with great care.[17]*

As the reform progressed, it became clearer that the College was pursuing its own agenda, to the detriment of other organisations in the Mental Health Alliance (which the College was purporting to represent). This is particularly clear concerning the government's proposals to change the nature of professional roles under the Mental Health Act 1983, specifically, the proposed widening of those who were approved to act in a legal capacity, and as a result, able to authorise continued compulsion. This was to be made open to non-medical professionals (eg nurses and psychologists).

The relationship between the College and the Alliance was, overall, mutually beneficial. It can therefore be seen metaphorically as two faces of the same coin. Both groups gained credibility through the arrangement. The Alliance gained political credibility and weight with the College within their ranks, as illustrated by Lord Carlile, emphasising the College's membership and consequently, the authority of the Alliance: *I suggest to the Government – and in this I have the support of the Mental Health Alliance, including the Royal College of Psychiatrists.*[18] The value of having the College within the Alliance was reinforced later in the same debate: *We all know perfectly well that if the college supported the Government, they would be holding up the flag of that college at every turn, saying, 'We have the Royal College of Psychiatrists – the representative body – behind us'.*[19]

The College also gained populist credibility from being a member of the Mental Health Alliance. No longer were they perceived as operating separately to, or above, service-user organisations, but standing shoulder to shoulder in a resolute movement of unity.

However, the stability of the Alliance was undermined during the House of Lords Committee stage of the 2006 Bill. The government's proposed widening of professional roles led to Lord Carlile tabling an amendment proposed by the Mental Health Alliance. The purpose of this amendment was to reject the legal authority of a non-medically qualified practitioner in making certain decisions concerning compulsion, and in doing so, to return the balance of power to the medical profession.[20] The introduction of this amendment caused internal conflict within the Alliance, leading to an agreement not to campaign on this particular issue (Sutton, 2007, p 340). It was the first significant breach of unity experienced by the Alliance; where consensus had been maintained, publicly at least, a visible and fundamental split occurred.

## Membership suspension

The consequence of the events surrounding this single amendment was the announcement that five organisations of the Mental Health Alliance were suspending their membership; together they constituted 85 per cent of the NHS mental health workforce. The organisations felt that through their membership of the Mental Health Alliance, several issues of high importance to them were not adequately represented during the Committee stage, and specifically that the Alliance had failed to brief clearly on the different views within the Alliance. They considered that it was essential that MPs and Lords received clear and unambiguous messages from all stakeholders and that the only way to achieve that was to remove themselves from the Alliance and set up a separate, flexible, campaigning group called the Mental Health Coalition (AMICUS-MHNA et al., 2007; BPS, 2007, para. 6.1.2; Carvel, 2007, p 2; Sutton, 2007, p 340).

It is noteworthy that the Royal College of Psychiatrists later commented in a public statement that they had *supported the Alliance amendment* tabled by Lord Carlile (Royal College of Psychiatrists, 2007, para. 4). Although, given the extant discourse which was so heavily dominated by the College's varied opposition to this widening of the professional roles (eg JCDMHB, 2005a, Ev 64, para 1–5, Ev 89, DMH 381; Royal College of Psychiatrists, 2000, para. 8, 2001, para. 5; Zigmond, 2003a, 2004b, p 162), it is more than likely that such an amendment would have emanated from the College, rather than any other Alliance member. Specifically, in their briefing prior to the second reading of the 2006 Bill in the House of Lords, the College explicitly announced their intention to oppose the government's proposal by the submission of an amendment.

*It is unclear how a psychologist or other person who is not medically qualified is able to satisfy the legal requirement of ensuring that the relevant conditions are still satisfied when the patient's section is to be renewed if they are unable to determine the presence or absence of these conditions in the first instance. This policy appears to rest on the erroneous assumption that the initial diagnosis is the most complex and difficult and that diagnoses and 'nature and degree' of mental disorder can be more easily resolved once a person's condition is stabilised. The College will be seeking to have the Bill amended to remove this anomaly.* (Royal College of Psychiatrists, 2006, para. 3.15)

The overall effect of the influence of the medical profession on the discourse was noted by Lord Soley, which, while undoubtedly an ideological tactic in itself, was nonetheless an accurate reflection of the conflict that transpired. Consistent with the discussion above, and as seen elsewhere, Lord Soley's comments correlated warfare-oriented metaphors with the discourse constituted by the union of the medical profession and politicians. His comments are particularly pertinent to the House of Lords, given the number of peers who were also medically trained:

*Part of the battle that troubles me is that there are too many psychiatrists speaking for psychiatry and not enough people speaking for the other professions involved.*[21]

As the English reform progressed into the House of Commons, and in particular, the hostile environment of the Public Bill Committee, the conflict over the changes to professional roles became more overt, and the ideological tactics more adversarial.

During the second reading of the 2006 Bill in the Commons, the Royal College of Psychiatrists and other medical organisations maintained their dominant position within the reform, being quoted more than any other group. This position of dominance remained so during the Public Bill Committee, although the situation shifted slightly, with the lobbyists becoming more clearly divided in the evidence to this Committee. The medical profession continued to argue that a consultant psychiatrist must have overall responsibility for an individual's care,[22] whereas the newly formed Mental Health Coalition contended that the amendments secured in the House of Lords greatly damaged the Bill in ways which undermined measures that could positively impact on patients and the expansion of professional responsibilities.[23]

It is noteworthy that the contest of evidential authority was not limited to inter-professional challenges (ie psychologist vs. psychiatrist), as intra-professional differences of opinion were brought to bear in apparent attempts to determine which view was to dominate the discourse. This very much reflected the divergences within psychiatry cited above, usually involving Professor Maden and other members of the Royal College of Psychiatrists (eg Professor Thornicroft). Typical of this during the Public Bill Committee was when Doug Naysmith brought into the discussion a letter from two psychiatrists (Vize and Humphries, 2007) who contended that the Royal College of Psychiatrists' opposition to extending the legal roles of non-medical professionals significantly devalued their multidisciplinary colleagues.[24] In response, Tim Loughton produced a private letter from the President of the Royal College of Psychiatrists, which denounced Vize and Humphries as purporting to represent the views of the College when they did not. In other words, the President's response appears to be both a rebuke to the authors and an advisory for the Committee that their letter should be ignored, as it had no authority.[25]

# Conclusion

This chapter has considered a selection of issues that influenced the reform of the Mental Health Act 1983. It is not exhaustive, or as detailed as is possible; that is simply a physical limitation. Nonetheless, it illustrates the tensions affecting the successful reform of such a powerful piece of statute.

The Richardson Committee was impeded by a very difficult set of circumstances. While the Department of Health was aware of the risks inherent in limiting consultation or imposing policy against the opposition of practitioners (Brown, 1998a, para. 9(iv), 1998b, para. 8 (iv), para. 21–22, para. 24), that is largely what transpired, and this negatively affected the completion of a successful reform programme. However, heavy-handed and top-down political Executives are not a new phenomenon, and consequently, should not be seen as such. This does not condone such potentially dominating practice, but rather acknowledges that Labour was not the first, nor will it be the last, government to try and control the agenda.

In contrast, the Home Office was prepared to follow a consensual lead, although it was uncomfortable with links between capacity and mentally disordered offenders, in case this became a barrier to detention. Despite the 'Scotland is better' rhetoric, Millan had similar concerns, and as an exception, legislated to ensure such offenders with capacity were excluded from their capacity principle (ie reflecting the Home Office's thinking).

The difficulties surrounding DSPD are largely rooted in the unresolved problem of psychopathic disorder. This has always created a professional divide, and was a significant influencing focus of the recent reforms in England. In the 1990s, the case of Christopher Clunis materialised as a moral panic within the news media, affecting legislative reform. Michael Stone's case was powerful, and added to the risk agenda being reported. It was not, however, the catalyst for reform, as was frequently claimed.

However, the dominant newspaper publications illustrate that a comparatively limited editorial group controlled the media influence. Rupert Murdoch's News International dominated reporting on Michael Stone and was only second to the *Independent* in reporting on the English reform in a campaign run by the Sunday edition. Consequently, the media discourse was a result of isolated editorial decisions rather than a broad media frame concerning any of the specific events. However, the sensationalist reporting proved to be very powerful and exerted significant influence on 'expert evidence', particularly in England (eg Home Affairs Committee, 2000c, para. 92; JCDMHB, 2005a; Ev 697: 1154, Ev 363: 499).

In the context of an adversarial and aggressive political process, the voice of the medical profession and, in particular, the Royal College of Psychiatrists, was a prevailing force throughout the whole of the English reform discourse. Evidence from the College pervades almost every single English consultation and political event. Committee and Parliamentary evidence, debates and reports are dominated by the opinions and desires of the College or its members. Towards the end of the English reform, the apparent consensual partnership between various professional and service-user groups (as represented by the Mental Health Alliance) was eroded by the very same aggressive and polarised lobbying strategy that had been used against the government throughout the course of the reform.

This brings into question the authenticity of the College's membership of the Mental Health Alliance, as the College's intent and ability was clearly to act in its own best interests (eg Fallon et al., 1999b, p 420). This also raises the question, if the circumstances for the expansion of professional roles had come about earlier, how long would the Alliance have lasted? Moreover, if it had fallen sooner, how would the course of the English reform have unfolded without the surface consensus that the world saw for so long?

# Notes

## 3  Exploring Shared Decision Making for Psychiatric Medication Management

1  This chapter includes data from independent research commissioned by the National Institute for Health Research under the Research for Patient Benefit programme (the 'ShiMME' project; PB-PG-0909–20054; April 2011–March 2014). The views expressed in this publication are those of the authors and not necessarily those of the NHS, the NIHR or the Department of Health.

## 4  The Recovery Concept: The Importance of the Recovery Story

1  Mental Health Act (1959), Mental Health Act (1983), Mental Health Act (2007).

## 5  The Part Can Never Be Well, Unless the Whole is Well

1  www.britishlegion.org.uk/branches/wootton-bassett/repatriation.

2  http://dxrevisionwatch.wordpress.com/tag/medicalising-grief.

## 10  The Mirage of Mental Health Law Reform

1  House of Commons (henceforth HC) Hansard 3 December 1997 col.395; HC Hansard 18 June 1997 col.345; House of Lords (henceforth HL) Hansard 18 December 1997 col.729.

2  HC Hansard 4 March 1998 col.676W; HC Hansard 19 March 1998 col.704W.

3  HC Hansard 29 July 1998 col.382.

4  HC Hansard 26 October 1998 col.8.

5  HC Hansard 15 February 1999 col.601; HC Hansard 18 January 1999 col.550; Department of Health, 1998: para. 4.31–4.34.

6  HC Hansard 11 November 2005 col.820; HL Hansard 10 January 2007 col.244; Watson, 2001, para. C.4; JCDMHB, 2005d, p 14: para. 29; McClelland, 2007, para. 2.28.

7   HC Hansard 29 July 1998 col.382; Boateng, 1998.

8   HC Hansard 15 February 1999 col.601–603.

9   HC Hansard 20 December 2000 col.365.

10   Eg HL Hansard 8 January 2007 col.36; HL Hansard 19 February 2007 col.891; MHA, 2004; JCDMHB, 2005a, Ev 239.

11   Eg HL Hansard 28 November 2006 col.708; JCDMHB, 2005d, para. 35.

12   Eg HC Hansard 19 June 2007 col.1304; Health Select Committee, 2000b, p lix; HL Hansard 28 November 2006 col.690; JCDMHB, 2005c, para. 71, 141, 404; JCDMHB, 2005d, Ev 119: para. 1.4, Ev 131: para. 4.15, Ev 183: 181, Ev 199: para. 4.4, Ev 242: para. 7.

13   Eg Scottish Parliament (henceforth SP) Official Report 11 December 2002 col.16212; SPCB, 2002, col. 3246.

14   SP Official Report 11 December 2002 col.16228; SP Official Report 11 December 2002 col.16239; SP Official Report 20 March 2003 col.19823.

15   SP Official Report 20 March 2003 col.19810; SP Official Report 20 March 2003 col.19814–19815; SP Official Report 20 March 2003 col.19816.

16   Eg HL Hansard 8 January 2007 col.38; HL Hansard 10 January 2007 col.240; HL Hansard 10 January 2007 col.240–243; HL Hansard 10 January 2007 col.280; HL Hansard 10 January 2007 col.303; HL Hansard 10 January 2007 col.313–314; HL Hansard 10 January 2007 col.316; HL Hansard 15 January 2007 col.441; HL Hansard 15 January 2007 col.442.

17   HL Hansard 10 January 2007 col.239.

18   HL Hansard 10 January 2007 col.303.

19   HL Hansard 10 January 2007 col.319.

20   HL Hansard 15 January 2007 col.439–441.

21   HL Hansard 19 February 2007 col. 916.

22   Public Bill Committee Debate 2007, Mental Health Bill [Lords], MH 48: para. 2.

23   Public Bill Committee Debate 2007 Mental Health Bill [Lords], MH 40: para. 3.

24   Public Bill Committee Debate 2007 Mental Health Bill [Lords], col.171.

25   Public Bill Committee Debate 2007 Mental Health Bill [Lords], col.171–172.

# Bibliography

Adebimpe, V. (1981) Overview: White Norms and Psychiatric Diagnosis of Black Patients. *American Journal of Psychiatry*, 138(3): 279–85.

Adebimpe, V. (1994) Race, Racism and Epidemiological Surveys. *Hospital and Community Psychiatry*, 45(1): 27–31.

Ahmed, S. (1996) Cultural Racism in Work with Asian Women and Girls, in Ahmed, S., Cheetham, J. and Small, J. (eds) *Social Work with Black Children and Their Families*. London: Batsford.

Aldhous, P. (2012) Psychiatry Is Failing Those with Personality Disorders. *New Scientist*, 5 December.

Ali, A. (2004) The Intersection of Racism and Sexism in Psychiatric Diagnosis, in Caplan, P.J. and Cosgrove, L. (eds) *Bias in Psychiatric Diagnosis*. Lanham, MD: Jason Aronson, pp 71–75.

Allen, D. (2005) Fatally Flawed? *Mental Health Practice*, 8(8): 6–7.

Alwin, N., Blackburn, R., Davidson, K., Hilton, M., Logan, C. and Shine, J. (2006) *Understanding Personality Disorder: A Report by the British Psychological Society*. London: British Psychological Society.

AMICUS-MHNA, BPS, BAOT/COT, RCN and Unison (2007) Health Groups Suspend Membership of Mental Health Alliance [online]: www.rcn.org.uk/newsevents/press_releases/uk/article2428. Accessed: 9 January 2013.

Andresen, R., Caputi, P. and Oades, L. (2006) Stages of Recovery Instrument: Development of a Measure of Recovery from Serious Mental Illness. *Australian and New Zealand Journal of Psychiatry*, 40: 972–80.

Andresen, R., Oades, L. and Caputi, P. (2003) The Experience of Recovery from Schizophrenia: Towards an Empirically Validated Stage Model. *Australian and New Zealand Journal of Psychiatry*, 37: 586–94.

Anonymous (2009) A Handkerchief for Parents' Wet Eyes upon the Death of Children, in Young, B. *Family Life in the Age of Shakespeare*. Westport: Greenwood, p 225.

Anthony, W.A. (1993) Recovery from Mental Illness: The Guiding Vision of the Mental Health System in the 1990s. *Innovations and Research*, 2: 17–24.

Anthony, W.A. (2003) The Decade of the Person and the Walls that Divide Us. *Behavioral Healthcare Tomorrow*, April: 23–30.

APA (1980) *Diagnostic and Statistical Manual of Mental Disorders*, 3rd edn. Washington DC: American Psychiatric Association.

APA (1994) *Diagnostic and Statistical Manual of Mental Disorders*, 4th edn. Washington DC: American Psychiatric Association.

Aristotle. Poetics. Trans. S. H. Butcher. Available at: http://classics.mit.edu/Aristotle/poetics.1.1.html. Accessed 8 February 2013.

Asch, Solomon (1952) *Social Psychology*. New Jersey: Prentice-Hall.

Axelson, J.A. (1985) *Counseling and Development in a Multicultural Society*. Belmont, CA: Brooks/Cole.

Bains, J. (2005) Race, Culture and Psychiatry. *A History of Transcultural Psychiatry*, 16: 39–154.

Baker, E., Fee, B., Bovingdon, L., Campbell, T., Hewis, E., Lewis, D., Mahoney, L. and Roberts, G. (2013) From Taking to Using Medication: Steps Towards a Recovery-Focused Approach to Prescribing and Medicines Management. *Advances in Psychiatric Treatment*, 19(1): 2–10.

Barker, P. (2008) *Psychiatric and Mental Health Nursing: The Craft of Caring*. London: Penguin.

Barker, P. and Buchanan-Barker, P. (2005) *The Tidal Model: A Guide for Mental Health Professionals*. London: Brunner-Routledge.

Barratt, R. (1996) *The Psychiatric Team and the Social Definition of Schizophrenia*. Cambridge: Cambridge University Press.

Barton, R. (1959) *Institutional Neurosis*. Bristol: Wright.

Baskin, D., Bluestone, H, and Nelson, M. (1981) Ethnicity and Psychiatric Diagnosis. *Journal of Clinical Psychology*, 39: 529–37.

Bateman, W.B. and Fonagy, P. (2004) Mentalization-Based Treatment of BPD. *Journal of Personality Disorders*, 18(1): 36–51.

Beatch, R. and Stewart, B. (2002) Integrating Western and Aboriginal Healing Practices, in Nash, M. and Stewart, B. (eds) *Spirituality and Social Care*. London: Jessica Kingsley.

Benson, H. (2000) *Socratic Wisdom*. Oxford: Oxford University Press.

Bentall, R.P. (2003) *Madness Explained: Psychosis and Human Nature*. London: Penguin.

Beresford, P. (2005) Developing Self-Defined Social Approaches to Madness and Distress, in Ramon and Williams, pp 109–26.

Bettleheim, B. (1950) *Love Is Not Enough*. New York: The Free Press.

Bhugra, D. and Bhui, K. (2007) *Textbook of Cultural Psychiatry*. Cambridge: Cambridge University Press.

Bhui, K., Stansfeld, S. A., Hull, S., Priebe, S., Mole, F. and Feder, G. (2003) Ethnic Variations in Pathways to Specialist Mental Health Care: A Systematic Review. *British Journal of Psychiatry*, 182: 5–16.

Bion, W.R. (1961) *Experiences in Groups*. London: Tavistock.

Bion, W.R. (1997) *War Memoirs*. London: Karnac Books.

Bleuler M. (1968) A 23-Year Longitudinal Study of 208 Schizophrenics and Impressions in Regard to the Nature of Schizophrenia, in Rosenthal, D. and Kety, S.S. (eds) *The Transmission of Schizophrenia*. Oxford: Pergamon.

Bloom, S. (1997) *Creating Sanctuary: Towards the Evolution of Sane Societies*. New York: Routledge.

Bloomfield, S. (2002) Top Authors Attack Bill as 'Terrifying'. *Independent on Sunday*, 11 August 2002, p 13.

Bluglass, R. (1984) The Origins of the Mental Health Act 1983: Doctors in the House. *Bulletin of the Royal College of Psychiatrists*, 8127–134.

Boardman, J. and Shepherd, G. (2012) *Making Recovery a Reality*. York: Sainsbury Centre for Mental Health.

Boateng, P. (1998) *Expert Advisor Appointed to Start Review of Mental Health Act*. Press Release Reference Number 98/391–22 September 1998. London: Department of Health.

Bogg, D. (2010) *Values and Ethics in Mental Health Practice*. Exeter: Learning Matters.

Bosseley, S. (2002) Psychiatrists to Join Protest over Bill – Mental Health Groups Plan to March on Whitehall. *Guardian*, 29 July 2002, p 6.

Bowlby, J. (1969) *Attachment and Loss*. London: Hogarth Press.

BPS (2007) *Minutes: Parliamentary & Policy Support Unit Steering Group* – Tuesday 17 April 2007 at 12.30pm.

Braun, V. and Clarke, V. (2006) Using Thematic Analysis in Psychology. *Qualitative Research in Psychology*, 3: 77–101.

Brindle, D. (1998) Care in the Community: Civil Liberty Row on Mental Health Law. *Guardian*, 9 December 1998, p 14.

Brown, D. (2006) Megan's Killer Told Nurse He Would Murder a Family Days before Attack; Factbox. *The Times*, 26 September 2006, p 25.

Brown, M. (1998a) Submission on a Review of the Mental Health Act: Draft – Mental Health Act 1983: Proposals for Review – Restricted Policy [Internal Policy Document], Document produced by Martin Brown HSD4 (5W08 QH – EXT 45256) to Alan Laglands, cc: S Shepherd, Y Moores, G Winyard, S Adam, T Luce, A McKeon, M Staniforth: Sent 6 February 1998.

Brown, M. (1998b) Mental Health Act 1983: Proposals for Review – Restricted Policy [Internal Policy Document], Produced by Martin Brown HSD4: 5W08 QH – Ext 45256: Sent 20 February 1998.

Brown, P. (2006) Risk Versus Need in Revising the 1983 Mental Health Act: Conflicting Claims, Muddled Policy. *Health, Risk & Society*, 8(4): 343–58.

Brown, W. and Kandirikirira, N. (2006) *Recovering Mental Health in Scotland*. Report on Narrative Investigation of Mental Health Recovery. Glasgow: Scottish Recovery Network, www.scottishrecovery.net/content/mediaassets/doc/Recovering%20Identity.pdf.

Burrell, I. (1999) Psychopath Units Plan Costs Millions. *Independent*, 14 July 1999, p 2.

Busfield, J. (2011) *Mental Illness*. Bristol: Polity Press.

Butcher, J. (2007) Controversial Mental Health Bill Reaches the Finishing Line. *The Lancet*, 370: 117–18.

Calton, T., Ferriter, M., Huband, N. and Spandler, H. (2008) A Systematic Review of the Soterial Paradigm for the Treatment of People Diagnosed with Schizophrenia. *Schizophrenia Bulletin*, 34: 181–92.

Campbell, J. and Davidson, G. (2012) *Post-Qualifying Mental Health Social Work Practice*. London: Sage.

Campbell, J., Stickley, T. and Bonney, S. (2008) Recovery as a Framework for Care Planning, in Hall, A., Kirby, S.D. and Wren, M.M. (eds) *Care Planning in Mental Health: Promoting Recovery*. Oxford: Blackwell, p 113–35.

Campling, P. (1999) Chaotic Personalities: Maintaining the Therapeutic Alliance, in Campling and Haigh, pp 127–39.

Campling, P. and Haigh, R. (eds) (1999) *Therapeutic Communities: Past, Present and Future*. London: Jessica Kingsley.

Carroll, M. (1998) Social Work's Conceptualization of Spirituality. *Social Thought: Journal of Religion in the Social Sciences*, 18(2): 1–14.

Carroll, S. (2006) Shame the Fools Who Left Stone Free to Kill. *Mirror*, 27 September 2006, p 13.

Carvel, J. (2004) Psychiatrists Condemn Draft Mental Health Bill. *Guardian*, 9 September 2004, p 8.

Carvel, J. (2007) Section Issue Splits Mental Health Unity. *Guardian*, 23 May 2007, p 2.

Carvel, J. and Ward, L. (2002) Detention Plan for 'Dangerous' Mental Patients. *Guardian*, 26 June 2002, p 9.

Castillo, H. (2003) *Personality Disorder: Temperament or Trauma?* London: Jessica Kingsley.

Castillo, H. (2010) The Person with a Personality Disorder, in Norman, I. and Ryrie, I. (eds) *The Art and Science of Mental Health Nursing*. Maidenhead: Open University Press.

Chamberlin, J. (1978) *On Our own: Patient-Controlled Alternatives to the Mental Health System*. New York: Hawthorn Books.

Chamberlin, J. (2005) Confessions of a Non-Compliant Patient. National Empowerment Centre website: www.power2u.org.

Charles, C., Gafni, A. and Whelan, T. (1997) Shared-Decision Making in the Medical Encounter: What Does It Mean? (or It Takes At Least Two to Tango). *Social Science & Medicine*, 44: 681–92.

Charles, C., Gafni, A. and Whelan, T. (1999) Decision-Making in the Physician–Patient Encounter: Revisiting the Shared Treatment Decision-Making Model. *Social Science & Medicine*, 49: 651–61.

Chiesa, M. (2000) At a Crossroad between Institutional and Community Psychiatry: An Acute Psychiatric Admission Ward, in Hinshelwood, R.D. and Skogstad, W. (eds) *Observing Organisations*. London: Routledge.

Chiesa, M., Bateman, A., Wilberg, T. and Friss, S. (2002) Patients' Characteristics, Outcome and Cost-Benefit of Hospital-Based-Treatment for Patients with a Personality Disorder: A Comparison of Three Difference Programmes. *Psychology and Psychotherapy: Theory, Research and Practice*, 75: 381–92.

Chiswick, D. (1999) Preventive Detention Exhumed – and Enhanced. *Psychiatric Bulletin*, 23(12): 703–704.

Chittenden, M. and Sheehan, M. (1998) Law to End Loophole That Let Stone Kill; Murder. *The Sunday Times*, 25 October 1998, p 6.

Ciompi, L. (1980) Catamnestic Long-Term Study on the Course of Life and Aging in Schizophrenics. *Schizophrenia Bulletin*, 6: 606–18.

Clare, A. (1976) *Psychiatry in Dissent: Controversial Issues in Thought and Practice*. London: Tavistock.

Clements, J. (2006) If Everyone Had Done Their Jobs Right Maybe Stone Wouldn't Have Murdered My Wife and Daughter. *Mirror*, 26 September 2006, p 17.

Cobb, M. and Robshaw, V. (1998) *The Spiritual Challenge of Health Care*. Edinburgh: Churchill Livingstone.

Cohen, S. (1972) *Folk Devils and Moral Panics*. London: McGibbon and Kee.

Coid, J. and Maden, A. (2003) Should Psychiatrists Protect the Public? A New Risk Reduction Strategy, Supporting Criminal Justice, Could Be Effective. *British Medical Journal*, 326(7386): 406–407.

Coid, J., Yang, M., Tyrer, P., Roberts, A. and Ulrich, S. (2006) Prevalence and Correlates of Personality Disorder in Great Britain. *British Journal of Psychiatry*, 188: 423–31.

Coleman, R. (1999) *Recovery: An Alien Concept?* Gloucester: Handsell.

Coles, R. (1990) *The Spiritual Life of Children*. New York: Random House.

Coulter, A. and Collins, A. (2011) *Making Shared Decision-Making a Reality. No Decision about Me, without Me*. London: The King's Fund.

Cox, J.L. (1977) Aspects of Transcultural Psychiatry. *British Journal of Psychiatry*, 130: 211–21.

Cressy, D. (1997) *Birth, Marriage and Death: Ritual, Religion and the Life-Cycle in Tudor and Stuart England*. Oxford: Oxford University Press.

Crichton, J. and Darjee, R. (2007) New Mental Health Legislation: A Decade's Deliberations Result in Confused Proposals. *British Medical Journal*, 334(7594): 596–97.

Crompton, M. (1996) *Children, Spirituality, Religion and Social Work*. London: CCETSW.

CSIP, RCPsych, SCIE (2007) *A Common Purpose: Recovery in Future Mental Health Services*. London: CSIP, RCPsych, SCIE.

Cutcliffe, J.R. and Hannigan, B. (2001) Mass Media, 'Monsters' and Mental Health Clients: The Need for Increased Lobbying. *Journal of Psychiatric and Mental Health Nursing*, 8(4): 315–21.

Darjee, R. and Crichton, J. (2002) The Maclean Committee: Scotland's Answer to the 'Dangerous People with Severe Personality Disorder' Proposals? *Psychiatric Bulletin*, 26(1): 6–8.

Darjee, R. and Crichton, J. (2003) Personality Disorder and the Law in Scotland: A Historical Perspective. *The Journal of Forensic Psychiatry and Psychology*, 14(2): 394–425.

Darjee, R. and Crichton, J. (2004) New Mental Health Legislation: Scottish Legislation, Based on 'Care and Treatment', Has Lessons to Offer. *British Medical Journal*, 329: 634–35.

Davidson, L. (2003) *Living outside Mental Illness: Qualitative Studies of Recovery in Schizophrenia*. New York: New York University Press.

Davidson, L., Borg, M. and Marin, I. (2005) Process of Recovery in Severe Mental Illness: Findings from a Multi-National Study. *Journal of Psychiatric Rehabilitation*, 8(3): 177–201.

Davidson, L., Miller, R. and Flanagan, E. (2008) What's In It for Me? The Utility of Psychiatric Treatments from the Perspective of the Person in Recovery. *Epidemiologia e psichiatria sociale*, 17(3): 177–81.

Davidson, L., Rakfeldt, J. and Strauss, J. (2010) *The Roots of the Recovery Movement in Psychiatry: Lessons Learned*. London: Wiley.

Davies, R. (1996) The Interdisciplinary Network and the Internal World of the Offender, in Cordess, C. and Cox, M. (eds) *Forensic Psychotherapy*, Volume 2. London: Jessica Kingsley.

Daw, R. and Zigmond, T. (2004) Clear as Mud [online]. Available: http://society.guardian.co.uk/mentalhealth/comment/0,8146,1301778,00.html. Accessed: 9 January 2013.

Day, J., Bentall, R. Roberts, C. et al. (2005) Attitudes towards Antipsychotic Medication: The Impact of Clinical Variables and Relationships with Health Professionals. *Archives of General Psychiatry*, 62: 717–24.

Daycare Trust (2000) *Ensuring Equality*. London: Daycare Trust.

Deegan, P.E. (1996) Recovery as a Journey of the Heart. *Psychiatric Rehabilitation Journal* 19, 3: 91–98.

Deegan, P.E. (1997) Recovery and Empowerment for People with Psychiatric Disabilities. *Social Work in Health Care*, 25(3): 11–24.

Deegan, P.E. (1990) *How Recovery Begins*. The Centre for Community Change through Housing and Support: VT, CI 25: Burlington: Trinity College.

Deegan, P.E. (2005) The Importance of Personal Medicine. *Scandinavian Journal of Public Health*, 33: 24–35.

Dell'Acqua, G. and Mezzina, R. (1998) *Shouldering the Burden (Providing Treatment for Persons with Schizophrenia Disturbances in the Community: The Deinstitutionalised Model)*. Schizophrenia Treatment Consensus Conference. Brussels, May 1998.

Department of Health (1998) *Modernising Mental Health Services: Safe, Sound, Supportive*. London: TSO.

Department of Health (1999) *Review of the Mental Health Act 1983: Report of the Expert Committee*. London: Department of Health.

Department of Health (2001) *The Journey to Recovery: The Government Vision of Mental Health Care*. London: Department of Health.

Department of Health (2007) www.personalitydisorder.org.uk/training/kuf.

Department of Health (2008) *Medication Is Everybody's Business*. London: Department of Health.

Department of Health (2009a) *New Horizons: A Shared Vision for Mental Health*. London: Department of Health.

Department of Health (2009b) *Recognising Complexity: Commissioning Guidance for Personality Disorder Services*. London: Department of Health.

Department of Health (2011) *Liberating the NHS: Greater Choice and Control*. Consultation paper. London: Department of Health.

Department of Health Commissioning Board (2012) *Compassionate Practice*. London: Department of Health.

Department of Health and Social Security and Office (1986) *Offenders Suffering from Psychopathic Disorders: A Joint Department of Health and Social Security/Home Office consultation document*. London: HMSO.

Department of Health for Scotland (1958) *Mental Health Legislation*. Report by a Committee Appointed by the Council (Dunlop Committee). Edinburgh: HMSO.

Dobson, F. (1998) *Frank Dobson Outlines Third Way for Mental Health*. Press Release Reference Number 98/311–29 July 1998. London: Department of Health.

Doka, K. J. and Martin, T. (2010) *Grieving beyond Gender: Understanding the Ways Men and Women Mourn*, Revised edn. London and New York: Routledge.

Dolan, M. and Doyle, M. (2000) Violence Risk Prediction: Clinical and Actuarial Measures and the Role of the Psychopathy Checklist. *British Journal of Psychiatry*, 177(4): 303–11.

Dominelli, L. (2008) *Anti-Racist Social Work*. Basingstoke: Palgrave Macmillan.

Donati, F. (1989) A Psychodynamic Observer in a Chronic Psychiatric Ward. *British Journal of Psychotherapy* 5: 317–29. Republished in Hinshelwood, R.D. and Skogstad, W. (2000) *Observing Organisations*. London: Routledge.

Doole, T. (2009) *Freedom of Information Act (Foia): Request for Internal Review*. Dh Case Ref: 413343 IR [Letter], Personal Communication: Sent 26 August 2009.

Doyle, C. (2002) Why I'll Battle against the Bill: The Royal College of Psychiatrists. *Daily Telegraph*, 10 September 2002, p 16.

Drum, P. and Lavigne, G. (1987) Extended State Hospital Treatment for Borderline Patients. *Hospital and Community Psychiatry*, 38: 515–19.

Duggan, C. (2005) Treatment of Severe Personality Disorder. *Psychiatry*, 4(3): 26–28.

Eastman, N. (1999a) Who Should Take Responsibility for Antisocial Personality Disorder?: Fallon Suggests Emphasising Custody, but Psychiatrists' Future Role Remains Unclear. *British Medical Journal*, 318(7178): 206–207.

Eastman, N. (1999b) Public Health Psychiatry or Crime Prevention?: Government's Proposals Emphasise Doctors' Role as Public Protectors. *British Medical Journal*, 318: 549–51.

Eastman, N. (2006) Reforming Mental Health Law in England and Wales: The Government's Recent Climb Down Is Not a Victory: The Real Battle Is About to Begin. *British Medical Journal*, 332(7544): 737–38.

Edelson, M. (1984) *Hypothesis and Evidence in Psychoanalysis*. Chicago: Chicago University Press.

Edwards, A. and Elwyn, G. (2009) *Shared Decision-Making in Healthcare: Achieving Evidence-Based Patient Choice*, 2nd edn. Oxford: Oxford University Press.

Edwards, R. (2006) Russells Would Be Here Now If Everyone Had Done Their Job. *Evening Standard*, 25 September 2006, p 5.

Eliot, T.S. (1975) *Selected Prose of T. S. Eliot*. Frank Kermode (ed). London: Faber and Faber; San Diego: Harcourt.

Engel, M. (1997) The British Began to Queue, in MacArthur, B. (ed) *Requiem: Diana, Princess of Wales 1961–1997: Memories and Tributes*. London: Pavilion Books, pp 26–29.

Entwistle, V.A. and Watt, I.S. (2006) Patient Involvement in Treatment Decision-Making: The Case for a Broader Conceptual Framework. *Patient Education and Counselling*, 63: 268–78.

Fallon, P., Bluglass, R., Edwards, B. and Daniels, G. (1999a) *Report of the Committee of Inquiry into the Personality Disorder Unit, Ashworth Special Hospital*, Volume I: Cmnd. 4194-ii. London: TSO.

Fallon, P., Bluglass, R., Edwards, B. and Daniels, G. (1999b) *Report of the Committee of Inquiry into the Personality Disorder Unit, Ashworth Special Hospital*, Volume II Expert Evidence on Personality Disorder: Cmnd. 4195. London: TSO.

Faulkner, A., Petit-Zeman, S., Sherlock, J. and Wallcraft, J. (2002) *Being There in a Crisis*. Mental Health Foundation and Sainsbury Centre for Mental Health.

Feeney, A. (2003) Dangerous Severe Personality Disorder. *Advances in Psychiatric Treatment*, 9(5): 349–58.

Fernando, S. (1988) *Race and Culture in Psychiatry*. London: Croom Helm.

Fernando, S. (2002) *Mental Health, Race and Culture*, 2nd edn. Basingstoke: Palgrave.

Fernando, S. (2003) *Cultural Diversity, Mental Health and Psychiatry: The Struggle against Racism*. London: Routledge.

Fernando, S. (2009) *Mental Health in a Multi-Ethnic Society*. London: Routledge.

Fernando, S. (2010) *Mental Health, Race and Culture*. Basingstoke: Palgrave.

Foucault, M. (1965; 1988) *Madness and Civilization: A History of Insanity in the Age of Reason*. New York: Random House.

Foulkes, S.H. (1946) On Group Analysis. *International Journal of Psycho-Analysis*, 27: 46–51.

Foulkes, S.H. (1983) *Introduction to Group Analytic Psychotherapy: Studies in the Social Integration of Individuals and Groups*. London: Karnac.

Francis, R., Higgins, J. and Cassam, E. (2006) *Report of the Independent Inquiry into the Care and Treatment of Michael Stone*. Kent: South East Coast Strategic Health Authority/ Kent County Council/Kent Probation Area.

Freire, P. (1970) *Pedagogy of the Oppressed*. New York: Herder and Herder.

Freud, S. (1909) *Analysis of a Phobia in a Five-Year-Old Boy*. London: Hogarth Press.

Freud, S. (1953) *General Works, Standard Edition* Vol VII, 33. London: Pelican.

Fulcher, L.C. (1999) Cultural Origins of the Contemporary Group Conference. *Child Care in Practice*, 6: 328–39.

Gabbard, G.O. (2000) On Gratitude and Gratification. *Journal of the American Psychoanalytic Association*, 48: 697–716.

Galton, F. (1869) *Hereditary Genius: Its Laws and Consequences*. London: Macmillan.

Ghuman, P. (2004) *Double Loyalties: South Asian Adolescents in the West*. Swansea: University of Wales Press.

Goffman, E. (1961) *Asylums: Essays on the Social Situation of Mental Patients and Other Inmates*. New York: Doubleday.

Golightley, M. (2011) *Social Work in Mental Health*, 4th edn. Exeter: Learning Matters.

Goodchild, S. (2006) Mental Health: The Bill Has Been Dropped but Has the Battle Been Won? *Independent on Sunday*, 26 March 2006, p 22.

Goody, J. and Poppi, C. (1994) Flowers and Bones: Approaches to the Dead in Anglo-American and Italian Cemeteries. *Comparative Studies in Society and History*, 36(1): 146–75.

Gordon, J. and Kirtchuk, G. (2008) *Psychic Assaults and Frightened Clinicians*. London: Karnac.

Greben, S. (1983) The Multi-Dimensional Inpatient Treatment of Severe Character Disorders. *Canadian Journal of Psychiatry* 28: 97–101.

Gunn, J. (2000) A Millennium Monster Is Born. *Criminal Behaviour and Mental Health*, 10(2): 73–76.

Guthrie, R.V. (2003) *Even the Rat Was White: A Historical View of Psychology*. New York: Harper & Row.

Hacking, I. (2001) *An Introduction to Probability and Inductive Logic*. Cambridge: Cambridge University Press.

Haigh, R. (1999) The Quintessence of a Therapeutic Environment: Five Universal Qualities, in Campling and Haigh, pp 246–57.

Hall, R. (2008) *Applied Social Research: Planning, Designing and Conducting Real-World Research*. South Yarra: Palgrave Macmillan.

Hamann, J., Langer, B. and Winkler, V. (2006) Shared Decision Making for In-patients with Schizophrenia. *Acta Psychiatric Scandinavica*, 114: 265–73.

Haney, C.W., Banks, W.C. and Zimbardo, P. (1973) Interpersonal Dynamics in a Simulated Prison. *International Journal of Criminology and Penology*, 1: 69–97.

Hardcastle, M., Kennard, D., Grandison, S. and Fagin, L. (2007) *Experiences of Mental Health Inpatient Care*. London: Routledge.

Harding, C.M., Brooks, G.W., Ashikaga, T. et al (1987) The Vermont Longitudinal Study of Persons with Severe Mental Illness: II. Long-Term Outcome of Subjects Who Retrospectively Met DSM III Criteria for Schizophrenia. *American Journal of Psychiatry*, 144: 727–35.

Harrison, G., Hopper, K., Craig, T. et al. (2001) Recovery from Psychotic Illness: A 15- and 25-Year International Follow-up Study. *British Journal of Psychiatry*, 179: 506–17.

Hay, D. (1990) *Religious Experience Today: Studying the Facts*. London: Mowbray/Cassell.

Health Committee (1993) *Fifth Report: Community Supervision Orders: Volume 1. Report, together with an Appendix and the Proceedings of the Committee*. London: HMSO.

Health Select Committee (2000a) *Fourth Report: Provision of NHS Mental Health Services: Volume II Minutes of Evidence and Appendices*. London: TSO.

Health Select Committee (2000b) *Fourth Report: Provision of NHS Mental Health Services*, Volume 1, Report and Proceedings of the Committee. London: TSO.

Healy, D. (2009) *Psychiatric Drugs Explained*, 5th edn. London: Elsevier.

Hennessy, P. (2001) *The Prime Minister: The Office and Its Holders since 1945*. Basingstoke: Palgrave Macmillan.

Hernstein, R. and Murray, C. (1996) *The Bell Curve: Intelligence and Class Structure in American Life*. New York: Free Press.

Hewitt, J.L. (2008) Dangerousness and Mental Health Policy. *Journal of Psychiatric and Mental Health Nursing*, 15: 186–94.

Highland Users Group (HUG) (2006) *Recovery: Our Thoughts on Recovery and What Helps Us to Recover from Mental Health Problems*. Inverness: HUG www.hug.uk.net.

Hinshelwood, R.D. (1987) *What Happens in Groups*. London: Free Association Books.

Hinshelwood, R.D. (1996) Communities and Their Health. *Therapeutic Communities*, 17: 173–82.

Hinshelwood, R.D. (1999a) The Difficult Patient: The Role of 'Scientific' Psychiatry in Understanding Patients with Chronic Schizophrenia or Severe Personality Disorder. *British Journal of Psychiatry*, 174: 187–90.

Hinshelwood, R.D. (1999b) How Foulkesian Was Bion? *Group Analysis*, 32: 469–88.

Hinshelwood, R.D. (1999c) The Difficult Patient. *British Journal of Psychiatry*, 32(4): 469–88.

Hinshelwood, R.D. (2002) Symptoms or Relationships (Comment on Jeremy Holmes', 'All You Need is CBT'). *British Medical Journal*, 324: 288–94.

Hinshelwood, R.D. (2004) *Suffering Insanity*. London: Routledge.

Hinshelwood, R.D. (2010) Psychoanalytic Research: Is Clinical Material Any Use? *Psychoanalytic Psychotherapy*, 24: 362–79.

Hinshelwood, R,D., Pedriali, E, and Brunner, L. (2010) Action as a Vehicle of Learning. *Organisational and Social Dynamics*, 10: 22–39.

Hodes, M. (2000) Psychologically Distressed Refugee Children in the United Kingdom. *Child Psychology and Psychiatry Review*, 5(2): 57–67.

Home Affairs Committee (2000a) *Managing Dangerous People with Severe Personality Disorder*. First Report – Volume 1: Report and Proceedings of the Committee: HC – 42. London: TSO.

Home Affairs Committee (2000b) *Managing Dangerous People with Severe Personality Disorder*. Government Reply to the First Report from the Home Affairs Committee Session 1999–2000: HC – 505. London: TSO.

Home Affairs Committee (2000c) *Managing Dangerous People with Severe Personality Disorder*. First Report – Volume 11: Minutes of Evidence and Appendices: HC – 42. London: TSO.

Home Office and Department of Health (1999) *Managing Dangerous People with Severe Personality Disorder: Proposals for Policy Development*. London: Home Office / Department of Health.

Houlbrooke, R. (1998) *Death, Religion and the Family in England, 1480–1750*. Oxford: Oxford University Press.

Houlihan, G.D. (2000) The Nurses' Power to Detain Informal Psychiatric Patients: A Review of the Statutory and Common Law Provisions in England and Wales. *Journal of Advanced Nursing*, 32(4): 864–70.

Huber, G., Gross, G. and Schuttler, R. (1975) A Long-Term Follow-Up Study of Schizophrenia: Psychiatric Course of Illness and Prognosis. *Acta Psychiatrica Scandanavica*, 52: 49–57.

Human Rights Commission (1997) *Bringing Them Home: Report of the Inquiry into the Separation of Aboriginal and Torres Straits Islander Children from Their Families*. Sydney: HR & EOC.

Hutton, J. (1998) *Review of the Mental Health Act* [private correspondence to Genevra Richardson] 17 November 1998. London: Department of Health.

Independent on Sunday (2005) A Bittersweet Victory on Mental Health. *Independent on Sunday*, 30 October 2005, p 37.

Independent on Sunday (2006) Mental Health Campaign. *Independent on Sunday*, 3 September 2006, p 16.

Jackson, R. (2004) Intercultural Education and Recent European Pedagogies of Religious Education. *Intercultural Education*, 15(1): 3–14

Jackson-Lowman, H. (2004) Perspectives on Afrikan American Mental Health: Lessons from Afrikan Systems, in Jones, R.L. (ed) *Black Psychology*. Berkeley, CA: Cobb & Henry.

Jaques, E. (1955) Social Systems as a Defence against Persecutory and Depressive Anxiety, in Klein, H. and Money-Kyrle, R.E. (eds) *New Directions in PsychoAnalysis*. London: Tavistock, pp 478–98.

JCDMHB (2005a) *Joint Committee on the Draft Mental Health Bill: Session 2004–05*: Volume II. HL Paper 79-II: HC 95-II. Norwich: TSO.

JCDMHB (2005b) *Mental Health Bill Needs Radical Overhaul*. Press Release – Session 2004–05, 23 March 2005 [online]. Available: www.parliament.uk/parliamentary_committees/jcdmhb/jcdmhb_07.cfm. Accessed: 9 January 2013.

JCDMHB (2005c) *Joint Committee on the Draft Mental Health Bill: Session 2004–05:* Volume III, HL Paper 79-III: HC 95-III. Norwich: TSO.

JCDMHB (2005d) *Joint Committee on the Draft Mental Health Bill: Session 2004–05:* Volume I, HL Paper 79–1: HC 95–1. Norwich: TSO.

Jensen, A. (1969) How Much Can We Boost I.Q. and Scholastic Achievement? *Harvard Educational Review*, 39: 1–23.

Jensen, A. (1987) Further Evidence for Spearman's Hypothesis Concerning Black–White Differences on Psychometric Tests. *Behavioral and Brain Sciences*, 10: 512–19.

Johnson, R. (1999) Exemplary Differences: Mourning (and Not Mourning) a Princess, in Kear, A. and Steinberg, D.L. (eds) *Mourning Diana: Nation, Culture and Performing of Grief*. London and New York: Routledge, pp 15–39.

Johnston, P. (2002) Psychopaths to Be Held before They Strike. *Daily Telegraph*, 26 June 2002, p 5.

Jones, E.E. and Korchin, S.J. (eds) (1982) *Minority Mental Health*. New York: Praeger.

Jones, R.L. (1981) *Black Psychology*, 3rd edn. Washington DC: Washington University Press.

Jones, R.L. (2004) (ed) *Black Psychology*, 4th edn. Berkeley, CA: Cobb & Henry.

Jordan, H. and Slade, M. (2012) The Development of Five Language Tools Looking at Clinical Decision-Making Involvement and Satisfaction (CDIS). Paper given at the ReFocus Conference on Recovery Research, London, 7 March 2012.

Jung, C.G. (1978) *Psychological Reflections*. Princeton: Bollingen.

Kalathil, J. (2010) *Recovery and Resilience. African, African-Caribbean and South Asian Women's Narratives of Recovering from Mental Distress.* London: Mental Health Foundation.

Katsakou, C., Marougka, S., Barnicot, K., Savill, M., White, H., Lockwood, K. and Priebe, S. (2012) Recovery in Borderline Personality Disorder (BPD): A Qualitative Study of Service Users' Perspectives. *PloS ONE*, 7, 5.

Katz, J.H. (1985) The Socio-Political Nature of Counseling. *The Counseling Psychologist*, 13: 615–24.

Kesey, K. (1962) One Flew over the Cuckoo's Nest. Victoria: Methuen.

Keval, N. (2003) Triangulation or Strangulation: Managing the Suicidal Patient. *Psychoanalytic Psychotherapy*, 17(1): 35–51.

Kisely, S. (1999) Psychotherapy for Severe Personality Disorder: Exploring the Limits of Evidence-Based Purchasing. *British Medical Journal*, 318 (7195): 1410–12.

Kofman, F. and Senge, P. (2001) Communities of Commitment: The Heart of Learning Organisations. Cambridge, MA: Organisational Learning Centre, Massachusetts Institute of Technology.

Kutchins, H. and Kirk, S. (eds) (1997) *Making Us Crazy: DSM – The Psychiatric Bible and the Creation of Mental Disorders.* London: Constable.

Laing, R.D. (1965) *The Divided Self: An Existential Study in Sanity and Madness.* London: Penguin Books.

Laing, R.D. (1967) *The Politics of Experience and the Bird of Paradise.* Harmondsworth: Penguin.

Larsen, L. and Plesner, I.T. (eds) (2002) *Teaching for Tolerance and Freedom of Religion and Belief.* Oslo: Oslo Coalition on Freedom of Religion and Belief, University of Oslo.

Laurance, J. (2004) Bill to Lock Mentally Ill Condemned as Unfair and Dangerous. *Independent*, 9 September 2004, p 15.

Law Society (2002) *The Draft Mental Health Bill 2002: The Law Society's Response to the Government's Consultation Process.* London: Law Society.

Leganger-Krogstad, H. (2000) Developing a Contextual Theory and Practice of Religious Education. *Panorama: International Journal of Comparative Religious Education and Values*, 12(1): 94–104.

Lehman, A.F., Lieberman, J.A., Dixon, L.B. et al. (2004) Practice Guideline for the Treatment of Patients with Schizophrenia, 2nd edn. *American Journal of Psychiatry* 161(sppl2): S1–S56.

Lewis, G., Croft-Jeffreys, C. and David, A. (1990) Are British Psychiatrists Racist? *British Journal of Psychiatry*, 157: 411–15.

Liberman, R.P. and Kopelowicz, A. (2002) Recovery from Schizophrenia. *International Review of Psychiatry*, 14: 245–55.

Liberman, R.P. and Kopelowicz, A. (2005) Recovery from Schizophrenia: A Concept in Search of Research. *Psychiatric Services*, 56(6): 735–42.

Lidchi, V.G. (2003) Cross Cultural Transferability in Child Protection: Challenges and Opportunities. *Child Abuse Review*, 12: 238–50.

Littlewood, R. (1992a) DSM-IV and Culture: Is the Classification Intentionally Valid? *Psychiatric Bulletin*, 16: 257–61.

Littlewood, R. (1992b) Psychiatric Diagnosis and Racial Bias: Empirical and Interpretative Approaches. *Social Science & Medicine*, 34(2): 141–49.

Littlewood, R. and Lipsedge, M. (1997) *Aliens and Alienists: Ethnic Minorities and Psychiatry*, 3rd edn. London: Routledge.

Livesley, W.J. (2010) Confusion and Incoherence in the Classification of Personality Disorder: Commentary on the Preliminary Proposals for DSM-5. *Psychological Injury and Law*, 3: 304–13.

Loh, A., Simon, D., Wills, C.E. et al. (2007) The Effects of a Shared Decision-Making Intervention in Primary Care of Depression: A Cluster – Randomised Controlled Trial. *Patient Education and Counseling*, 67: 324–32.

Loring, M. and Powell, B. (1988) Gender, Race and DSM-III: A Study of the Objectivity of Psychiatric Diagnostic Behaviour. *Journal of Health and Social Behaviour*, 29: 1–22.

McClelland, R.J. (2007) *The Bamford Review of Mental Health and Learning Disability (Northern Ireland): A Comprehensive Legislative Framework – Consultation Report*. Belfast: NI Executive.

McDonald, C. (2009) *Response to Request for Internal Review*. DH Case Reference DE00000413343 [Letter], Personal Communication: Sent 5 November 2009.

MacDonald, M. (1981) *Mystical Bedlam: Madness, Anxiety and Healing in Seventeenth-Century England*. Cambridge and New York: Cambridge University Press.

McKenzie, K. and Bhui, K. (2007) Better Mental Health Care for Minority Ethnic Groups – Moving Away from the Blame Game and Putting Patients First. Commentary on Institutional Racism in Psychiatry. *Psychiatric Bulletin*, 31: 368–69.

McDougall, W. (1921) *Is America Safe for Democracy?* New York: Scribner.

Maclean, R. (2011) *A Gift of Time*. London: Constable.

McLuhan, M. (1964) *Understanding Media*. London: Routledge.

Maden, A. (2001) Practical Application of Structured Risk Assessment. *British Journal of Psychiatry*, 178(5): 479.

Maden, A. (2005) Violence Risk Assessment: The Question Is Not Whether but How. *Psychiatric Bulletin*, 29(4): 121–22.

Maden, A. (2007a) Mental Health Law: Real Doctors Should Not Become Spin Doctors: Rapid Response. *British Medical Journal* [online]: www.bmj.com/rapid-response/2011/11/01/mental-health-law-real-doctors-should-not-become-spin-doctors. Accessed 31 January 2013.

Maden, A. (2007b) Dangerous and Severe Personality Disorder: Antecedents and Origins. *British Journal of Psychiatry*, 190(suppl. 49): s8–s11.

Main, T.F. (1946) The Hospital as a Therapeutic Institution. *Bull Menninger Clinic*, 10: 66–70. Republished 1989 in T.F. Main, *The Ailment and Other Psychoanalytic Essays*. London, Free Association, pp 7–11.

Makoul, G. and Clayman, M.L. (2009) An Integrative Model of Shared Decision Making in Medical Encounters. *Patient Education and Counseling*, 60(3): 301.

Malpass, A., Shaw, A., Sharp, D. et al. (2009) 'Medication Career' or 'Moral Career'? The Two Sides of Managing Antidepressants: A Meta-Ethnography of Patients' Experience of Antidepressants. *Social Science and Medicine*, 68: 154–68.

Martin, D. (1955) Institutionalisation. *Lancet* 2: 1188–90.

Martin, D. (2007) Ministers Retreat on Law to Lock up Mental Patients. *Daily Mail*, 14 June 2007, p 19.

Martslof, D.S. and Mickley, J.R. (1998) The Concept of Spirituality in Nursing Theories: Differing World-Views and Extent Focus. *Journal of Advanced Nursing*, 27: 294–303.

Matthias, M.S., Salyers, M.P., Rollins, A.I. and Frankel, R.M. (2012) Decision Making in Recovery-Oriented Mental Health Care. *Psychiatric Rehabilitation Journal*, 35: 305–14.

Mental Welfare Commission for Scotland (2002) *Comments on Mental Health Bill*, Med/DrMO/A0214102–22.10.02. Edinburgh: Mental Welfare Commission for Scotland.

Menzies Lyth, I. (1959) The Functioning of Social Systems as a Defence against Anxiety: A Report on a Study of the Nursing Service of a General Hospital. *Human Relations*, 13: 95–121. Republished 1988 in Menzies Lyth (ed) *Containing Anxiety in Institutions*. London: Free Association Books; and in Trist and Murray (eds) 1990 *The Social Engagement of Social Science*. London: Free Association Books.

MHA (2004) *Revised Mental Health Bill Is Unfit for the 21st Century*. London: Mental Health Alliance.

Milgram, S. (1964) Group Pressure and Action against a Person. *Journal of Abnormal and Social Psychology*, 64: 137–43.

Miller, E. and Gwynne, G. (1972) *A Life Apart*. London: Tavistock.

Miller, L.J. (1989) Inpatient Management of Borderline Personality Disorder: A Review and Update. *Journal of Personality Disorders*, 3: 122–34.

Mind: The Mental Health Charity (2002) *Roads to Recovery*. London: Mind.

Moncrieff, J. (2009) *A Straight Talking Introduction to Psychiatric Drugs*. Ross on Wye: PCCS Books.

Montori, V.M., Gafni, A. and Charles, C. (2006) A Shared Treatment Decision-Making Approach between Patients with Chronic Conditions and Their Clinicians: The Case of Diabetes. *Health Expectations*, 9 (1): 25–36.

Moran, P. (1999) *Maudsley Discussion Paper No. 7: Should Psychiatrists Treat Personality Disorders?* [online]. Available: www.iop.kcl.ac.uk/iopweb/blob/downloads/locator/l_600_ Maudsley_Discussion_Paper_7.pdf. Accessed: 9 January 2013.

Morant, N. (2006) Social Representations and Professional Knowledge: The Representation of Mental Illness among Mental Health Practitioners. *British Journal of Social Psychology*, 45 (4): 817–38.

Morris, M. (2000) Tyrannical Equality, in Hinshelwood, R.D. and Skogstad, W. (eds) *Observing Organisations*. London: Routledge.

Morrison, A.P., Hutton, P., Shiers, D. and Turkington, D. (2012) Antipsychotics: Is It Time to Introduce Patient Choice? *British Journal of Psychiatry*, 201: 83–84.

Moules, N. (2000) Postmodernism and the Sacred: Reclaiming Connection in Our Greater-Than-Human Worlds. *Journal of Marital and Family Therapy*, 26: 229–40.

Mullen, P.E. (2007) Dangerous and Severe Personality Disorder and in Need of Treatment. *British Journal of Psychiatry*, 190(suppl 49): s3–s7.

Murray, H.A. (1938) *Explorations in Personality*. New York: Oxford University Press.

Nash, M. and Stewart, B. (2002) Spirituality and Social Care: Contributing to Personal and Community Well-Being. London: Jessica Kingsley.

Nash, O. (1935) Professional Men, in *I Wouldn't Have Missed It: Selected Poems of Ogden Nash (1975)*. New York: Little, Brown.

National Institute for Mental Health in England (NIMHE) (2005) *NIMHE Guiding Statement on Recovery*. London: NIMHE.

Nehls, N. (2000) Recovering: A Process of Empowerment. *Advanced Nursing Science*, 22(4): 62–70. Aspen Publishers.

NICE (2009a) *Borderline Personality Disorder: Treatment and Management*. NICE Clinical Guideline 78. National Institute for Health and Clinical Excellence.

NICE (2009b) *Medicines Adherence: Involving Patients in Decisions about Prescribed Medication and Supporting Adherence*. London: NICE.

Norman, I. and Ryrie, I. (2009) *The Art and Science of Mental Health Nursing*. Maidenhead: Open University Press.

Norton, K. and Bloom, S.L. (2004) The Art and Challenges of Long-Term and Short-Term Democratic Therapeutic Communities. *Psychiatric Quarterly*, 75(3): 249–61.

Norton, K. and Hinshelwood, R.D. (1996) Severe Personality Disorder: Treatment Issues and Selection for Inpatient Psychotherapy. *British Journal of Psychiatry*, 168: 723–31. Republished 2009, in Adshead, G. and Jacob, C. *Personality Disorder: The Definitive Reader*. London: Jessica Kingsley.

Nose, M., Barbui, C. and Tansella, M. (2003) How Often Do Patients with Psychosis Fail to Adhere to Treatment Programmes? A Systematic Review. *Psychological Medicine*, 33: 1149–60.

Nouwen, H.J.M. (1979) *The Wounded Healer*. London: Darton, Longman and Todd.

Oades, L., Walker, R. and Fisher, N. (2011) Staff Wellbeing Predicting Positive Attitudes towards Mental Health Recovery. *The International Journal of Person Centred Medicine*, 1(3) no.4070: 250–58.

Obholzer, A. and Roberts, V. (eds) (1994) *The Unconscious at Work*. London: Routledge.

Oborne, P (2005) *The Rise of Political Lying*. London: Free Press.

Ogawa, K., Miya, M., Watarai, A. et al. (1987) A Long-Term Follow-Up Study of Schizophrenia in Japan with Special Reference to the Course of Social Adjustment. *British Journal of Psychiatry*, 151: 758–65.

O'Keeffe, G. and Scott-Moncrieff, L. (2000) The Mental Health Act: From Review to Reform. *The Journal of Forensic Psychiatry*, 11(3): 667–81.

Oliver, M. (1996) *Understanding Disability: From Theory to Practice*. London: Macmillan.

Onyango, R.S. (1986) Cannabis Psychosis in Young Psychiatric Inpatients. *British Journal of Addiction*, 81: 419–23.

Owusu-Bempah, K. and Howitt, D. (2000) *Psychology beyond Western Perspectives*. Leicester: BPS.

Paloutzian, R.F. (1996) *Invitation to the Psychology of Religion*, 2nd edn. London: Allyn & Bacon.

Patel, S.R., Bakken, S. and Ruland, C. (2008) Recent Advances in Shared Decision Making for Mental Health. *Current Opinion in Psychiatry*, 21(6): 606–12.

Paterson, B. (2006) Newspaper Representations of Mental Illness and the Impact of the Reporting of 'Events' on Social Policy: The 'Framing' of Isabel Schwarz and Jonathan Zito. *Journal of Psychiatric and Mental Health Nursing*, 132: 94–300.

Pedersen, P.B. (2003) Culturally Biased Assumptions In Counseling Psychology. *The Counseling Psychologist*, 20(10): 3–10.

Peplau, H. (1952) *Interpersonal Relations in Nursing: Patients and Other Inmates*. New York: Random House.

Pilgrim, D. (2007) New 'Mental Health' Legislation for England and Wales: Some Aspects of Consensus and Conflict. *Journal of Social Policy*, 36(1): 79–95.

Pilgrim, D., Rogers, A. and Gabe, J. (2011) Social Aspects of Psychotropic Medication, in Pilgrim, D., Rogers, A. and Pescosolido, B. (eds) *The Sage Handbook of Mental Health and Illness*. London: Sage.

Pinel, P. (1801) Personality Disorder, in Gelder, M., Gath, D. and Mayou, R. (eds) (transl. Kauka, 1949) *Oxford Text Book of Psychiatry*, 2nd edn. Oxford: Oxford Medical Publications.

Pines, M. (1978) Group Analytic Psychotherapy with Borderline Personality Disorder. *Group Analysis* 11: 115–26.

Pollock, L. (1983) *Forgotten Children: Parent–Child Relationships from 1500 to 1900*. Cambridge and New York: Cambridge University Press.

POST (2003) *Postnote: Number 204: Reform of Mental Health Legislation*. London: Parliamentary Office of Science and Technology.

Prins, H. (2008) Counterblast: The Mental Health Act 2007 (a Hard Act to Follow). *The Howard Journal*, 47(1): 81–85.

Purves, L. (2012) Why Must Grief Be a Sign of Mental Illness? *The Times*, 20 February 2012, p 21.

Ramon, S. (2003) *Users Researching Health and Social Care: An Empowering Agenda?* Birmingham: Ventura.

Ramon, S. (2011) Organisational Change in the Context of Recovery-Oriented Services. *Journal of Mental Health Training, Education and Practice*: Issue for Workforce Development, 6(1): 37–45.

Ramon, S. and Williams, J.E. (2005) *Mental Health at the Crossroads – the Promise of the Psychosocial Approach*. Aldershot: Ashgate.

Ramon, S., Castillo, H. and Morant, N. (2001) Experiencing Personality Disorder. *International Journal of Social Psychiatry*, 47, 4: 1–15.

Rapp, C.A. (1998) *The Strengths Model: Case Management with People Suffering from Severe and Persistent Mental Illness*. New York: Oxford University Press.

Rapp, C.A. and Goscha, R.J. (2012) *The Strengths Model: A Recovery-Oriented Approach to Mental Health Services*. Oxford: Oxford University Press.

Raval, H. (1996) A Systemic Perspective on Working with Interpreters. *Child Clinical Psychology and Psychiatry*, 1: 29–43.

Ravazzola, M.C. (1997) Historia Infames: Los Malatros en las Relaciones. Buenos Aires: Paidos Terapia Familiar.

Rawnsley, A. (2000) *Servants of the People: The Inside Story of New Labour*. London: Hamish Hamilton.

Rayner, J. (2007) Legal Mindfield [online]. Available: www.lawgazette.co.uk/features/legal-mindfield. Accessed: 8 February 2013.

Reason, P. and Bradbury, H. (2001) *Handbook of Action Research*. London: Sage.

Rees, J. (2000) Food for Thought: The Canteen of a Mental Hospital, in Hinshelwood, R.D. and Skogstad, W. (eds) *Observing Organisations*. London: Routledge.

Repper, J. and Carter, T. (2011) A Review of the Literature on Peer Support in Mental Health Services. *Journal of Mental Health*, 20(4): 392–411.

Repper, J. and Perkins, R. (2003) *Social Inclusion and Recovery: A Model for Mental Health Practice*. Edinburgh: Balliere Tindall.

Resnik, M.D., Harris, L.J. and Blum, R.W. (1993) The Impact of Caring and Connectedness on Adolescent Health and Wellbeing. *Journal of Paediatrics and Child Health*, 29: 1–71.

Richardson, G., Chiswick, D. and Nutting, I. (1997) *Report of the Inquiry into the Treatment and Care of Darren Carr*. Reading: Berkshire Health Authority, Berkshire County Council, Oxfordshire Health Authority, Oxfordshire County Council.

Ridgeway, P. (2001) Restorying Psychiatric Disability: Learning from First Person Recovery Narratives. *Psychiatric Rehabilitation Journal*, 24(4): 335–43.

Ridley, C. (2005) *Overcoming Unintentional Racism in Counseling and Therapy: A Practitioner's Guide to Intentional Intervention*, 2nd edn. Thousand Oaks, CA: Sage.

Roberts, M. (2008) Facilitating Recovery by Making Sense of Suffering: A Nietzschean Perspective. *Journal of Psychiatric and Mental Health Nursing* 15: 743–48.

Robinson, L. (2009) *Psychology for Social Workers*. London: Routledge.

Romme, M., Escher, S., Dillon, J., Corstens, D. and Morris, M. (eds) (2009) *Living with Voices*. Nottingham: PCCS Publishing.

Rorschach, H. (1942) *Psychodiagnostics*. Berne: Huber.

Rosenhan, D.L. (1973) On Being Sane in Insane Places. *Science*, 179: 250–58.

Royal College of Psychiatrists (1999) *Offenders with Personality Disorder: CR71*. London: The Royal College of Psychiatrists/ Gaskell.

Royal College of Psychiatrists (2000) *Re: Reform of the Mental Health Act 1983 – Proposals for Consultation*, Letter to Will Niblett, Department of Health, sent 28 March 2000.

Royal College of Psychiatrists (2001) *White Paper on the Reform of the Mental Health Act 1983*. Response from the College's Mental Health Law Sub-Committee.

Royal College of Psychiatrists (2004) *Draft Mental Health Bill: Royal College of Psychiatrists Anxious about Civil Liberties, Ethics, Practicality and Effectiveness*. London: Royal College of Psychiatrists.

Royal College of Psychiatrists (2006) *Briefing on the Mental Health Bill 2006: House of Lords Second Reading: 28th November 2006*. London: Royal College of Psychiatrists.

Royal College of Psychiatrists (2007) The Mental Health Bill and Renewal of Detention [online]: www.rcpsych.ac.uk/pdf/MHB and renewal.pdf. Accessed: 9 January 2013.

Royal College of Psychiatrists and Law Society (2002) *Reform of the Mental Health Act 1983: Joint Statement by the Royal College of Psychiatrists and the Law Society*. Press Statement 25 June 2002.

Rushton, J.P. (1988a) Race Differences in Behaviour: A Review and Evolutionary Analysis. *Personality and Individual Differences*, 9: 1009–24.

Rushton, J.P. (1988b) The Reality of Racial Differences: A Rejoinder with New Evidence. *Personality and Individual Differences*, 9: 1035–40.

Ryan, P., Ramon, S. and Greacen, T. (eds) (2012) *Recovery, Empowerment and Lifelong Learning: Towards a New Paradigm*. Basingstoke: Palgrave Macmillan.

Sainsbury Centre for Mental Health (SCMH) (2002), *Breaking the Circles of Fear: A Review of the Relationship between Mental Health Services and African and Caribbean Communities*. London: SCMH.

Santos, A. and Hinshelwood, R.D. (1998) The Use at the Cassel of the Organisational Dynamics to Enhance the Therapeutic Work. *Therapeutic Communities*, 19: 29–39.

Sapsted, D. (2006) Stone 'Might Not Have Killed Lin and Megan If People Had Done Their Jobs'; Attacker Had Told His Psychiatric Nurse: 'I Want to Kill a Family'; Father Says He Has Relied Greatly on Josie to Give Him Strength. *The Daily Telegraph*, 26 September 2006, p 13.

Sashidharan, S. (2001) Institutional Racism in British Psychiatry. *Psychiatric Bulletin*, 25(7): 244–47.

Sashidharan, S. (2003) *Inside Outside: Improving Mental Health Services for Black and Minority Ethnic Communities in England*. London: National Institute for Mental Health in England.

Scanlon, C. and Adlam, J. (2012) The (Dis)Stressing Effects of Working in (Dis)Stressed Homelessness Organisations. *Housing, Care and Support*, 15 (2): 74–82.

Schauer, C., Everett, A., del Vecchio, P. and Anderson, L. (2007) Promoting the Value and Practice of Shared Decision-Making in Mental Health Care. *Psychiatric Rehabilitation Journal*, 31: 54–61.

Seale, C., Chaplin, R., Lelliott, P. and Quirk, A. (2006) Sharing Decisions in Consultations Involving Anti-Psychotic Medication: A Qualitative Study of Psychiatrists' Experiences. *Social Science & Medicine*, 62: 2861–73.

Secker J. (2010) Mental Health Problems, Social Inclusion and Social Exclusion: A UK Perspective, in Pilgrim, D., Rogers, A. and Pescosolido, B. (eds) *The SAGE Handbook of Mental Health and Illness*. London/Thousand Oaks, CA/Delhi: Sage.

Segall, M.H., Dasen, P.R., Berry, J.W. and Poortinga, Y.H. (1990) *Human Behaviour in Global Perspective*. New York: Pergamon.

Seikkula, J., Alkare, B. and Aaltonen, J. (2011) The Comprehensive Open Dialogue Approach in Western Finland II: Long-Term Stability of Acute Psychosis Outcomes in Advanced Community Care. *Psychosis*, 3(3): 192–204.

Seldon, A. (2005) *Blair's Britain*. London: The Free Press.

Shakespeare, W. (1997) *The Riverside Shakespeare: The Complete Works*. Evans, G. Blakemore and Tobin, J. J. M. (eds), 2nd edn. Boston and New York: Houghton Mifflin.

Shepherd, G. and Perkins, R. (2012) *Im-Roc Project*. London: Centre for Mental Health.

Sherif, M. and Sherif, C.W. (1956) *An Outline of Social Psychology*. New York: Harper.

Shorter, E. (1997) A History of Psychiatry: From the Era of the Asylum to the Age of Prozac. Chichester, New York: Wiley.

Simons, J. (2001) The Child Death Helpline, in Hockey, J., Katz, J. and Small, N. (eds) *Grief, Mourning and Death Ritual*. Buckingham: Open University Press, pp 158–73.

Sinha, D. (1983) Cross-Cultural Psychology: A View from the Third World, in Deregowski, J.B., Dziurawier. S. and Annis. R.C. (eds) *Explorations in Cross-Cultural Psychology*. Lisse: Swets & Zeitlinger.

Sinha, C. (1998) *Language and Representation: A Socio-Naturalistic Approach to Human Development*. London: Harvester Wheatsheaf.

Skogstad, W. (2000) Working in a World of Bodies, in Hinshelwood, R.D. and Skogstad, W. (eds) *Observing Organisations*. London: Routledge.

Slade, M. (2009) *Personal Recovery and Mental Illness: A Guide for Mental Health Professionals*. Cambridge: Cambridge University Press.

Slade, M. (2010) Measuring Recovery in Mental Health Services. *Israel Journal of Psychiatry and Related Sciences*, 47(3): 260–71.

Slade, M., Amering, M. and Oades, L. (2008) Recovery: An International Perspective. *Epidemiolofia e Psychatria Sociale*, 17, 2: 128–37.

Spaniol, L., Wewiorski, N., Gagne, G. and Anthony. W.A. (2002) The Process of Recovery from Schizophrenia. *The International Review of Psychiatry*, 14(4): 327–36.

SPCB (2002) *Health and Community Care Committee*, 18th Report 2002: Stage 1 Report on the Mental Health (Scotland) Bill: Volume 2: Evidence: SP Paper 708. Norwich: TSO.

Stalker, K., Ferguson, I. and Barclay, A. (2005) 'It Is a Horrible Term for Someone': Service User and Provider Perspectives on 'Personality Disorder'. *Disability and Society*, 20, 4: 359–73.

Stickley, T. and Wright, N. (2011) The British Research Evidence for Recovery, Papers Published between 2006 and 2009 (Inclusive). Part One: A Review of the Peer-Reviewed Literature Using a Systematic Approach. *Journal of Psychiatric and Mental Health Nursing*, 18: 247–56.

Sue, D.W. and Sue, D. (2008) *Counseling the Culturally Diverse: Theory and Practice*. New Jersey: John Wiley & Sons.

Sue, D., Ivey, A. and Penderson, P. (1996) *A Theory of Multicultural Counselling and Therapy*. New York: Brooks/Cole Publishing.

Sutton, J. (2007) Society Suspends Mental Health Alliance Membership. *The Psychologist*, 20(6): 340.

Swinton, J. (2003) *Spirituality and Mental Health Care*. London: Jessica Kingsley.

Szasz, T.S. (1961; 1984) *The Myth of Mental Illness: Foundations of a Theory of Personal Conduct*. New York: Harper and Row.

Szasz, T.S. (1970; 1997) *The Manufacture of Madness: A Comparative Study of the Inquisition and the Mental Health Movement*. New York: Syracuse University Press.

Szmukler, G. (2001) Violence Risk Prediction in Practice. *British Journal of Psychiatry*, 178(1): 84–85.

Taylor, J., DeFrain, J. and Ernst, L. (1986) Sudden Infant Death Syndrome, in Rando, T.A. (ed) *Parental Loss of a Child*. New York: Research Press.

Taylor, P.J., Leese, M., Williams, D., Butwell, M., Daly, R. and Larkin, E. (1998) Mental Disorder and Violence. A Special (High Security) Hospital Study. *British Journal of Psychiatry*, 172 (3): 218–26.

Tee, S., Lathlean, L., Coldham, T., East, B. and Johnson, T. (2007) User Participation in Mental Health Nurse Decision-Making. *Journal of Advanced Nursing*, 60: 135–45.

Tewfik, G.I. and Okasha, A. (1965) Psychosis and Immigration. *Postgraduate Medical Journal*, 41: 603–12.

Theakston, K. (2003) Political Skills and Context in Prime Ministerial Leadership in Britain, in Hargrove, E.C. and Owens, J.E. (eds) *Leadership in Context*. Oxford: Rowman & Littlefield.

Theophrastus (290 BC) *Characters* 16.

Thomas, A. and Sillen, S. (1972) *Racism and Psychiatry*. Secaucus, NJ: The Citadel Press.

Thomson, L., Bogue, J., Humphreys, M., Owens, D. and Johnstone, E. (1997) The State Hospital Survey: A Description of Psychiatric Patients in Conditions of Special Security in Scotland. *Journal of Forensic Psychiatry and Psychology*, 8(2): 263–84.

Thorndike, E.I. (1940) *Human Nature and the Social Order*. New York: Macmillan.

Thornicroft, G. (2006) *Shunned: Discrimination against People with Mental Illness*. Oxford: Oxford University Press.

Thornicroft, G., Brohan, E., Rose, D., Sartorius, N. and The INDIGO Study Group (2009) Global Pattern of Experienced and Anticipated Discrimination against People with Schizophrenia. *The Lancet*, 373(9661): 408–15.

Thorp, A. and Wright, K. (1999) *The Mental Health (Amendment) (Scotland) Bill: Finances of Incapable Adults – Bill 14 of 1998–99*. Research Paper 99/25: 10 March 1999, London: House of Commons Library.

Tillich, P. (1963) *Christianity and the Encounter of the World Religions*. Washington DC: Columbia University Press.

The Times (2004) Mental Health Bill 'To Disappear'. *The Times*, 15 June 2004, p 4.

Tsuang, M., Woolson, R.F. and Fleming, J. (1979) Long-Term Outcomes of Psychoses: Schizophrenia and Affective Disorders Compared with Psychiatrically Symptom-Free Surgical Conditions. *Archives of General Psychiatry*, 36: 1295–1301.

Turner, K., Lovell, K. and Brooker, A. (2011) ... And They All Loved Happily Ever After: 'Recovery' or Discovery of the Self in Personality Disorder? *Psychodynamic Practice*, 17: 3.

UNICEF (2011) *The State of the World's Children*, London, UNICEF.

Valentine, C.A. (1971) Deficit, Difference and Bicultural Models of Afroamerican Behaviour. *Harvard Educational Review*, 41(2): 137–57.

Valentine, L. and Feinauer. L.L. (1993) Resilience Factors Associated with Female Survivors of Childhood Sexual Abuse. *American Journal of Family Therapy*, 21(3): 216–24.

van de Vijver, F.J.R. and Poortinga, Y.H. (1997) Towards an Integrated Analysis of Bias in Cross-Cultural Assessment. *European Journal of Psychological Assessment*, 13(1): 29–37.

van Dijk, T. (1993) Principles of Critical Discourse Analysis. *Discourse & Society* 4(2): 249–83.

van Dijk, T. (2006) Ideology and discourse: A Multidisciplinary Introduction [online]. Available: www.discourses.org/UnpublishedArticles/Ideology and discourse.pdf. Accessed: 9 January 2013.

Vize, C. and Humphries, S. (2007) Rights and responsibilities in mental health care [letter]. *Guardian*, 1 May 2007, p 33.

Voltaire, François-Marie Arouet (1764) *Dictionnaire philosophique*.

Walker, M.T. (2006) The Social Construction of Mental Illness and Its Implications for the Recovery Model. *International Journal of Psychosocial Rehabilitation*, 10(1): 71–87.

Walker, S. (2003) *Social Work and Child and Adolescent Mental Health*. Lyme Regis: Russell House.

Walker, S. (2005) *Culturally Competent Therapy: A Guide to Working with Young People*. Basingstoke: Macmillan.

Walker, S. (2010) Young People's Mental Health: The Spiritual Power of Fairy Stories, Myths and Legends. *Mental Health Race and Culture*, 13(1): 81–94.

Walker, S. (2011) *The Social Workers Guide to Child and Adolescent Mental Health*. London: Jessica Kingsley.

Walker, S. (2012) *Effective Social Work with Children, Young People and Families: Putting Systems Theory into Practice*. London: Sage.

Wallcraft, J. (2005) The Place of Recovery, in Ramon, S., Williams, J.E. (eds) *Mental Health at the Crossroads: The Promise of the Psychosocial Approach*. Aldershot: Ashgate Publishing, pp 127–36.

Watson, A. (2001) *Detained: SSI Inspection of Compulsory Mental Health Admissions*. London: Department of Health.

Whaley, A.L. (2001a) Cultural Mistrust: An Important Psychological Construct for Diagnosis and Treatment of African Americans. *Professional Psychology: Research and Practice*, 32(6): 555–62.

Whaley, A.L. (2001b) Cultural Mistrust and the Clinical Diagnosis of Paranoid Schizophrenia in African American Patients. *Journal of Psychopathology and Behavioral Assessment*, 23(2): 93–100.

White, S.M. (2002) Preventive Detention Must Be Resisted by the Medical Profession. *Journal of Medical Ethics*, 28: 95–98.

Whiting, L. (1999) Caring for Children of Differing Cultures. *Journal of Child Health Care*, 3(4): 33–38.

Whittaker, R. (2010) *Anatomy of an Epidemic: Magic Bullets, Psychiatric Drugs and the Astonishing Rise of Mental Illness in America*. New York: Crown.

WHO (2010) *Mental Health*. Geneva: World Health Organization.

Wilkinson, R.G. and Pickett, K. (2009) *The Spirit Level*. London: Allen Lane.

Winnicott, D. (1960) The Theory of the Parent–Infant Relationship. *International Journal of Psychoanalysis*, 41: 585–95. Republished 1965 in *The Maturational Processes and the Facilitating Environment*. London: Hogarth.

Winnicott, D. (1965) *The Maturational Process and the Facilitating Environment*. London: Hogarth.

Wirtz, V., Cribb, A. and Barber, N. (2006) Patient–Doctor Decision-Making about Treatment within the Consultation: A Critical Analysis of Models. *Social Science & Medicine*, 62(1): 116–24.

Wober, J.M. (2000) A Feeding Frenzy, or Feeling Friendsy? Events after the Death of Diana, Princess of Wales. *Journal of Popular Culture*, 34(1): 127–34.

Wolfensberger, W. (1972) The Principle of Normalization in Human Services. Toronto: NIMR.

Wolff, N. (2002) Risk, Response, and Mental Health Policy: Learning from the Experience of the United Kingdom. *Journal of Health Politics, Policy and Law*, 27(5): 801–32.

Wooding, D. (2006) Dangerous Patient Bill Is Scrapped. *The Sun*, 24 March 2006, p 32.

Wrench, M. (2012) Annihilating the Other: Forensic Aspects of Organisational Change, in *The Therapeutic Milieu under Fire*. London: Jessica Kingsley.

Yanos, P.T., Roe, D., Marcus, K. and Lysaker, P.H. (2008) Pathways between Internalized Stigma and Outcomes Related to Recovery in Schizophrenia Spectrum Disorders. *Psychiatric Services*, 59: 1437–42.

Yanos, P.T., Roe, D. and Lysaker, P.H. (2011) Narrative Enhancement and Cognitive Therapy: A New Group-Based Treatment for Internalized Stigma among Persons with Severe Mental Illness. *International Journal of Group Psychotherapy*, 61(4): 576–95.

Yeo, S. (2003) Bonding and Attachment of Australian Aboriginal Children. *Child Abuse Review*, 12: 292–304.

Young Minds (2010) *Annual Report*. London: Young Minds.

Zanarini, M.C., Frankenburg, F.R., Reich, D.B. and Fitzmaurice, G. (2012) Attainment and Stability of Sustained Symptomatic Remission and Recovery among Patients with Borderline Personality Disorder and Axis II Comparison Subjects: A 16-Year Prospective Follow-up Study. *American Journal of Psychiatry*, 169: 476–83.

Zigmond, A. (1999) A Time to Keep Silent and a Time to Speak: Reviewing the Mental Health Act. *Psychiatric Bulletin*, 23(12): 705–706.

Zigmond, A. (2002) *Draft Mental Health Bill*, Letter from Campaign Headquarters, Number 1.

Zigmond, A. (2003a) *Draft Mental Health Bill*, Letter from Campaign Headquarters, Number 3.

Zigmond, A. (2003b) Draft Mental Health Bill, Letter from Campaign Headquarters, Number 2.

Zigmond, A. (2003c) *Draft Mental Health Bill*, Letter from Campaign Headquarters, Number 4.

Zigmond, A. (2004a) *Draft Mental Health Bill*, Letter from Campaign Headquarters, Number 6.

Zigmond, A. (2004b) A New Mental Health Act for England and Wales. *Advances in Psychiatric Treatment*, 10(3): 161–63.

Zigmond, A. (2005a) *Draft Mental Health Bill*, Letter from Campaign Headquarters, Number 7.

Zigmond, A (2005b) *Draft Mental Health Bill*, Letter from Campaign Headquarters, Number 8.

Zigmond, A., Eastman, N. and Freeman, R. (2003) No Way to Treat the Mentally Ill. *Sunday Telegraph*, 13 July 2003, p 20.

Zimbardo, P. (2008) *The Lucifer Effect: How Good People Turn Evil*. London: Rider Books.

Zubin, J. and Spring, B. (1977) Vulnerability: A New View of Schizophrenia. *Journal of Abnormal Psychology*, 86: 260–26.

# Index

Page numbers in italics are figures